Raphael Semmes
The Philosophical Mariner

Raphael Semmes
The Philosophical Mariner

Warren F. Spencer

The University of Alabama Press
Tuscaloosa

The University of Alabama Press
Tuscaloosa, Alabama 35487-0380
uapress.ua.edu

Hardcover edition published 1997.
Paperback edition published 2015.
eBook edition published 2015.

Inquiries about reproducing material from this work should be addressed to the
University of Alabama Press.

Manufactured in the United States of America
Cover photograph: Statue of Raphael Semmes, Mobile, Alabama;
courtesy of the author
Cover design: Gary Gore

∞

The paper on which this book is printed meets the minimum requirements of American National Standard for Information Science–Permanence of Paper for Printed Library Materials, ANSI Z39.48-1984.

Paperback ISBN: 978-0-8173-5839-6
eBook ISBN: 978-0-8173-8893-5

A previous edition of this book has been
catalogued by the Library of Congress as follows:

Library of Congress Cataloging-in-Publication Data
Spencer, Warren F., 1923–
Raphael Semmes : the philosophical mariner / Warren F. Spencer.
p. cm.
Includes bibliographical references (p.   ) and index.
ISBN 0-8173-0844-X (alk. paper)
1. Semmes, Raphael, 1809–1877. 2. Admirals—Confederate States of America—
Biography. 3. Confederate States of America. Navy—Biography. 4. United States—
History—Civil War, 1861–1865—Naval operations. I. Title.
E467.1.S47S64   1997
973.7'57—dc20   96-9580

British Library Cataloguing-in-Publication Data available

To Elizabeth Toth Spencer
Wife, Critic, and Friend

Contents

Illustrations

Maps

Preface

I first encountered Raphael Semmes as a historical figure while writing *The Confederate Navy in Europe*. Fascinated by his career, I later took the time to read both of his *Memoirs* and several of the published biographies. It occurred to me that the man was important historically for much more than his Civil War career. At a time when both Europe and the United States were in an uproar, Semmes made a career for himself first in the U.S. Navy, then in the C.S. Navy. As I studied him further I concluded that he was a unique figure and that he deserved a more thorough biography than any in existence. I was, perhaps, most impressed with his intellect. And besides, we both had the good sense to marry an Elizabeth Spencer!

My interest in Semmes was aroused by Dr. Charles Grayson Summersell shortly before his death. He kindly offered me all of his books and notes on Semmes's career. Mrs. Frances Sharpley Summersell graciously invited me to work in his home office. Those papers provided much of the material for Semmes's pre–Civil War career and inspired me to undertake this biography. I thankfully acknowledge the contributions of Dr. and Mrs. Summersell to the completion of this work.

Three other people have been instrumental in the writing of this book. First there is my wife Elizabeth Spencer, who has proofread every word and whose advice was, I soon learned, always correct. She has been an inspiration for me during these last three years.

Then there is Mrs. America Abbott. Her keen eyes always spotted misspellings and repetitions; her impeccable typing made my job much easier.

Finally, I owe to my former mentor at the University of Pennsylvania, Lynn M. Case, the training that has sustained me through the last few years that I have lived so closely with my subject. He shared his thoughts with me as we talked on the telephone, thoughts that solved a particular problem, or led me to a new approach, or simply inspired me to finish the job!

These people have unknowingly been the sparks that led me to complete the book. I owe them more than I can ever repay. Although they are of the kind who expect no acknowledgment, I happily give it to them nonetheless.

One other person inspired me to complete this writing: Raphael Semmes. His personality comes through all of his writings; his strong intellect constantly challenged me. I have learned from him the meaning of honor and the value of sacrificing one's self for the sake of one's convictions. My travel through Raphael Semmes's life has, in the sunset of my career, given me a new meaning to this period of my own existence. And for that, I thank Raphael Semmes.

Raphael Semmes
The Philosophical Mariner

Introduction

Why write a sixth biography of Raphael Semmes? Because no previous biographer has attempted to place him within his times, nor to delve into his personality and intellect, nor to relate his Civil War experiences within the context of his whole naval career. No previous biographer has touched upon his compassion as a family man. Manuscripts, previously unused, reveal much more about the complete Raphael Semmes than has heretofore been published.

Raphael Semmes matured and rose to his greatest achievements at the height of nineteenth-century romanticism and nationalism. He was a navy officer, a historian, a naturalist, a lawyer. A romantic and a nationalist, his best-known book, *Service Afloat during the War Between the States*, embodies and reflects these main characteristics of the mid-nineteenth century.

That era, roughly 1848 to 1870, saw monumental changes in Europe and the United States. It was the period of the "great man" theory of history, and Semmes played that role in his life; it was a period of extensive social reforms, and Semmes recognized them—and opposed them during his service in the Confederate States Navy; it was a time of the birth of new nation-states, and Semmes fought to create such a state.

The decade of the 1860s produced more wars and created more new national states than any era since the fall of Napoleon (1815). Camille Cavour used France to rid the Italian states of Austrian dominance and to establish the new Kingdom of Italy (1859–61). Otto von Bismarck fought three wars to establish Prussian dominance over the Germanies and to create the German Empire (1864, 1866, 1870–71). In 1861 Emperor Napoleon III began an intervention in Mexico to establish French dominance there, and he placed Maximilian on the throne of the Empire of Mexico. That endeavor came to a sad end with the execution of Maximilian by the Mexican republicans in 1867. And in 1861, Southern states in the United States seceded from the Union and fought the American Civil War to establish their independence. The 1860s were the years that Raphael Semmes reached the height of his naval career—fighting as did Cavour and Bismarck to establish a new nation.

The first stage of industrialization in western Europe, especially in Great Britain and France, and in the United States, especially in the Northern states, reached its peak in the 1860s. Textile factories in Europe depended on the long staple cotton from the Southern states, and this dependence created a one-crop agrarian economy in the South. The science of metallurgy had also advanced, producing the iron for the cotton textile machines. In France and Great Britain, iron was applied to naval architecture, first in France with the ironclad warship, the *Gloire* (1859), then in England with the ironclad *Warrior* (1860). The improved metal was also applied to rifles and artillery pieces, a development that in turn led to larger standing armies and navies. By 1861, Great Britain and France were dependent on the South's long staple cotton to clothe not only their people but also their soldiers and sailors. They also realized that a shortage of cotton would result in widespread unemployment that could destabilize their societies. Great Britain, especially, also depended on the import of northern and western American wheat to feed its people. Both American governments, but especially the Confederate one, depended also on English and French production of arms and munitions.

This economic interdependency led to a lively diplomatic relationship between Richmond and Washington, on the one hand, and London and Paris on the other hand. Those two American cities, then, joined the two western European ones and Rome, Berlin, and Saint Petersburg as wartime capitals in the war-torn decade of the 1860s. The United States already had diplomatic representatives in those European cities, but the Confederate States had to establish diplomatic ties with them. They sent diplomatic "agents" who were received by the ministers of foreign affairs in both Paris and London and to a lesser extent in Saint Petersburg.

The countries on each side of the Atlantic Ocean remained neutral in the wars on the other side of the water. But the commercial and naval shipping raised questions of international maritime law, questions that generally have been overlooked by most scholars and popular writers on the Civil War, questions covered by two acts of international law: the Paris Declarations of 1856 and the Geneva Tribunal of 1870–73.

The Paris Declarations of 1856 covered the matters of wartime rights and obligations of neutrals and belligerent use of privateers. The American Civil War became an international event almost from the first days of the conflict. When President Jefferson Davis of the Provisional Government of the Confederate States of America announced (April 17, 1861) that the Confederate States would issue letters of marque for use against Northern commercial shipping, and President Abraham Lincoln two days later proclaimed a blockade of Southern ports and harbors, the internal dispute between North and South became an international question. Other maritime nations had to respond. After some exchange of correspondence, Great Britain and France announced their neutrality in the American conflict, and other nations around the world soon followed. The Civil War had become a worldwide event; the provisions of the Paris Declarations applied immediately.

Those declarations provided that a blockade to be legal must be real, thus outlawing paper blockades. The North would have to have sufficient maritime force to prevent any ship from entering or leaving any Southern port. Also, neither side could use letters of marque for privateers to act against the other side. Finally, neutral goods (except contraband goods) in any ship, even a belligerent one, and belligerent goods (except contraband goods) in a neutral ship would be exempt from capture. Because the United States had not adhered to the 1856 Paris Declarations, the South could issue letters of marque for privateers to capture enemy commercial ships. It was, however, an unsuccessful venture.

One final aspect of international law played a part in the Geneva deliberations. A naval tradition dating back several centuries and followed by the European powers stipulated that a neutral country must enforce its neutrality upon its own citizens by "local" or "domestic" laws. Furthermore, should those laws be too weak to enforce the government's neutrality, that government would then be responsible for its citizens' unneutral acts. It was on this tradition that Great Britain was found guilty of unneutral acts by the Geneva Tribunal (1873) and was required to pay to the United States fifteen and a half million dollars in gold. The British domestic law to enforce neutrality upon its subjects was too weak to prevent British-built Confederate ships, unarmed and unmanned, from getting to sea. For Great Britain it was a question not of the government acting in an unneutral fashion but of the British law being "insufficient" to restrain British subjects from doing so. It was that insufficiency of British law that allowed the Confederacy to obtain such ships as the *Alabama* from the British shipbuilders.

In Great Britain, and to a lesser extent in France, individuals who had personal interests in the war either circumvented or tried to circumvent their governments' neutrality laws. Their motivation during the early years was cotton. In both countries the Union blockade of Southern ports created a shortage of cotton, and this shortage resulted in high unemployment and much higher prices of cotton cloth. Unemployment, especially in France, created social unrest. The French government acted swiftly to relieve the plight of the workers: It enacted unemployment compensation; it established retraining centers and provided funds to relocate the retrained workers and their families; it encouraged the creation of private foundations to relieve the workers' plight. Furthermore, both governments sought new sources for raw cotton. By 1863, with alternate cotton sources and unemployment reduced, both governments began to restrict the activities of individuals who aided the Confederacy and to oversee the application of their neutrality laws with greater diligence. Still, there were private individuals who for large profits were willing to act in behalf of the South: shipbuilders, cotton brokers, and bankers. As late as early 1865, Southern agents were building and receiving ships from yards in England and Scotland and were sailing them loaded with arms and munitions to the remaining ports still open to them.

Confederate government leaders well knew that they would be unable to sustain the war effort without aid from the industrial nations of Europe. They therefore consciously attempted to internationalize the war. Confederate Secretary of the Navy Stephen R. Mallory took the first step to maintain contact with Europe. He devised a navy policy to weaken the Union blockade: so destroy Northern merchant shipping as to force the Union navy to withdraw ships from blockade duty in order to protect the merchant ships on the high seas. To take the first step in the internationalization of the American domestic dispute, Mallory, almost by accident, selected Commander Raphael Semmes, Confederate States Navy.

Commander Semmes sailed the newly commissioned Confederate States Steamer *Sumter* from New Orleans, down to the mouth of the Mississippi River, and on June 30, 1861, slipped past the Union blockaders and began a career of destroying Union merchant ships. His specific orders were "to show the Confederate flag" in ports around the world and to prey upon Northern merchant shipping. He did the deed so well on the CSS *Alabama* as well as the *Sumter* that in twenty-two months he captured more enemy merchant ships than any other cruiser captain in maritime history. He showed the Confederate flag in ports on six of the world's seven seas, and he publicized his actions in papers of several ports he visited. He wrote letters to the *Times* of London justifying his actions and explaining his methods in condemning a prize. Because he could not take a captured ship into a neutral port, he called upon his legal training and formed a prize court aboard his ship and acted as an admiralty judge. Finally, he cultivated and exploited sympathizers in Europe, South Africa, Central and South

America, and even Singapore. Semmes's career at sea was a calculated and successful attempt, in accordance with Confederate government policy, to internationalize the American Civil War. It was the activities of Semmes aboard the *Alabama* that led the Geneva Tribunal in 1873 to order Great Britain to pay the "Alabama Claims" to the United States.

Born in Maryland to a slaveholding family, Raphael Semmes entered the United States Navy in 1826 at the age of seventeen years. His career was not unusual for that interwar era: Promotions were slow in coming with long periods of official leaves during which he supported his family through the practice of law; he moved his family to Mobile, Alabama, to be near the Pensacola, Florida, Navy Base. He was an astute student not only of international law but also of weather patterns; astronomy; flora and fauna; naval, social, and cultural history; and the classics. It was his study of constitutional law that led him to side with his adopted state in 1861. He was convinced that if the people of a state so voted, the state then had a right to secede from the Union because they had voted to enter it in the first place.

Born in 1809 and living until 1877, Semmes lived through not only that period of most intense change, 1848–70, but through most of the nineteenth century. His youth, early social environment and education, his dual vocations, his family life, his participation in two wars, his struggles to survive in the postwar years in the South are all mirrored in his public writings and his private correspondence. His experiences create a living slice of Western civilization in the nineteenth century.

1

The Student Mariner-Philosopher

Raphael Semmes was a product of his time. In an age of nationalism and romanticism, he was both a nationalist and a romanticist; but he was also very much more. He had almost no formal education, yet he was an intellectual and an avid reader. A strong family man, he was orphaned at an early age and spent most of his married life at sea. An observer of man and nature, of which he wrote movingly, he never quite understood himself.

In both his private and his public writings—he wrote two books of his experiences, one a best-seller in the 1850s—Semmes unconsciously revealed more of himself than of his topics. He has been the subject of five biographies that concentrate on his Civil War experiences and thus fail to reveal his developing intelligence and the complexity of his nature.

Raphael was born into the sixth generation of a Roman Catholic, slave-holding family that had settled in southern Maryland as early as 1662. The progenitor of the Semmes family in America was Marmaduke Semme (the *s* was added in the second generation), 1635–93.[1] Marmaduke's origins in England are uncertain, but he received 50 acres of land, indicating he was gentleman enough to have paid his fare across the Atlantic Ocean. He was also listed as an "innholder" and by the time of his death had accumulated some 800 acres of additional land.

Raphael's descent was through Marmaduke's second son, James (1671–1728), who inherited "Middle Plantation" in Cecil County, Maryland. James soon sold his land and moved westward to Chandler's Town, later known as Charles Town, then Port Tobacco. Presumably from the proceeds of the sale of "Middle Plantation," he bought several plantations from the Chandlers. He had eight children by his wife, Mary Goodrich Semmes. By his will he distributed his lands among seven of his eight children, leaving to his fourth son, James (1713–87), only 3,000 pounds of tobacco. This son, known in the family as Lieutenant James for his military service during the American Revolution, was Raphael's great-grandfather by his second wife, Mary Simpson, who was the great-granddaughter of Maryland's second governor, Thomas Green. Their eldest son, Benedict Joseph (1753–1824), was called Joseph by the family. Born in Charles County, he inherited several large tracts of land and married Henrietta Thompson. They were Raphael's grandparents.

Joseph and Henrietta Thompson Semmes had seven children. Their fourth child and third son was Richard Thompson (1784–1823), Raphael's father, who married Catherine Taliaferro Middleton Winter. Richard's three brothers—Alexander (1780–1816), Raphael (1786–1846), and Benedict Joseph (1789–1863)—were to play important roles in young Raphael's life.

Richard Thompson Semmes and Catherine Middleton, daughter of Samuel Middleton and Catherine Taliaferro Hooe, were married in 1808. Catherine, a widow, brought to the marriage the home and lands of Efton Hills, Charles County, Maryland. They had two sons, Raphael, September 27, 1809, and Samuel Middleton, March 5, 1811, and a daughter who died in childhood, all born at Efton Hills. Upon Catherine's death Richard Thompson married another widow, Kitty Brawner, who contributed to the union eleven slaves and other real and personal property. When Richard Thompson Semmes died in 1823, his two sons were placed under the guardianship of their uncles Raphael Semmes and Alexander Semmes, both of Georgetown, D.C.

Within a few years after Richard Thompson Semmes's death, executors acting in behalf of the boys' parents petitioned the court for the sale of lands that had belonged to the parents. The records do not reveal the value or the sale price of the lands, nor do they reveal to whom the proceeds were to go. Perhaps Uncle Raphael, in whose home the boys lived, compensated himself from those funds for their education and upkeep. It is also possible that the money provided the boys with an income in their early manhood years. Raphael never mentioned financial difficulties during his bachelorhood. It is possible, even likely, that young Raphael, fourteen years old when his father died, and young Samuel, twelve years old at the time, enjoyed an income that helped to sustain them until their professional incomes became sufficient to do so. Young Raphael's income during his navy training, and even after his commissioning as a passed midshipman, was insufficient to support him during unpaid leaves and while he studied law. And a lieutenant's salary was insufficient to allow him in 1837 to invest in land speculations. Even as a lieutenant he would have needed outside income to support a growing family.

Uncle Raphael sent the boys to a private school for a short time and later provided them with individual tutors. But their real education came at the dinner table where Uncle Raphael led discussions on the interpretation of the United States Constitution, especially the relationship between the individual states and the central government, and on politics. Later the uncle claimed as close friends such leaders as President Franklin Pierce, Senator Henry Clay, and Congressman Alexander Stephens of Georgia. As time passed, Uncle Raphael prospered, becoming a well-known merchant and businessman. By 1831 he was a popular tavern keeper, a director of the Farmers and Mechanics Bank, and a commissioner of the Potomac Insurance Company of Georgetown, and in the early 1830s he and a partner operated Semmes and Company, a wholesale grocery business. The table talk also must have centered on life at sea, for in his youth Uncle Raphael had sailed for a maritime company to ports throughout the world, having crossed the Atlantic Ocean nineteen times. Uncle Alexander Semmes owned a fleet of merchant ships based in Georgetown, in one of which young Raphael's father had held half-interest. But his influence on the orphaned boys was slight because they lived in Uncle Raphael's home and because Alexander was frequently at sea, where he was lost sometime between September 21, 1826, and December 1827.

His education, such as it was, led Raphael to become an avid, if lonely reader. He became introverted: His memoirs make no mention of a childhood friend other than his brother and cousins. He began to read classical history and philosophy, natural science, and biographies of the great seafarers, such as Christopher Columbus, and of great leaders, such as Genghis Khan and Julius Caesar. He was familiar with Shakespeare, eighteenth-century rationalism, and early nineteenth-century romanticism.[2]

During those years in Georgetown—1823 to 1826—he must also have learned of his various ancestors who had served the young republic: Through his grandmother, he was fourth cousin to Francis Scott Key, author of "The Star Spangled Banner"; on his mother's side he was a direct descendant of Arthur Middleton, a signer of the Declaration of Independence; and Uncle Raphael himself had served as a captain in the army during the War of 1812. The quiet boy-scholar undoubtedly dreamed of his own contributions to his country's history—but how? He and his brother Samuel, close in age and thrown even closer together by their parents' deaths, undoubtedly discussed their future. The table talk about the United States Constitution led Samuel to decide upon the practice of law, and Raphael was drawn to it also. But he was more influenced by their uncles' talk of life at sea. At the age of fourteen or fifteen he decided to enter the United States Navy and also to study law.

He turned to the political influence of Benedict Joseph Semmes (1789–1863). This youngest uncle had studied medicine at Philadelphia Medical College, then at Baltimore Medical College, from which he graduated in 1811. Despite a successful practice in Piscataway, Prince George's County, Maryland, he also was drawn to politics. In 1823 he won a seat in the Maryland House of Delegates, serving as Speaker for a number of years, and later became a notable Maryland senator. From 1829 to 1833 he was a Democratic representative in Congress. It was Uncle Benedict Semmes who in 1826 used his political influence in Maryland to secure from President John Quincy Adams an appointment as midshipman in the United States Navy for young Raphael Semmes.

Prior to the establishment of the United States Naval Academy at Annapolis (1845), officer appointees learned their trade by on-the-job training. A midshipman was an officer-trainee, not an officer. Young Raphael's career was typical of the training process.[3]

The presidential appointment was effective April 1, 1826. Five months later, on September 8, Raphael was called to active duty. Now, almost seventeen years old, he reported to the USS *Lexington* in New York City. For some reason, not in the records, on September 11 he was given unlimited leave; then on October 15 he was ordered aboard the USS *Erice,* on which he served until August 7, 1829. Again granted leave until January 7, 1830, he was assigned to the USS *Brandywine,* on which he served until November 7, 1831. He had two leaves of one month each while aboard the *Brandywine.*[4] On the two ships, he sailed in the waters of the West Indies, along the eastern coast of South America, and across the Atlantic Ocean into the Mediterranean Sea—waters and places he would later visit as captain of the CSS *Sumter* and *Alabama.* During one of his leaves from the *Brandywine* he visited Cincinnati, Ohio, with the ship's surgeon, where he met Anne Elizabeth Spencer, whom he would later marry.

At sea a midshipman's duties were varied and often menial: He had to awaken the various officers for their watch tours and perform any other duty the captain or lieutenants ordered. Apart from such tasks, the trainee learned about the ship's rigging, the tides and currents, and the prevailing winds. He also learned mathematics, astronomy, artillery management, and navigation from a tutor who was aboard to teach the midshipmen. His sleeping quarters were small and damp. All in all, the midshipman's life was hard: He could sleep only in short snatches; he was always at the beck and call of the officers; and his mess was the same as that of the enlisted sailors.

Semmes spent most of his off-duty time reading and studying naval regulations, natural science, and history. He never participated with his fellow midshipmen in their pranks, and he seldom went ashore with them. They considered him to be reserved and aloof—a reputation that would follow him throughout his service in navies of both the United States and the Confederate States.

In 1831, five years after his appointment, Semmes was assigned with other midshipmen to the Navy School at the Norfolk, Virginia, Navy Yard. For almost three months they studied intensive courses in the subjects they had practiced at sea, and then they were examined by an officer board. Not all midshipmen were approved by the officers, but Raphael passed second in his class. On April 28, 1832, almost exactly six years after his presidential appointment, he was commissioned a passed midshipman in the United States Navy. He was almost twenty-three years old. Except for a short tour (October 8–30, 1833) as keeper of the U.S. Navy chronometers, he was on leave from February 6, 1832, until July 25, 1835.[5]

The frequent extended leaves were suffered by all officers. It was a matter of the navy having more officers than it could use at one time, but the unpaid leaves placed a financial burden on the officers. To support himself, not to mention any family he might have, a navy officer needed some additional source of income. Many, such as John McIntosh Kell, Semmes's first lieutenant on both the *Sumter* and the *Alabama*, came from families with large land holdings and could simply return home and participate in the operation of the land. That fact explains why so many pre–Civil War officers were from the South. But Semmes had no land to fall back on and his legacy, if it existed, probably would be insufficient; what to do? This time his younger brother, Samuel, came to his rescue.

Samuel had early decided on a career in law. By 1832, still a bachelor, he had already established his practice in Cumberland, Maryland. Raphael simply went to Cumberland and read law in Samuel's office. He was admitted to the Maryland bar in 1835. So at the age of twenty-six he was both a navy officer and a qualified lawyer. Through the years prior to the Civil War, he came to be called the "sea-lawyer."

In July of the same year he was recalled to navy duty and assigned as acting master of the frigate USS *Constellation*, which was participating in the Seminole Indian War (1832–42) in Florida. In 1836 Semmes was given temporary command of a small steamer, the *Lt. Izard*, to transport troops and supplies to join General C. K. Call's planned attack against the Seminoles in the Everglades. But first he had to explore the Withlacoochee River to determine whether he could tow the supply barge about twelve miles upriver. Unfortunately, during the night of October 11 the *Lt. Izard* ran aground and was wrecked; Semmes had to abandon the steamer. It was the first of three ships under his command that he would lose. He and his men, tired and worn by the ordeal, were sent to the Pensacola Navy Base. According to one newspaper account, twenty-four of *Lt. Izard*'s twenty-eight crew members were "enfeebled and worn down by disease." As would occur two more times in his naval career, Semmes received a promotion or a better assignment after losing a ship to the waters. In March he was promoted to the rank of lieutenant, effective February 9, 1837, and received a three months' leave.[6]

The rank of lieutenant was a milestone in an officer's career. Only three higher ranks existed—commander, captain, and admiral. Should an officer fail to achieve a lieutenancy by the age of thirty, his chances of further promotion would be slight. And although the annual salary was quite small, it was considerably larger than a passed midshipman's. The frequent unpaid leaves placed further strains upon an officer's financial condition. In Semmes's case, however, his law practice in Cincinnati—and perhaps his legacy—afforded him a comfortable income. In early 1837, he purchased four lots at $200 each in a real estate development called the "New City of Pensacola." The terms provided that he pay one-fifth cash and one-fifth a year for four years. A month after the purchase, he sold three of the lots back to the developers and received $128 above the price he had paid for them. Thus he reduced the cost of the lot he retained to only $72. Unfortunately, before he completed payment on the remaining lot, the panic of 1837 forced the "New City of Pensacola" into bankruptcy; thus he lost $72 in the venture.[7]

Before the collapse of the "New City of Pensacola," however, Semmes had returned to his law practice in Cincinnati. But law was not his primary interest. He earlier had begun to court Anne Elizabeth Spencer, who at the age of eighteen was a "stately, handsome woman with regular chiseled features, brilliant brunette complexion and hazel eyes." Her grandfather, a colonel in the revolutionary army, had been among the first to settle in Cincinnati, and her parents—Oliver Marborough Spencer and Electra Ogden—were prominent citizens.[8] Anne Elizabeth had just made her debut when Raphael arrived. Although ten years his junior and an Episcopalian, Anne accepted his proposal and agreed to a Roman Catholic ceremony. They were married on May 5, 1837. Anne later embraced Raphael's church. Despite Raphael's frequent sea assignments that would mar their marriage, it nonetheless was a happy union, blessed with six children. The births came almost in pairs, determined it seems by Lieutenant Semmes's sea duty assignments. The first pair were both sons, born soon after his marriage to Anne Elizabeth: Samuel Spencer (1838–1912) and Oliver John (1839–

1918), the latter born at the Norfolk Navy Yard where Lieutenant Semmes was serving his first assignment after the wedding. The second pair were daughters: Electra Louise (1843–1925), born shortly after Semmes was assigned to the Pensacola Navy Base while on survey duty, and Katherine Middleton (1845–1937), born after a three-month leave just prior to the lieutenant's *Porpoise* cruise. The last pair—a daughter and a son—were born further apart: Anna Elizabeth (1847–1936), early during the Mexican War, and Raphael, Jr. (1849–1918), after the lieutenant's return from the war. All the children received good educations and grew into constructive and creative adulthood. More important, each child played a distinct role in Semmes's life, as will be seen later in his story.

Raphael Semmes in 1840 was thirty-one years old. He had reached manhood and had a wife and children to support. He had achieved progress in his chosen profession. What sort of person was he? Physically, he was slightly below medium height but held himself erect. He had a broad forehead, wore his black hair long to his ears, had an almost Roman nose and a waxed, up-turning mustache with a goatee. But his piercing black eyes that seemed to penetrate into one's very soul were his most striking physical characteristic. His appearance demanded obedience. With his legally trained mind, broadened by his wide reading, he was equal to almost any task. He was very proud and reacted sharply to any aspersion on his character or ability. He was impatient with inappropriate or slovenly acts, expecting everyone to be as precise and correct as he was.

It is not surprising, then, that Semmes became involved in several controversies with the navy hierarchy. In 1842 while stationed at the Pensacola Navy Base he alleged that the base commander, Captain A. J. Dallas, issued orders to him that Semmes considered to be a personal affront. Semmes wrote to the secretary of the navy accusing Dallas of conduct unbecoming an officer and a gentleman by using certain threats "while in a balcony in a loud tone, as if in a rostrum." The captain responded by placing Semmes under house arrest and even threatened to put him in the guardhouse. In a second letter to the Navy Department, Semmes claimed that Dallas suspended him because Dallas "did not like to meet him [Semmes] on duty." The Navy Department, basing its action on Semmes's accusations, ordered that Dallas be tried by court-martial. The captain was acquitted but transferred to another station, while Semmes remained at Pensacola for several years.[9] Semmes's fierce pride, knowledge of navy regulations, and lawyer's mind undoubtedly had served him well.

While assigned at the Pensacola Navy Base, Semmes in 1841 rented a house on land in Baldwin County, Alabama, where there was a settlement of navy officers. The property, known as Prospect Hill, was across the Perdido River from the base. His family joined him there. Between navy assignments he cut timber from the land, directing rented slaves. Most of his navy service had been in the South—Florida and Virginia—and having his family with him in Alabama was a kind of symbol of passing for him: He ever afterwards considered himself a citizen of the state of Alabama. Later, to provide his children with better educational opportunities, he moved the family to the city of Mobile. He bought three household slaves to help Anne Elizabeth with their growing family. Raphael Semmes was now committed to the Southern way of life.

The remainder of his navy duties prior to the Mexican War primarily involved coastal survey work. Between September 1840 and April 1845 he served on three different ships—the *Consort, Warren,* and *Poinsett,* which he commanded—all on survey duty and based in Pensacola. He then was transferred to the Home Squadron (September 9, 1845) and assigned to the USS *Porpoise.* During the five years of survey duty he learned the prevailing winds and currents of the Gulf of Mexico and much of the Caribbean Sea, knowledge he later would use during the Mexican and American Civil Wars.

During his service on the *Porpoise* as first lieutenant he kept a journal, which he did not publish. It is important as a forerunner of his Mexican War and Civil War journals, which were the raw materials of his two books. The *Porpoise* journal, rather primitive when compared to the later ones, contains phrases and expressions that would appear in his books as well as in the *Sumter* and *Alabama* logs. The early journal's observations reflect Semmes's mental attitudes, intellectual development, and reading habits. It is expressed in the flowery language of romanticism and draws descriptive pictures as reflected in his mind's eye. Written when he was thirty-six years old, the journal reveals Raphael Semmes's broad knowledge, despite his scanty formal education, of nature, humankind, architecture, history, and religion. It seems to be a rehearsal for his later journals and books.[10]

The *Porpoise* journal establishes Semmes's technique and methodology used in his later writings. Wherever he went he took copious notes—notes of mountain scenery, street vendors, military reviews, modes of dress, social customs, religious practices, conditions of life, political systems—to which he later referred as he wrote the journal. He also had various books with him or notes made from books he had read prior to sailing, and he frequently compared his subject to some historical precedent. The journal reveals his own prejudices and concepts of social virtues, political systems, and comparative racial characteristics. Finally, this handwritten, unedited journal contains many scratched-over phrases, additions, and changes, as he sought more precise expressions. It thus reveals more of Semmes's own concepts and prejudices than do his later published journals and books.

Semmes was assigned to the *Porpoise* on September 9, 1845, as first lieutenant, or second in command. It was to be his last cruise before the outbreak of the Mexican War (May 13, 1846). Events leading ultimately to the war—Texan independence, U.S. efforts to buy California, the annexation of Texas, and John Slidell's mission to Mexico City—were well under way.[11] A fleet of U.S. ships under the command of Commodore David Conner was stationed off the coast of Mexico at Vera Cruz. The *Porpoise* served as carrier of "official documents with their formidable yellow envelopes and seals of state" between the Home Fleet Headquarters at Pensacola and the commodore. So urgent was the situation in the "state of quasi war" that "no one was permitted to stretch his legs" at either end of the run, and the ship hardly had time to "wood and water" in Pensacola. For seventy days she plied the Gulf waters between Pensacola and Conner's fleet, and for seventy days the crew—officers and sailors—had been "cribbed and confined" in their narrow quarters aboard the small brig.

In December 1845 the *Porpoise* and her crew were relieved from their boring duty as a result of events in another area of Spanish America. The successful revolt of the "Dominican or Spanish portion" of the island of Santo Domingo had declared independence from the "Black" Republic (Haiti) on the western end of the island and sought recognition from the United States. At the request of the U.S. State Department, Secretary of the Navy George Bancroft sent Lieutenant David D. Porter, "a young officer of intelligence," to Domingo to gather information on the situation there. The USS *Laurence* was designated to convey Porter, but it was absent from Pensacola, and the mission was delegated to the *Porpoise*. The officers and crew were so delighted to be relieved of their mail carrier duties that sailors and officers all worked together to prepare the brig for the new assignment.

The *Porpoise* cruise included a stop in Havana, Cuba, then on to Santo Domingo City, on the southern coast of the island, and the capital of the "White" Republic. Lieutenant Porter was scheduled to make an inland trip through the republic, and the *Porpoise* was to meet him at Puerto Plata, on the northern coast close to the Haitian border. Similar stops in Haiti were scheduled, but the beginning of the Mexican War cut the cruise short and the ship briefly visited only one Haitian port. Throughout the cruise, at sea or on land, Semmes jotted observations in his journal.[12]

As the ship approached the island of Cuba, Semmes, then thirty-six, mused that it had been ten years since he had last seen that coast and that "from a youth with the warm blood rushing joyously through his veins, with the field of life, as painted by his imagination, spread out before him, like a garden of the *houris*, tempting him to ramble at pleasure amid its seductive walks, and pluck the flowers that seemed most fair, he had sobered down to the demure habits and temperate views of middle age." Later, aboard the *Alabama*, he again would reflect upon himself in the third person as if he stood outside himself and examined his own feelings. In the same breath, as it were, he described the approaching coast of Cuba: "Just abreast of us stood the giant Spanish Saddle, as though it had been fashioned for some spirit of air . . . to the westward rose the serrated summits and craggy sides of the Cock's Combs, whilst stretching away towards Havana, lay in hazy indistinctiveness the table lands of Muriel, all robed in the azure tints of distance, and forming together one of the softest and most poetical of tropical landscapes. . . . The sea lay in placid beauty, spread out like a sheet of molten silver; its gentle undulations flashing back the pure and soft rays of the moon." Throughout his life, Semmes remained fascinated with landscapes seen as they reached to the seas or to the heavens.

Some of the more fascinating observations and experiences that Semmes noted in the journal concerned Christopher Columbus. They reflect not only a young seaman's veneration for the great discoverer but also the impact of reading history on a young man's mind-set. His knowledge of Columbus was derived from Washington Irving's biography of Columbus, published in 1829. Widely read in the United States, the book "contributed to the idealized image of the discoverer that dominated literature for more than a century."[13] Its "soaring fancy produced a romance more than a judicious biography." Despite the fact that no portrait of Columbus "was drawn, carved, or painted from life," Irving described him as being "tall, well-formed, muscular, and of an elevated and dignified demeanor" and as a man whose countenance "had an air of authority." Irving had created "a hero in the romantic mold favored in the [nineteenth] century's literature." That romantic role fit Raphael Semmes's concepts of the "great man" in history and fed his romantic views of the Great Discoverer. The *Porpoise* cruise to Cuba and on to the island Columbus had called Hispaniola afforded Semmes an opportunity to indulge himself to walk in the steps of Columbus.

Semmes was impressed with the cathedral in Havana, which he described in detail: the eight variegated marble Doric columns, the checkered blue and white marble floor, the raised marble altar. But he and some fellow officers from the *Porpoise* were most attracted to the tomb of Columbus, "whose ashes repose in this fitting mausoleum." The ashes, he wrote, "are deposited in a niche in the wall, on the right of the grand altar, and are covered with a slab of white marble, on which the bust of the great navigator is sculptured in bas relief, and beneath which one reads the following inscription," which Semmes translated:

> May the remains of the great Columbus
> Repose in this urn, and his image be
> Enshrined in the hearts of our nation forever!

Semmes considered the New World the most fitting place for the repose of Columbus's ashes because it is "the theatre of his glory and the everlasting monument of his fame." He then reviewed the migratory history of Columbus's ashes, from Seville in Spain to the city of Santo Domingo, then "the most flourishing city of the New World and the metropolis of the Spanish colonial power." But when the French captured the island in 1796, "with much pomp and ceremony and escorted by a large squadron of Spanish and French ships of war, they were removed to Havana, and deposited in their present resting place." Semmes felt that Spain had appropriated Columbus too much to itself when of right "he belonged to the whole civilized world." Further, he reflected, "We Americans, viewing him as we are accustomed to, through the medium of Washington Irving's beautiful and romantic history of his life and voyages almost regard him as a countryman, and feel as proud of his great fame, as the most zealous Spaniard." As he and his shipmates stood reverently before the bas relief effigy of Columbus and "breathed upon his sacred ashes, we felt all our school-boy enthusiasm for the old navigator return upon us, and naturally ran over in our minds the principal events of his sacred career—his tiresome life, and almost neglected death!" Semmes was, indeed, a product of the age of romanticism— a true observer, yet romantic.

Semmes attended a service in the Havana cathedral and was impressed that no racial or social distinction existed in the seating arrangements. He was particularly impressed with the women in attendance: "A lovely woman in prayer! What spectacle can be more beautiful? I have gazed upon many a Spanish maid, with her lovely madonna face upturned in prayer, whilst she was seemingly abstracted from all things of earth, with a feeling akin to veneration. Religion, instead of being the cold creature of reason, is a sentiment with a Spanish woman, in which there is more love than fear. . . . There is a sublimity in all grand and beautiful objects, whether in nature or art, that tends to raise us . . . from the groveling thoughts of earth, and lead us to the contemplation of holier and better things. . . . Sinner that I am, I bow down, in all Christian humility before the Most High, and always think I come away a better man." Throughout his life, Semmes remained a loyal attendant to the Roman Catholic faith of his ancestors.

Semmes summarized the history of Cuba and the social customs of its people. He commented favorably upon the disappearance of the slave trade ("a nefarious" practice), described the racial relations existing on the island, and then entered into a geopolitical discussion of the relationship between Cuba, still a Spanish possession, and the United States. He reflected upon the strategic value of the island to the United States: the proximity between the two, Cuba's control over the sea entrances into the Gulf of Mexico, and the value of those waters that wash so much of the U.S. shorelines. Within this geopolitical context, almost prophetically, he stated that possession of Cuba would provide the United States Navy with a base from which it could "harass the enemy's commerce and pick up his single ships," thus unintentionally describing the onerous duty he would perform during the American Civil War and forecasting the establishment of a U.S. Navy Base at Guantanamo Bay, near the Windward Passage into the Gulf of Mexico.

These strategic advantages to the United States, he wrote, could best be accomplished if the people of Cuba voluntarily petitioned for statehood in the United States. It could be accomplished, he suggested, by purchase of Cuba from Spain as the United States had purchased Louisiana from France. Advantages of the Cuban people would be the abolition of the decadent and exploitative rule of Spain and the acquisition of freedoms, such as freedom of speech and separation of church and state. To the United States the advantage would be the control of the sea passages to the Gulf of Mexico by the establishment of a naval base in Cuba. Both peoples would benefit from the free trade existing between the states of the United States. The economies of both peoples would be stimulated, thus improving the standards of living. The Cuban state could retain the institution of slavery but, as in the United States, the import of additional slaves would be abolished and the racial balance in Cuba could be maintained.

Semmes's reflections upon Cuba reveal his unspoken views on Manifest Destiny.[14] They differed from the more generally expressed transcontinental ones only because they emanated from a seaman's mind.

From Cuba the *Porpoise* sailed to Santo Domingo, on the eastern end of the island of Hispaniola. During the short voyage Semmes described the *Porpoise* and her crew. As second in command of the ship, he did not directly criticize the captain, but he did consider the frequent calls to quarters as unnecessary and suggested better treatment of the sailors. He reported his own seasickness, a malady he was never able to escape while on the high seas. Drawing upon his experience of coastal survey and lighthouse inspection duties, he criticized the poor conditions of the West Indies lighthouses.

Semmes recounted the history of the island: the arrival of Columbus in 1492; the later treatment of the native Indians; the import of Africans as slaves; the intermingling of the races; the interventions of European powers, especially the French; and the recent—and still ongoing—revolution of the White Republic of the eastern part of the island from the Black Republic of the west. He described in detail the poverty of the majority of the people: their cohabitation without benefit of clergy, their shanty houses, their indolence, their social customs, their political systems. He was almost obsessed by the racial mixtures and noted that although whites were in the minority, they were economically better off than those of mixed blood. Nonetheless they socialized with mulattoes and blacks. He accepted these social amenities and at social affairs danced with ladies of color, some of whom he found to be quite beautiful. "As for myself," he wrote, "I never regarded the circumstance, of a little more, or a little less pigment, in a lady's complexion, of any particular consequence—outside of the family."[15] Indeed, wherever he went, he found some ladies of color to be graceful, intelligent dancing partners.

One day while Semmes and the ship's doctor were viewing a parade in the city they were "accosted, in good English, by an old negress . . . who claimed to be our countrywoman." She had lived in Baltimore and "was right glad to see some of her own people once more, having been in the island twenty-two years." The two officers congratulated her "on her rise in the world—her ability to move here in the best society, the positions attainable by her children in a community where there were no distinctions of color, and so forth." But the old woman interrupted: "Lord bless your souls, honeys, I've bin alonging to git back ever since I bin here. I can't learn the outlandish language, except a few words here and there, I can't git no money, I can't do nothing, I can't." If she could get back to Market Street in Baltimore, she said: "I should holler right out. I couldn't stand it, indeed, I couldn't." She claimed the food they had on the island was no good: "If you want a nigger to *be* strong, you must give him corn and hog, indeed you must." The two officers ended the conversation by giving the woman a dollar, for which she was very grateful.[16] Semmes seemed to have taken some consolation in this ex-slave's desire to get back to her former U.S. home.

While in the city of Santo Domingo, Semmes saw a great citadel built on the sheer cliff on the east side of the city, overhanging the river. He recognized it as the place in which Columbus had been incarcerated prior to being returned to Spain in chains. Prompted by his recent emotional ex-

perience in the Havana cathedral, he decided to visit the very cell in which
the Great Discoverer had been detained. It was the topmost room of the
citadel's tallest tower. After ascending spiral stone steps, Semmes and his
friend, the ship's doctor, arrived, exhausted, at the top. They were in "a room
of some twelve feet square, with a single, grated window facing to the Westward. In the wall are the remains of the ring bolts to which the old admiral
was chained." These relics thrilled and saddened Semmes.

Throughout the journal Semmes recounted the history and the present
condition of the areas he visited. In the case of Hispaniola, he not only
described the racial, social, and political conditions but included a running
account of the revolution, then in progress, that eventually resulted in the
division of the island into two states: the Dominican Republic, which he
referred to as the White Republic, and Haiti, which he called the Black
Republic. He actually found little good in either state; but in both he was
completely enthralled by the racial intermixture of the people, as he had
been in Cuba. Although he met many whites in the eastern state, he met
none in Haiti. In both areas he commented on the beauty of many of the
mulatto women.

The *Porpoise* sailed back through the Mona Passage to the northern side
of the island and stopped at the town of Puerto Plata, near the Haitian
border. Here, too, Semmes observed and recorded his impressions of the
place and the people. He was, as in all cases, precise in describing the mountains, trees, and people. In the coastal city of Cape Haitien, he described the
mountain summer houses of rich merchants as "sleeping in mid-air, a thousand feet or more above the city." In the Black Republic he referred to "the
slave revelling in the halls of his master." In reference to the same area, he
criticized historians of the previous 250 years for "unfortunately dealing
alone in the comparatively dry and unimportant political and military details of nations leaving untouched the far more fruitful and philosophical
theme of human passions and emotions, and vicissitudes of our race as ex-
emplified in private life." This is an insight into historiography that historians began to rectify only in the mid-twentieth century.

In one sense, Semmes was a typical racist of his time. He later wrote that
he "didn't hold much with slavery," but he accepted it as a fact of life in
the Southern states. He had rented slaves to cut timber on his rented land
in Alabama, and he had purchased three household slaves to help Anne
Elizabeth. In his comments on Cuba, he did not advocate the abolition of
slavery. He did oppose the slave trade then existing in Spanish America,
and he did criticize the importation of additional slaves into Cuba. He was
born into a family of slaveholders, and his uncles in Georgetown had had

household slaves. His experiences with the mixture of races in Cuba and on the island of Santo Domingo and his willingness to dance with mulatto women were new racial experiences for him. He seemed fascinated with the successes of some mulatto men—fascinated with their intelligence and achievements in business or government. At times he seems to have been on the edge of accepting these people for their achievements on an equal basis with himself. He always treated blacks with respect. But in the long run, he could not overcome his own heritage. He remained a racist.

A few days after the *Porpoise* had arrived in Puerto Plata (Semmes gave no dates in his narrative), he learned of the outbreak of war between Mexico and the United States and that the brother of one of his fellow officers aboard the ship was killed in one of the early skirmishes. The captain decided to cut the cruise short after visiting only two ports of Haiti "before squaring off for Pensacola and the Home Squadron. Then, hurrah! for the Gulf and the Mexican War."[17]

Semmes's opinions on the causes of the war were typically those of Manifest Destiny: Mexico was in the wrong and the United States was in the right. He had been in the navy since 1826 and had experienced war only once—the Seminole Indian War—and that experience had been brief. Now, too, he saw the role of the navy against Mexico as very limited: "Our only regret in the Navy is that as Mexico has neither commerce nor fleet we shall be little more than idle spectators of the gallant deeds of our more fortunate brethren of the army."[18]

Lieutenant Raphael Semmes had come a long way since being orphaned. His slow rise in the navy was common for most officers of his era. Still, he had managed somehow to become a well-educated, articulate man. He had married well and, despite his frequent absences, was a strong and happy family man. As the *Porpoise* sailed toward Pensacola, little could he have anticipated that of all the navy officers in the Mexican War he would be among the few to participate in the "gallant deeds" of his "more fortunate brethren of the army."

2

The Mexican War: Navy Duty

The transition from the peaceful Hispaniola voyage to the war in Mexico was quick and easy. The *Porpoise* sailed to the navy base at Pensacola, Florida, where it arrived on July 1, 1846. After "eight or ten days replenishing our water and provisions," the *Porpoise* sailed with essentially the same crew to rejoin the squadron off the coast of Vera Cruz, Mexico. The port of Vera Cruz was Mexico's deepest and its only one capable of handling large vessels. A blockade of the port by the United States Navy, under command of Commodore David Conner, was already in place. The *Porpoise* immediately resumed her place among the other U.S. vessels in the monotonous duty.

Lieutenant Semmes continued the habit of daily jotting down his experiences, and from that Mexican War journal he published in 1851 *Service Afloat and Ashore during the Mexican War*.[1] It was a best-seller in 1852. The purpose of the book, as Semmes wrote, was to record "many interesting social and political questions" that he personally experienced as he "contemplated the great disparity" between the people of the United States and Mexico "in their civilization and the progress they had severally made in the arts." His object was to sketch "the physical and moral condition of Mexico," to "review her . . . manners, customs, religion, and laws," and to trace "accurately . . . the principal events of our naval operations, and of General Scott's campaign." He claimed also to have "sketched persons and things as he saw them." His success is affirmed not only by the popularity of *Service Afloat and Ashore* in his own day but also by the frequency with which twentieth-century historians cite the work.[2]

The book consists of 479 pages divided into twenty-two chapters. It is at once a social, political, and military history of Mexico from the days of Cortez to those of Santa Anna and a history of the war as Semmes personally experienced it.

The first three and a half chapters deal with the climate and geography of Mexico, its political and military leaders, and the origins of the war of 1846. He described the social classes of the country and, although a devout Roman Catholic, criticized the Roman Catholic clergy for its ownership of large properties and the great wealth of the upper clergy while the vast majority of Mexicans were landless and lived in abject poverty. He compared the workers of the land, whether clerical or secular, to the serfs and peasants of the Old Regime in Europe. Without racial prejudice he described the racial intermixtures between the native Mexican Indians, African blacks brought to Mexico as farm laborers, and poor Spanish-descended farmers, as well as those of mixed blood, all of whom had been suppressed by Spanish rule that provided Spanish military leaders with large land grants. Indeed, he specifically referred to Mexican society as being equal to or worse than eighteenth-century prerevolutionary Europe.

The Mexican eleven-year struggle to win independence from Spain finally succeeded with the establishment of the Republic of Mexico in 1821. However, Semmes noted, it failed to create a strong central government that could lead the people from the eighteenth century into the nineteenth. A political and sometimes military tug-of-war ensued between the several states on the one hand and the central government on the other. He described in detail the adverse effect of this struggle on the central government's efforts to establish an effective rule throughout the country, or to effect social change, or even to defend the people against foreign invaders.

This social and political analysis of Mexico is in accord with modern historians, some of whom frequently quote Semmes for their specific examples. The book is exciting to read because of Semmes's descriptive power and his nineteenth-century romantic writing style. The content and style acquire even greater significance because he wrote as he sailed on warships and as he served with the army in Mexico.

In his discussion of the causes of the U.S. war with Mexico, Semmes blamed the politicians in both countries, but especially the former:

> Nothing is more difficult than to arrive at the true state of any question in the United States, having a political aspect. Such is the habitual rancor of politicians, that even facts are often distorted to suit party prejudices. The accounts we have of the origins of the Mexican War are a remarkable illustration of this want of political morals on the part of the mass of those who seek political office in our country; and that politicians, with a few honorable exceptions, have descended to the position of mere office seekers is a fact as humiliating to our pride, as it is obvious to our senses.
>
> Not being a politician, and having heard both parties, I will endeavor to give a succinct narrative of the circumstances which preceded the Mexi-

can War, without reference to either. As "history is philosophy teaching by example," I shall endeavor not to spoil the philosophy, by falsifying the example.[3]

Semmes remained true to his word throughout his analysis of the causes of the war. He began with Mexico's independence from Spain in 1821 and described the Mexican republican form of government, dwelling at length on the powers of the individual states as they successfully opposed the central government's effort to increase its own power. "Mexico was a federal republic—the several states choosing their own rulers, framing their own laws, and managing all their concerns, precisely as did the states of the American Union." So similar were the two countries, he maintained, that there was no intention of the United States to expand its territory at the expense of Mexico. This attitude held even when Stephen Austin accepted Mexico's offer of free land in Mexico's territory of Texas, which bordered the state of Louisiana at the Sabine River. Other settlers from the United States soon followed Austin and "being of a superior race soon began to make their weight felt in local affairs." Friction developed, Semmes maintained, between the Anglo-Americans and the Mexican natives of the area, and the Mexican government in 1830 prohibited further immigration of American citizens. Still, Semmes wrote that except for political events, harmony could have been preserved, and "in a generation or two, the radical differences of the two races would entirely have disappeared—the flaxen hair and blue eyes of the Anglo-Saxon taking a darker shade, and more brilliant light from the Hispano-Mexican. We thus would have conquered Texas—and ultimately all Mexico—as Greece conquered Rome, by civilization and the arts, instead of the sword."

Semmes also wrote of the frequent changes in the presidency of Mexico, changes that were effected not by national voting but by a series of coups. He used the checkered career of Santa Anna, who first became president of Mexico in 1833, to illustrate the Mexican inability to establish a democracy based upon the votes of the people. In 1835 Santa Anna dissolved the federal system and proclaimed the adoption of a central system of government. The several states of Mexico opposed the change. Texas, now with a majority of American settlers, proclaimed its independence in March 1836. When Santa Anna invaded the state to impose his federal powers, he was defeated and deposed from the Mexican presidency. The Texans established their independent Republic of Texas and applied to Washington for annexation. Disputes in the United States over the extension of slavery, however, delayed any action and Texas remained a sovereign republic for ten years. It was recognized not only by the United States but also by France and Great Britain. Intrigues in Texas by the two European powers, disputes with Great Britain over the northwest boundary, and growing American expansionist feelings finally enabled President John Tyler in June 1845 to gain congressional approval for the annexation of Texas.

The government of Mexico, which had never recognized the independence of Texas, rejected the notion that it could be annexed by the United States. In early March 1846 on orders from the president of the United States, General Zachary Taylor advanced his American troops from Corpus Christi to the mouth of the Rio Grande, an act considered by many authorities to be the immediate cause for the outbreak of warfare. Semmes, however, maintained that Mexico did not consider Taylor's action as a cause for war because "she considered the occupation *of any part* of Texas as an invasion." Mexico, according to Semmes, considered Taylor's movement as an indication on the part of the United States "to seize *some one or more* of her departments." Nonetheless, Semmes also wrote that although war seemed inevitable between Mexico and the United States, he had "but little doubt that if General Taylor had remained at Corpus Christi, the war might have been postponed for several years." The Republic of Texas, Semmes argued, could claim only that boundary "she had marked out with the sword"; but "she had never exercised over it [the area between Corpus Christi and the Rio Grande] any other than a paper jurisdiction"—the Mexican inhabitants remaining in the country and the Mexican officers performing their "functions." He further claimed that Taylor's movement "was unquestionably a false step in the administration of Mr. Polk." The war, he thought, could have been delayed for many years, except for the army's march to the Rio Grande. He condemned that march "not because . . . it had any important agency in controlling events, but because it weakened somewhat a very strong case."

The causes of the Mexican War, he maintained, were "far above and beyond the theater of events, on which the fleeting generation of politicians play hide-and-go-seek and then pass away and are forgotten." The real origin of the war was

the passage of our own race into Texas, New Mexico and California [which] was but the first step in that great movement southward, and which forms a part of our destiny. An all-wise providence has placed us in juxtaposition with an inferior people, in order, without doubt, that we may sweep over them, and remove them (as a people) and their worn-out institutions from the face of the world. We are the northern hordes of the

Alani, spreading ourselves over fairer and sunnier fields, and carrying along with us . . . the newness of life, and the energy and courage of our prototypes, letters, arts and civilization. How insignificant, then, will appear the acts of all those who played a part in the bringing about of the Mexican War; how unimportant the saying and doings of Mr. Tyler or Mr. Polk, of General Herrera, or General Paredes, and of the scores of subordinate politicians who have figured in speeches and dispatches?[4]

These words reflect, despite his broad self-education and high degree of intelligence, Raphael Semmes's total submersion in the ideology of his times: racism and the destiny of a superior race to dominate the inferior ones. Do they sound more harsh to the late-twentieth-century ear than they did to the mid-nineteenth-century ear? Possibly.

While criticizing the U.S. leaders for forcibly acquiring territory from Mexico, perhaps unconsciously on racial grounds, Semmes approved their support of the Texan republic and their ultimate defeat of the "inferior" Mexicans. Indeed, he supported U.S. expansion at the Mexicans' expense; he was, in the final analysis, a strong adherent to Manifest Destiny.

Semmes's account of these various activities remained centered in Mexico. He wrote of the Mexican leaders, especially Santa Anna and Herrera. The former, despite his defeat in 1836, regained the presidency in 1841 and through his military forces so thoroughly exploited the country that in 1844 he was overthrown and banished from Mexico. Semmes while in Cuba during the *Porpoise* cruise, it will be recalled, had visited Santa Anna. General Herrera, who saw the inevitability of the annexation of Texas, succeeded to the presidency. But his policy was unpopular among the military leaders, and in December 1845 General Paredes seized the government. The war with the United States began during his administration.

Semmes analyzed the moral and social conditions of Mexico in order to explain the country's lamentable political life. The military disorders, he wrote, led to the "demoralization and debasement" of the people. "The several classes have become distrustful of each other, and that individual confidence of man in his fellow man, which rests upon morals, and is one of the finest cements of well organized societies, has ceased almost entirely to exist." Large landowners, even where "the lands are good and the climate one of the most favorable in the world for agricultural pursuits, employ administrators who are very inefficient," he wrote, "and only a few of them are able at the end of the year to balance their accounts." Wheel carriages, he noted, are "almost unknown," and produce is carried to the markets "on the backs of mules and asses." Mechanical arts, he observed, "are in an equally depressed condition, owing in great measure to the unsettled state of the country, and the insecurity of property." He concluded with the maxim: "Where neither the arts nor agriculture flourish, there can, of course, be but little commerce."

No less valuable are his analyses of military strategies, his detailed accounts of battles in which he participated, and his evaluations of the military leaders, both American and Mexican. These accounts are enhanced through his personal experiences during the war, and thus they should be revealed as he served with the navy on blockade duty and on several raids ashore and with the army from Puebla to Mexico City.

As a navy officer Semmes had a unique opportunity to be in Mexico in April 1844. At that time, before his *Porpoise* cruise, he commanded a small navy vessel based at Pensacola. Immediately after the United States and the Republic of Texas signed the treaty of annexation (April 12, 1844), Secretary of State John C. Calhoun sent a messenger to the government of Mexico with a letter explaining the position of the United States. It fell to Semmes to convey the messenger to Vera Cruz, where the U.S. Navy under command of Commodore David Conner had already established its position off the port of Vera Cruz. Semmes accompanied the messenger overland from Vera Cruz to Mexico City, giving him, he wrote, "an opportunity of becoming acquainted with the temper and feelings of the country on the occasion."

> The great mass of the inhabitants . . . neither knew nor cared anything about the matter. But the utmost exasperation prevailed upon most of the other classes, and particularly among the military. The annexation of Texas was denounced by them, as indeed it was by the government—as a robbery unparalleled in the annals of nations, and one which merited and should receive a severe chastisement. They boasted boldly of their ability to drive us back to the Sabine, and in their ignorance and vanity, I have no doubt, many of them believed the boast.[5]

This little known prewar trip through the country of Mexico gave Semmes an understanding unique among U.S. Navy officers of the Mexican society and of that country's ability to wage war. His later trip, a repetition of this one in 1844, only reinforced his low opinion of the Mexican warlords and of their ability to conduct a successful war against the United States. It also provided him with a preliminary knowledge of Mexican society and gave him a preview of the beautiful Mexican mountains and valleys about which he wrote so movingly.

Shortly thereafter, while serving on the USS *Porpoise* prior to her Hispaniola cruise, Semmes had the opportunity to observe the movement of General Zachary Taylor's U.S. troops from the mouth of the Neuces River, the present-day site of the city of Corpus Christi and the southern boundary claimed by the Texas republic, to the mouth of the Rio Grande. Taylor took up a position opposite the Mexican city of Matamoras. The *Porpoise* was lying just offshore. Semmes "witnessed the firing by the Mexicans of their customhouse and other buildings, as they retired before the army." In the context of his notation, this comment reflects Semmes's disapproval of such a show of military force, implying his agreement with Lieutenant Ulysses S. Grant's *Memoir*'s characterization of the Mexican conflict as his country's "most unjust war."

Upon the return of the *Porpoise* to Mexican waters, about July 1, 1846 (the war had officially begun on May 13, 1846), Semmes was appointed Commodore Conner's flag officer and boarding officer aboard the USS *Cumberland*. It was the flagship of the thirteen-ship fleet assigned to blockade the whole eastern coast of Mexico. Lieutenant Semmes's duty as boarding officer was to board enemy ships as well as neutral vessels to assure that no contraband of war reached Mexico. The duty was not pleasant: "No duties could have been more irksome than those devolved upon the navy. During the whole of this period we were confined to our ships, and engaged in the most arduous and active cruising. . . . During the parching heats of summer and the long and boisterous nights of winter, our vigilance was expected to be, and was, unremitting."[6]

The officers had to live off the ship's rations, and "our only clean shirts were such as Jack rinsed out for us in a bucket of salt water." The flagship lay most of the time at Anton Lizardo, "a harbor formed by several small barren islands, rising no more than a foot or two above sea level—which was even more irksome than active service on the blockade." It was for the navy, he wrote, "a war . . . of toils and vigils, without the prospect of either excitement or glory," for the enemy had no navy and almost no maritime commerce. A war without an enemy bored the sailors and officers of the blockading fleet, and boredom coupled with "the wearing and harassing nature of our service, in a pestilential climate, had a powerful effect upon the constitutions of the officers and men." Many more Americans died of disease than in battle, and Semmes saw many friends die or become incapacitated by tropical diseases. "Their requiem was sung, not by the booming of cannon on the battlefield, but by the solemn sounding surge, and the moaning of the norther, as it charitably heaped up fresh piles of sand on their newly-made graves."

The "northers" arose suddenly, without warning. The gales occur during the Mexican dry season, from October to May, and are "the most furious periodical winds known anywhere in America." The winds follow the range of mountains from the northern polar area, along the Rocky Mountains, and down the eastern coast of Mexico.

> The northers rage with peculiar violence in the vicinity of Vera Cruz. . . . The severest gale I ever experienced, in any part of the world, I encountered in the brig *Somers*. It blew for three days and nights, the usual time for their duration, with such violence that we could not show ourselves above the hammock-rail, without imminent danger of being taken off our feet. . . . As the waves would strike the vessel, every timber and plank in her would tremble and quiver as though she were being shaken in pieces.

While Semmes served in various assignments with the Vera Cruz blockading fleet, he constantly noted the beauties of the Mexican topography. He especially was intrigued by the Mexican mountain range called the Cordilleras, and he described the "Prince" of the mountains belonging to the Cordilleras range. Known as Orizaba, the mountain rises

> with the regularity of a faultless cone, to the height of seventeen thousand four hundred feet above the level of the sea, and having its hoary summit covered, for a distance of five thousand perpendicular feet, with perpetual snow. . . . While cruising on the blockade, I have seen this noble mountain distinctly, from a distance of one hundred and ten miles—so distinctly that the various ravines, down which they have thundered, from time to time, avalanches of snow were clearly visible.

Semmes's boring blockade duties were spiced by occasional leaves for what we today call Rest and Recreation (R & R) and by commands of several different ships. The former duty was made possible by Commodore Matthew C. Perry, who had been assigned to the fleet as second in command. Commodore Conner ordered Perry to attack the city of Laguna del Carmen on the peninsula of Yucatan. The state of Yucatan, being remote from Mexico City, had for the previous ten years declared itself, on and off, to be independent from the Republic of Mexico. It had even fought on the side of Texas during its war for independence from Mexico. When Perry's three small ships arrived at Laguna del Carmen, they were greeted as friends and even entertained by the wealthier citizens. With the enthusiastic approval of the inhabitants, Perry appointed one of his officers as military and civil governor of the city. The inhabitants were happy with American rule, and Conner sent officers and men to the city to relieve them from the boredom of blockade duties. Semmes visited Laguna del Carmen on at least two occasions. As usual, Semmes was interested in the people and their customs. He was "highly amused" when he learned the method of establishing the price of admission to the local theater. "The population was divided into two parts, the aristocrats and the plebeians; the former included those who wore shoes, and the latter those who went barefoot." Those who wore shoes had to pay two *reals* for a ticket, while the barefoot ones paid only one. So pleased were the inhabitants of the city with the American occupation that at war's end they petitioned Commodore Perry to remain and protect them from the refugees who were flooding into the city. Semmes concluded that had the United States desired to annex the whole peninsula of Yucatan, "there would scarcely have been a dissenting voice among the inhabitants."

This highly successful foray against an enemy coastal city was but one of three ordered by Commodore Conner. His purpose in doing so was twofold: to provide relief from the tedium of blockade duty for at least some of the navy personnel, and to give the people at home some knowledge and excitement about the navy's role in the war. Lieutenant Semmes participated in a similar action against the small port of Alvarado, located about thirty miles southeast of Vera Cruz. He was aboard the steamer *Vixen* with Commodore Conner; Commodore Perry commanded the steamer *Mississippi,* a larger and a more heavily armed ship. Apparently, Conner had failed to order any reconnaissance of the small port's protective defenses. Alvarado is located about two miles up the Alvarado River. The river is narrow, with a fast-flowing current, and its mouth is protected by a sandbar over which the larger U.S. vessels could cross only at high tide and with a strong wind. Also, as Conner and Perry discovered, Alvarado's defenses "were formidable."

Although the *Mississippi* was able to shell the town, the lower river defenses slowed the advance of Conner and Semmes in the *Vixen,* which received several shots in her hull and had her light rigging destroyed. This foray was doomed to failure when the steamer towing three gunboats ran aground on the bar and was unable to proceed. Conner had no alternative but to withdraw; he had failed to give the people at home encouragement in the progress of the war.

Semmes, in his account of this failed navy effort, praised Conner for realizing he could not succeed and for ordering the withdrawal of the small fleet; he never mentioned Conner's failure to reconnoiter the town's defenses prior to ordering the attack. Later in the war, when Semmes was with the army, he did not hesitate to criticize several generals for unnecessarily exposing their men to injuries and even death. It was typical of Semmes, once he served under an officer, to emphasize that officer's successes and to over-look his failures.

His loyalty to Conner was apparent, once again, in his account of Com-modore Perry's successful raid, in which Semmes did not serve, upon the town of Tobasco. Perry, with only small vessels that could cross the bar, sailed some sixty miles up the Tobasco River, bombarded the town, captured it, seized the vessels he found there, and retired in good order. That was all Semmes recounted about the event.

The reason he gave such a brief description of the Tobasco foray might well be that he did not participate in it. During Perry's Tobasco raid, Semmes was transferred from Conner's flagship to command of the USS *Somers* (sometime between October 16 and 23, 1846). She was Semmes's first command during the war. The *Somers,* assigned to blockade duty, was "a fast and active vessel, a very efficient blockader; and she was consequently continued on this service, before Vera Cruz, sometimes assisted by other vessels, but for the most part, alone." It was the season of the northers and Semmes handled his ship in such a way as to assure that he would always be in position to stop any other ship that might try to enter Vera Cruz harbor. He "would get the *Somers* underway every morning at daylight, stand off and on, in front of the city during the day, and toward sunset, run into our anchorage again under Green Island. But this means we were always at our post, ready to intercept anything that might appear off the harbor, without running the risk of being blown off by the northers, and leaving the city exposed while regaining our station."

It was unlike Semmes to fail to describe his ship in greater detail. During the Civil War he gave dimensions, number of crews, and various charac-teristics of his two commands, the CSS *Sumter* and the CSS *Alabama.* Per-haps it was the seaman's superstition that caused him to avoid giving the history of the *Somers,* for the ship had an unfortunate history, dating from its second voyage in 1842, involving both Commodore Perry and a brother of John Slidell, who later served the Confederate States in Europe and whom Semmes knew and corresponded with in France when he took the CSS Alabama into the harbor of Cherbourg. For whatever reason, the Mexican War commander wrote nothing of the ship's past history.

The *Somers* was built in 1841. She was "a little beauty," newly rigged and outfitted as of August 1842.[7] Her assigned captain was a brother of John Slidell who had taken their mother's maiden name, Alexander Slidell Mackenzie. Slidell Mackenzie in the 1830s and 1840s was an intimate of such intellectuals as James Fenimore Cooper, Richard Henry Dana, Jr.,

Washington Irving, Henry Wadsworth Longfellow, and Herman Melville. Mackenzie was himself a writer of note, especially because of his biographies of navy officers, such as Oliver Hazard Perry, John Paul Jones, and Stephen Decatur. He also wrote popular travel books on Spain, Ireland, and England. There can be little doubt that Semmes, an ardent reader, had read some of Mackenzie's books on the famous U.S. Navy figures. Still, he did not mention Mackenzie or his writings.

The *Somers* was only 103 feet in length overall and weighed 266 tons. Her two masts were slanted away from the bow, giving the ship a racy look. The main mast stood 130 feet above the deck carrying five separate tiers of canvas, and the foremast, rising 90 feet above deck, accentuated the bowsprit that jutted almost 50 feet beyond the bow. Even when tied to a dock the ship appeared to be cutting swiftly through the ocean waves. But there were drawbacks to her design: The length of her beam was only 25 feet, about half that of the bowsprit. There were other problems with *Somers*. Even for her designed number of crew—ninety men and officers—she was small. Living space for the crew was only 105 feet in length and 25 feet in width: about as long as a basketball court and as wide as a singles tennis court. Furthermore, her top-heavy masts and sails and the weight of her cannon on the top deck made her roll heavily in the sea.

The purpose of Captain Slidell Mackenzie's voyage in 1842 was twofold: to patrol off the eastern African coast in order to prevent ships from carrying slaves to the coasts of South America, and to train young officers. One such young officer was Philip Spencer, the son of John Canfield Spencer, who in 1842 was secretary of war in President John Tyler's administration. The elder Spencer had had a distinguished career in the state of New York, having served in both state and federal legislative bodies, been a member of the New York State Supreme Court, active in state politics, and now a member of the president's cabinet. Both father and grandfather were men of achievement and distinction. Young Philip, however, was a rebel. He had failed out of two colleges (but nonetheless had mastered both Latin and Greek), was a heavy drinker, and had been sent into the navy by an angry father. Commander Mackenzie soon learned that Midshipman Spencer earlier had been dismissed from the service because of drunkenness. Indeed, the young Spencer seemed intent upon destroying all that the two previous Spencer generations had accomplished.

After performing its duty off the African coast, the *Somers* headed back to New York by way of the Caribbean Sea. Throughout the crossing, young Spencer began to talk with other young officers and even the higher non-commissioned officers. Evidence brought to Commander Mackenzie's attention convinced him that Spencer was planning a mutiny. He chained Spencer and two others on the stern top deck while he gathered material to charge them with mutiny. The trial was held on *Somers's* top deck, before the main mast; Spencer and one other admitted to scheming to take over the ship. They were hanged from the main mast arm, and their bodies were buried at sea.

Some of the ship's officers felt the evidence too little to justify the hangings. When *Somers* returned to New York, Mackenzie requested a Court of Inquiry. The hearing attracted newspaper reporters, and the procedures and hearings appeared in the New York City press. They were the talk of the town for weeks. Finally, Commander Mackenzie was exonerated of any wrongdoing and the hanging of Philip Spencer was justified. Mackenzie, however, was put on extended leave. The *Somers* remained in service.

Knowledge of the ship's past history was common among navy officers: She was a bad luck ship. Semmes apparently considered any command of his own to be an opportunity to be his own master and to further his navy career. The "bad luck" *Somers,* however, prevailed over the ambitious officer. Two incidents occurred that decisively affected Semmes's career in the Mexican War.

During the nights when Semmes took *Somers* close into Vera Cruz, his officers sought reprieve from the monotonous blockade duty. On one occasion three officers—Lieutenant James L. Parker, Passed Midshipman R. C. Rogers, and Passed Midshipman Hynson—with five seamen "performed the clever exploit of burning the Mexican merchant brig *Creole*" virtually under the walls of the massive castle that overshadowed the harbor, San Juan de Ulloa. It was a feat that Semmes thoroughly appreciated.

Another nocturnal activity by the adventuresome Passed Midshipman Rogers and the ship's acting surgeon, Major George Wright, did not turn out so well. The two men often visited the English warship *Sacrificios* and talked with the English officers who, as neutrals, daily visited the Mexican coast to hunt. They told the Americans that a building, often seen from the *Somers,* was occupied by the Mexicans as a powder magazine. The good doctor and the young officer thought that it would be "an easy matter to surprise it and blow it up." After examining the building through his field glasses, Semmes gave his approval for a reconnaissance of the approaches to the building. "The moon was near her full, and the nights serene and cloudless." They found the approaches nearly impassable and tried twice again to find a passage to the back of the building. On the third attempt, the *Somers's* bad luck struck once again: Rogers and an enlisted man were captured, but

Dr. Wright made a clean escape. The capture of Rogers would soon change Lieutenant Semmes's role in the war.

That change, however, awaited an even greater bad luck strike from the *Somers*. Counting his loss of a riverboat during the Seminole Indian War, the *Somers* became the second ship under his command that Semmes would lose. Semmes tells the story directly: "On the 8th of December [1846], while endeavoring to cut off a vessel which was apparently intending to run the blockade, I was struck by a heavy norther, and capsized and sunk in ten minutes, losing about one half my crew, which consisted of seventy-six persons all told."

Two days later, on December 10, Semmes submitted his official report to Commodore M. C. Perry, who in the absence of Commodore Conner was in command of the fleet off Vera Cruz. It was a long report, over four and a half pages. Semmes was careful to point out to the commodore that the *Somers* had been constantly on blockade duty for forty-five days and that it had been his practice "to take shelter from the north-west gales, that blow with such frequency and violence along this coast, at this season of the year." Sighting a vessel in the distance, he moved to identify her despite a falling barometer and a changing wind. Having discovered that she was the USS *John Adams,* sent actually to relieve the *Somers,* and fearing a gale, Semmes turned back to seek the shelter of Verde Island. The "look-out at the masthead cried 'sail-ho!' a second time."

> I immediately abandoned my intention of anchoring, as the gale had not yet set in, and hauling on a wind, under topsails and courses, commenced beating up the passage, a second time, with the view of placing myself between the strange sail and the port, to prevent the possibility of running the blockade, if she should be so inclined. I made one tack toward the *Paxaros* reef, and at the time of the catastrophe . . . we were standing under topsails, courses, jib, spanker. . . . I was myself standing on the lee-arm-chest, having just passed over from the weather quarter . . . when Lieutenant James L. Parker remarked to me that it looked a little squally to windward. I immediately passed over to the weather side, and as it looked a little darker than it had done, I ordered him to haul up the main sail, and brail up the spanker, and directed the helm to be put up.

But before these orders were completed "the squall struck us": "It did not appear to be very violent, nor was its approach accompanied by any foaming of the water, or other indications, which usually mark the approach of heavy squalls."

However, the brig, "being flying-light, having scarcely any water or provisions, and about six tons of ballast on board, was thrown over almost instantly, so far as to refuse to obey her helm." Despite Semmes's efforts to right the ship, "the brig was on her beam ends, and water pouring into every hatch and scuttle." Semmes ordered the mast to be cut away. "But as this was a forlorn hope, the brig filling very fast, and her mast and yards lying flat upon the surface of the sea," Semmes had little faith the ship could be saved. "I accordingly turned my attention to saving as many lives as possible." He ordered Midshipman Francis G. Clarke to take charge of the only boat, a small one pulling but five oars, not already underwater. He ordered the purser, the surgeon, and seventeen men into the boat. "I cannot refrain from expressing . . . my admiration of the noble conduct of several of the men, embarked in this boat, who implored the officers by name to take their places, saying they would willingly die by the wreck, if the officers would but save themselves." The officers refused and none of "those generous fellows were permitted to come out, and they were all subsequently safely landed as they deserved to be." Midshipman Clarke had pulled away only about twenty paces when the brig sank. "When she was on the point of sinking beneath us, and engulfing us in the waves, I gave the order: 'Every man save himself who can!'" About sixty officers and men immediately plunged into the sea, each reaching for some frail object that had drifted from the wreck: "Some reached a grating, some an oar, some a boat's mast, some a hen coop." Semmes and Parker, both good swimmers, reached an "arm-chest grating," which helped them survive until "an upper half-port came drifting by us." They lashed it to the grating and "got along much better." They were picked up by Midshipman Clarke, who was making his second of three trips in the brig's boat. Still, about half the ship's crew was lost in the tragedy.

Semmes, two days after the sinking, was still amazed that "there cannot have elapsed more than ten minutes, between our being struck by the squall, and the total disappearance of the *Somers*." In all of his writing on the loss of *Somers* he never mentioned that the ship's masts and the weight of her cannon on her top deck made her roll heavily in the sea, nor did he refer to the light ballast she carried the day she went down. Did he simply refuse to excuse his loss of the ship, or did he fear that he as captain of the ship would be blamed for carrying such light ballast? Some officers thought heavier ballast would have prevented the sinking. In any case, the question was never raised.

A Court of Inquiry was later held to determine Lieutenant Semmes's role in the loss of the brig. He was more fortunate than Commander Mackenzie, whose Court of Inquiry had been reported daily in the New York press; Semmes's court lasted only one day. Unlike Mackenzie, Semmes's *Somers*-related tragedy occurred during wartime; a Court of Inquiry exonerated the much-needed navy officer, despite the ship's lack of proper ballast. Mackenzie waited four years for another navy assignment, but Semmes was immediately appointed flag officer to Commodore Connor aboard first the USS *Cumberland* and then, when the commodore changed flagships, aboard the USS *Raritan*. Mackenzie, on the other hand, did not receive another navy assignment after his Court of Inquiry in 1842 until July 1846, and then only with the influence of his brother, John Slidell, who had just returned from a failed diplomatic mission to Mexico City. John Slidell persuaded President James Polk that if the United States would help Santa Anna return to power in Mexico (he was then in exile in Cuba), that former president of Mexico would sign a treaty favorable to the United States. Mackenzie was recalled to active duty and successfully carried out the secret mission. Although he completed his assigned duty, Santa Anna refused to sign a treaty with the United States; indeed, he became the leader of a renewed Mexican determination to resist the United States. In the worst battles of the war, the most U.S. casualties were suffered from the Santa Anna–led forces.

There is no indication that Semmes and Mackenzie ever met. Semmes, in writing about his command of the *Somers*, never mentioned the ship's career, nor did he ever mention Philip Spencer or Mackenzie. Later during the Civil War Semmes did have several occasions to communicate with Mackenzie's brother, John Slidell. The *Somers*, somehow, created two dramatic events that bound Slidell and Semmes together through two wars.[8]

After the Court of Inquiry found no fault with Semmes in the sinking of the *Somers*, he was once again attached as flag lieutenant on Commodore Conner's staff aboard the USS *Cumberland*. When that ship returned to the United States, Conner transferred his flag and staff to the frigate *Raritan*. In the meantime, the United States finally adopted General Winfield Scott's proposal to open a second front against Mexico. Zachary Taylor was still fighting in northern Mexico with some success but, in Semmes's words, "had accomplished but little in bringing the war to a close." Scott's plan was to effect an amphibious landing at Vera Cruz, capture the city and port, and then proceed overland northward through the Valley of Mexico to Mexico City. Semmes was delighted with Scott's plan because he considered "the campaign, in the north of Mexico" to be "an error brought about by the easy credulity with which the administration of Mr. Polk listened to ignorant men, who pretended to be well informed on Mexican affairs." Semmes knew from his extensive reading that Cortez had captured Mexico by invading in the vicinity of the site of modern Vera Cruz, then taking "his departure for the capital of Montezuma." He also theorized that the U.S. victories in the north accomplished little to convince the Mexican people that they were defeated; but "the moment the stripes and stars were unfolded from the cupola of the government house in Mexico City, the war was ended: the enemy, having been stabbed to the heart, was dead."

Other members of the blockading fleet, officers and seamen alike, also welcomed Scott's planned invasion at Vera Cruz. It would, after all, break the monotony of blockade duty and give the navy a chance to participate in the military actions against the enemy.

Scott took only a little over two months, from January 1, 1847, to March 9, 1847, to mobilize the invading forces, both army and navy. Scott himself arrived on March 6, and the next day with Commodore Conner made a reconnaissance of the waters off Vera Cruz. Conner had already selected the spot for the invading forces to land: a smooth sand beach that was near enough to the city but distant enough from its guns. Scott concurred with the selection. Because of the small harbor it would have been impossible to land the soldiers from the many small transport vessels, so Scott and Conner decided "to throw most of the troops on board the larger ships of war, and make them the transports. . . . Between eleven and twelve o'clock [on the morning of March 9] the fleet—Commodore Conner, leading in the flag-ship *Raritan*, whose decks like those of the other ships, were crowded with troops, and General Scott following at a short distance in the steamer *Massachusetts*—got under way, in gallant style, and filed, one by one, out of the narrow pass leading from the anchorage." The first amphibious landing of a U.S. army was under way.

It took two hours to reach the landing point. Semmes, aboard the *Raritan*, was as excited as the rest. For Semmes, scholar that he was,

> Every step of our progress was fraught with the associations of three hundred years; and the mind as it recognized object after object, famous in the history of the conquest, became tinctured with the romance of that period, and emulous of the deeds which had characterized its actors. . . . Time with its scythe and hour glass had brought another and a newer race, to sweep away the moldering institutions of a worn out people, and replace them with a fresher and more vigorous civilization. . . . The descendant of the Dane and the Saxon, with "progress" inscribed on his helmet, had come to supplant the never-changing Visigoth in his halls, and to claim that superiority for his lineage, which an all-wise Providence has so indelibly stamped upon it.

Previous Semmes racist comments have been noted, but this is the most blatant one of them all. Did he consider the Mexicans, many of them of various racial mixtures, to be so inferior to the Americans? He had never to this point expressed so strongly a racial superiority. While in Cuba during the *Porpoise* cruise he had referred to the beauty of the women—black, mulatto, or white—whom he saw praying in the Havana cathedral. And in the Dominican Republic he had expressed compassion for the blacks and he had even danced with mulatto women. What did he see in the Mexicans that moved him to such claims of superiority? Was it the lack of a stable government? Was it the suppression of Mexican farm laborers? Was it the eighteenth-century class structure of Mexican society? For whatever reason, this expression of the "Dane and the Saxon" linked with the "all-wise Providence" is the most extreme racist statement to appear in his early writings.

In this "first major joint amphibious operation of the navy and army of the United States," the key to landing the soldiers was the surf-boats that conveyed the soldiers from ship to shore.[9] The boats had been designed and built specifically for this particular operation. Both ends were pointed alike so that they could move handily in either direction, and they were almost flat-bottomed. They were shipped to the fleet in "nests" of three. The bottom boat of each nest was the largest at forty feet long, twelve feet wide, and four feet deep. Each of the others was about two feet shorter and one foot narrower than the one below it, so that three boats formed a neat nest. "The surf-boats, 67 in number, and each one manned by experienced seamen of the navy, were hauled alongside the ships, and the soldiers with their arms and accoutrements" boarded them directly from the larger vessels; as each boat received her complement, "she shoved off, and laid on her oars, at a little distance, until the others should be ready." Commodore Conner assigned the USS *Spitfire* and the *Vixen* "to cover the landing in case any opposition should be made."

General Scott had chosen Brevet Brigadier General William J. Worth, who commanded the First Division of Regulars and who had distinguished himself in the north of Mexico in the battle of Monterey, to command the invasion forces. When the surf-boats were all ready, General Worth "descended into one of the man-of-war's boats, prepared for him, and placing himself at the head of his troops, moved in a semi-circle toward the shore." Standing aboard the poop deck of the flagship, Semmes felt that "nothing could exceed the beauty of this spectacle." As was his habit, as the surf-boats pulled toward the shore, he noted the beauties of nature: "The magnificent mountain of Orizaba, with her snow-capped summit, which had been hid from view most of the day, suddenly revealed itself with startling distinctness and grandeur; the distant Cofre of Perote loomed up, also, in blue and mystic beauty, and the bold and rugged outline of the coast, seemed more bold and rugged still, from the refracting power of the atmosphere."[10] The boats soon reached the shore, unopposed, and "unfurled the American flag . . . and planted it in the land of Cortez."

The whole force, "consisting of about twelve thousand men," landed without mishap; it was, Semmes wrote, "an event unparalleled in the annals of similar operations, and of which any naval commander might well be proud." Indeed, the whole U.S. Navy could be proud of the success of this largest of U.S. amphibious operations.

Shortly after this historic army-navy operation, Commodore Conner was relieved from duty because of illness, and Commodore Perry then became the commanding navy officer. He remained aboard the *Raritan* and so did Raphael Semmes.

The army had begun the laborious job of establishing a semicircular investment of the city of Vera Cruz. Because of the loose sand and the many sand hills, all covered by thorny mimosa, prickly pear, and other plants, the movement of men and guns was slow and laborious. There also were frequent pools of water between the sand hills through which the soldiers had to wade or if possible go around, all the time dragging guns, ammunition, and other supplies. On top of it all a norther set in, "sweeping the foundation of sand" from beneath the soldiers' feet and "almost stifling them in their progress." The norther also delayed the delivery of food and other supplies to them. Not until March 14, four days after the landing, could additional supplies, draft horses, and ammunition be delivered to the army. Even when the army was fully supplied and dug in, the relatively small army cannon could not penetrate the city's walls. Its mortars could only fire over the walls, destroying civilian homes and stores and killing civilians instead of the defending soldiers. General Scott was compelled to ask for assistance from Commodore Perry.

Perry willingly agreed to transfer his larger naval guns from ships to shore, but he insisted that navy personnel should operate them. By March 24 the heavier naval guns were in place, about 700 yards from a gate in the city walls. Semmes participated in the off-loading and delivery of the navy guns, "after running the gauntlet of the enemy's fire, on a portion of the route," and he remained to serve, in effect, as an artillery officer. That first night he slept "on the off-slope of the sand-hill on the brow of which the battery was placed; [we] cooked an excellent supper, with plenty of hot coffee; smoked a cigar, and went to bed; that is to say, each one of us made a hole in the sand, to conform to the angularity of his figure, and pulled a blanket over his head." Throughout the night "an occasional shell, thrown at random in our direction exploded in fearful proximity to us." But Semmes could not sleep. About midnight he wandered onto a small nearby hill "to look forth upon the scene":

> It was perfectly calm. . . . The castle of San Juan de Ulloa, magnified out of all proportion by the uncertain starlight, and looking ten times more sombre and defiant than ever, appeared to enjoy [its] repose. Even the sea seemed to have gone to sleep, after the turmoil of the recent norther, as the only sound that reached the ear, from that direction, was a faint, very faint murmur, hoarse and plaintive, as the lazy swell, with scarcely energy enough to break, stranded itself on the beach. The cricket and the catydid, and myriads of other insects . . . chirped in a sort of inharmonious melody, reminding one of his far-off home and of fireside scenes. But if nature were thus inclined to repose, man was not, for Death still held his carnival within the walls of the beleaguered city.

The army's "horrid mortars" were still in "awful activity": "I sat and watched those missiles for an hour or more, and I shall never forget the awful scream, apparently proceeding from female voices, which came ringing on the night air, as one of those terrible engines of destruction exploded—carrying death and dismay, no doubt, to some family circle."

Semmes also criticized the army's use of cannon against the city. Because they were too weak to destroy the city's walls, the army used them as mortars. The army had been "throwing shells [and mortars] into the city for two days," succeeding only "in destroying a beautiful city and killing the inoffensive, because unarmed, portion of the population." The purpose of a siege "is to reduce the *armed* portion of the population to submission, and thus insure the surrender of the place: humanity in the present century revolts at the destruction of private property and the unnecessary effusion of blood." He continued his critique of the army's activity:

> Instead of throwing shells from a safe distance into a fortified city, and thus making war upon the private domicile of the citizen, killing his wife and children, and destroying his property, we should erect batteries against his fortified points and assail its military defenders, breaching the walls, and carrying the bayonet, if necessary, in order, that if blood flow, it may flow in the right quarter.[11]

The next morning at sunrise, the cannon from both sides opened fire once again. Semmes, in charge of a 32-pounder navy gun was opposite a

Mexican navy gun commanded by Lieutenant Sebastian Holzinger, whom Semmes recognized as "an intelligent young German" who had been several years in the Mexican service. "We of the *Raritan*," he continued, "paid our particular respects to this young gentleman." Semmes's gun "fired with the accuracy of a rifle," and he was constantly able to place his "heavy metal right into him and destroyed his flag twice, but each time the gallant fellow replaced it." The big U.S. Navy guns continued to fire into the gate guarded by the German. "We [the navy guns] continued our fire until two o'clock P.M., when the enemy's fire ceased. . . . The city was beaten, and on the same afternoon we had the satisfaction of seeing a white flag pass into General Scott's camp."

A norther delayed the formalities of the surrender of Vera Cruz, and the terms of the city's capitulation were completed only on March 27. The formalities of the Mexican evacuation of Vera Cruz took place the next day on a meadow just outside the city walls: The Mexican soldiers, in dress uniforms, marched out of the city, laid down their arms, and were given written pardons.

Semmes, an eyewitness, described the scene:

> The Mexicans were about five thousand strong. They were arrayed in their dress uniforms—many of those of the officers being covered with the stars and embroidery of which this people is so fond—and marched, with music playing, beneath the standards of their respective corps. Accompanying the soldiery were many women and children—the women loaded down with their simple household effects, and the children trudging by their sides, looking with amazement and wonder upon the spectacle before them. Our men, on whose bronzed features were visible the joint emotions of pride and conquest, and sympathy for the fallen, were drawn, under arms, in two lines, between which their late enemies passed. . . . General Worth was the "observed of all observers," sitting his horse as proud as a marshal of France, in the best days of the republic, and receiving the submission of the enemy, with mingled dignity and grace, which he knew so well how to assume, and which became him so well. Thus ended the surrender of Vera Cruz.[12]

A few days after the fall of Vera Cruz, General Scott, in a kind of clean-up exercise, organized a sortie against Alvarado, a small town about thirty miles southeast of Vera Cruz. Commodore Perry had earlier sent two ships to the bar of the Alvarado River to cruise in observation until the army should arrive. When Lieutenant Hunter in the steamer *Scourge* fired a few shots into a Mexican fort at the mouth of the river, the fort immediately surrendered. Hunter then went upriver to the town of Alvarado, which also surrendered to him. When the army arrived there was nothing for it to do. Hunter, however, was censured by a court-martial for exceeding his orders. The Mexicans surrendered as they did because of the fall of Vera Cruz.

The story was a bit different, however, when Semmes, aboard the *Raritan*, participated in a similar raid on Tuxpan, a town about a hundred miles northwest of Vera Cruz, where the USS *Truxton* had earlier been lost. Tuxpan was the only port city on the east coast of Mexico not yet in American hands. On April 18, 1847, aboard the small steamer *Spitfire* with Commodore Perry, Semmes moved up a narrow river toward the town. Despite sharp opposition from Mexican soldiers along the banks of the river and cannon shots from forts on either side of the river, the navy captured Tuxpan. The American losses were greater than the navy's losses in the siege of Vera Cruz: Fourteen sailors and officers were killed or wounded. Among the wounded officers were Commander Josiah Tattnall and Lieutenants William C. Whittle, Henry J. Hartstene, and James L. Parker. Parker died later of yellow fever, but all the other wounded officers would later see service in the Confederate States Navy.

After the capture of Tuxpan, Semmes was assigned to an expedition that was sent up the river "to seize any vessels or launches the enemy might have secreted." He noted that "with the exception of occasional corn fields, the growth of which rivaled that of our richest bottom lands . . . the country seemed an unbroken wilderness. . . . The Indian built his thatched hut of reeds on the bank of the stream, and paddled his primitive canoe, precisely as he had done in the days of the 'conquest'; and with a little assistance from fancy we might have transported ourselves back three centuries, without doing violence, except in point of time, to historical propriety."[13]

The Americans bivouacked in a cornfield and availed themselves of the "privileges of conquest" to eat the corn, "just then in the milk." They hoped to compensate the owner, but he had fled before they arrived. They examined the farmer's single-room hut, built of reeds. "The pot was simmering away on the hearth, with the evening meal, and the cat sat dozing as quietly over the embers as though there had been no enemies about." The soldiers availed themselves "of the very nice turkey eggs . . . and made free with contents of the pot" but disturbed nothing else.

The next day they explored the plain where they saw "herds of fat cattle and horses apparently wild, feeding in droves of ten or a dozen, on the river banks." Semmes thought that the man of "progress," with a plow, could make the Tuxpan valley "a sort of Sicilian storehouse for the supply of Indian corn and other products of the *tierra caliente*."

Leaving several small ships, including the *Porpoise* on which Semmes had sailed to Hispaniola, Commodore Perry returned to the anchorage off Vera Cruz. A message from Secretary of the Navy John Y. Mason awaited the commodore that was to change the role Lieutenant Raphael Semmes would play in the remainder of the war. Semmes was to join the army and follow the route of Cortez, up the Valley of Mexico, and participate in the capture of Mexico City. He had played a role in all of the navy's activities: He had served in blockade duty and the first large-scale U.S. amphibious landing; he had commanded a ship and lost her in a gale; he had manned a gun in the siege of Vera Cruz; and he had participated in several raids upon smaller Mexican coastal cities. His account of the navy duty not only is consistent with all the official reports but is used by historians as an original source for their analyses of U.S. Navy activity during the Mexican War.

> I was thrilled! I was up betimes, next morning, forthwith summoned the gunner to prepare me revolving pistols, cartridges, cutlasses, and other murderous instruments, and sent for my lazy lout of a boy, directed him to pack up my kit in double quick time, as I was off to the "Halls of the Montezumas!"[14]

3

Off to the "Halls of the Montezumas!"
U.S. Army Duty

The Halls of the Montezumas! "There was romance in the idea, which fired my imagination," Semmes wrote. The secretary of the navy instructed Commodore Perry to send a special messenger to Mexico City to secure the release of Passed Midshipman R. C. Rogers. Rogers, it will be recalled, had been captured while serving under Semmes's command aboard the *Somers*. Reports indicated that he was being treated as a spy; the U.S. government lodged a protest and demanded his exchange. Perry selected Semmes to deliver that message to the Mexican authorities. "I was but too happy . . . to be made the means of wresting my late gallant subordinate from the clutches of the enemy."[1]

Semmes was up early the next morning and immediately ordered the gunner to prepare his revolving pistols, cartridges, "and other murderous implements." As an attendant and "sort of a sub-aide-de-camp," Semmes chose a young seaman from the ship's crew, Francis Seymour. Seymour was a "shrewd and courageous lad of about nineteen, who accompanied me in all my wanderings, passed through various adventures 'on his own hook' beside, and finally returned with me to the squadron." Indeed, Seymour was a resourceful and faithful attendant to Semmes during all of their shared adventures with the army.

Perry sent a letter with Semmes addressed to "Major-General Winfield Scott, General-in-Chief, U.S. Army," in which he requested the general's cooperation in sending Semmes to the seat of the Mexican government, if possible, to secure the release of Rogers.

Armed with Perry's letter and with the pistols and cutlasses, Semmes on April 28, 1847, left the squadron for the duration of the war. He and Seymour went to Vera Cruz to secure horses and "other necessaries" for the trip to Scott's headquarters in Jalapa. He was given a "detachment of twenty

mounted Tennessee rifles" as an escort to protect him from Mexican guer-
rilla action. He dined that night at the Casa de Diligencias, operated by
"a surly old Scotsman who had scarcely regained his good humor since
the bombardment." His table was crowded with officers; the old Scotsman
seemed to be making up for what little he had suffered by reaping a rich
harvest from his late enemies, "all of whom he charged war prices, and to
whom he gave war fare."

Semmes and Seymour, with their escort, departed the next day, April 29,
1847, at about 5:00 P.M., riding "heavy war cavalry horses, with warlike-
looking holsters in front of our saddles, cutlasses girded around our waists,
and a bountiful supply of *serapes,* blankets fancifully figured, and edibles
for the road." In the village of Santa Fe they overtook a wagon train that
Semmes and his soldiers were to escort to Scott's headquarters.

Semmes had scarcely dismounted his horse "when a villain stole one of
my revolvers, which I had carelessly laid down on a bench." Semmes seized
the man and made him return the revolver. "I am sorry to add that the
scamp was one of our Anglo-Saxon teamsters, picked up, perhaps, some-
where in the 'Bowery.' " Out of consideration for his blood, Semmes released
him with a sharp reprimand, "enjoining him to remember for the future,
however, his long and honorable descent all the way from the Danish pirates,
who were robbers of land only." Before falling asleep that night, Semmes
jotted down, with the aid of candlelight, "these veritable memoirs," a habit
he followed throughout the war.

The next morning Seymour brought Semmes a steaming cup of coffee
and a cigar, both of which he enjoyed. As they rode slowly, because of the
wagon train, Semmes noted various aspects of nature—trees, streams, and
the landscape. Indeed, little escaped his eye; his mind was like a sponge,
absorbing all that he saw. Herds of cattle were grazing quietly in the distance, contrasting with the ugly reminders that an army had recently passed
through the area: dead mules and horses, broken army wagons on the side of
the road. He was impressed, unfavorably, by the debris of army quartermaster property scattered along the way. He attributed this loss of army material
to "the incompetency of wagon-masters, the carelessness and drunkenness
of teamsters, and the general want of organization and accountability in
the corps." He concluded that such waste and carelessness with government
military property "was one of the penalties which republics pay, more than
other forms of government" for the lack of standing armies; "the penalty,"
he concluded, "is no doubt the lesser evil of the two."

The wagon train passed two "fair Jalapenas, mother and daughter," riding without escort. He asked them, in his fluent Spanish, if they were not

afraid "to travel on a road infested with the *barbaros del norte*." One of the women replied that she was not, which he noted "was highly gratifying to me, as an American." In stark contrast, soon after leaving the women, Semmes's train passed the dead body of an American soldier, "who had been killed in a skirmish a few days before, while escorting a train." Semmes's writing style frequently relied upon such stark contrasts as the beautiful and gracious woman and the soldier's dead body. They camped that night, still only eighteen miles from Vera Cruz. Semmes was not well, yet he and Seymour slept on the ground with only the interlacing limbs of small trees for protection, and Semmes slept as "comfortably as I could have done in my state room, aboard the *Raritan*." The sailor, it seems, was becoming acclimated to the soldier's life-style.

As they passed through small villages, Semmes found that he, or rather his horse, "was an object of admiration." The mount was

> indeed a monster, standing, I am afraid to say, how many hands high, and with legs little less in circumference than those of an elephant. . . . Sitting astride his monster, with a most uncomfortable expansion of crotch, armed with a small battery of artillery in front, and having a huge roll of blankets and pea-jackets strapped on behind, the Indians would gather around me as children are wont to do around an elephant. . . . They invariably ran out to me with the largest and coolest calabashes of water, and senored me with a deference of which my horse would, no doubt, have been exceedingly proud, could he have understood what was going on.[2]

This humorous sense of the ridiculous served Semmes well during the remainder of the Mexican War and indeed throughout his life.

On the third evening the train stopped at the Puente Nacional, an arched stone bridge that spanned the confluence of two rivers, which then formed the Antigua River. A hacienda owned by Santa Anna, "an elegant stone mansion, with tesselated marble floors," was situated near the Antigua River. Semmes and his Tennessee riflemen spent the night there. "Toward sunset, although still quite feverish, I descended the steep bank of the river in the rear of my new quarters, and enjoyed a most luxurious bath in the classic Antigua; a stream which has been indissolubly associated, by the pen of Cortez, with the renown of the conquerors." Even though the house was nearly stripped of furniture, Semmes found an elegant mahogany bedstead in which to sleep. But he was awakened at four in the morning by the Tennesseans riding their horses through the marble halls of "Santa Anna." That morning, being only twenty-eight miles from Jalapa, Semmes abandoned the wagon train and with the guard of riflemen rode on to the city.[3]

On the road to Jalapa, Semmes passed a burial plot for American soldiers who had died in the battle at Cerro Gordo. The poor fellows in the unmarked graves had already been forgotten. "The shout of glory, that had gone up in the United States, over the battle of Cerro Gordo, recked not of them. They were of the humble rank and file, who bear the brunt of war, and are crushed beneath the wheels of the chieftain's car, to which they are harnessed!"[4]

Despite his aversion to war and death, Semmes could not restrain himself from riding over the extensive battle area of what has come to be called the battle of Cerro Gordo. He described the battle in detail and in more understandable language than most military historians have presented it. For a navy officer, he had a remarkable grasp of land warfare.[5]

From Cerro Gordo Semmes and his Tennessee guards rode toward Jalapa. For two miles just before entering the city, the roadway was lined by trees and vines, loaded with flowers. The song of birds greeted the ear and the sweetness of the blossoms refreshed the air; even the rough riflemen were impressed by the experience, and Semmes, referring to his 1844 trip to Mexico City, remarked that "although I had beheld it before, I too enjoyed it with a keen relish."[6]

During the two weeks the Americans had been in the city, Jalapa had become "almost Americanized." American merchants and tradesmen of all sorts had descended upon the city of five to six thousand inhabitants. There was an American newspaper and an American dramatic troupe. Semmes hardly recognized the city he had last visited in 1844. He drew word-pictures of the scene: "American soldiers swaggering with lighted cigars in their mouths, or squirting their tobacco juice from side to side," while the "inhabitants wormed their way timidly between and around their more robust conquerors." American "teamsters and volunteer horsemen were the constant theme of admiration among the natives—the men with their stalwart limbs, unshaven and uncombed beards and hair, slouchy dress, and devil-may-care air, presenting no mean personification of the barbarians whom they believed them to be—and the horses, by contrast with their little barbs, seeming to be weird steeds, befitting only such gigantic and uncouth riders."

The navy officer did not fail to comment upon the Mexican women of the middle and upper classes; many had fled before the arrival of the Americans, but enough remained for Semmes to compare them with American women in towns the size of Jalapa: The fair Jalapenas want "the fairness and freshness of our women. To be sure, their soft black eyes, that

'Now melt into love, now madden to crime' and their hair
'Whose glossy black would bring
Shame to the raven's wing,'

are beautiful features; but nothing can compensate, in female beauty, for the absence of the lily and the rose."[7] These comments on female beauty cannot compare in detailed description with those of the woman in prayer in the Cuban or Dominican cathedral. During the *Porpoise* cruise he seldom mentioned the men he saw in Cuba or the Dominican Republic. In Jalapa, however, he was struck by the fact that "while the women were sufficiently robust in figure, and well developed, the men were puny and delicate looking."

Semmes in great detail described the public bathhouses, where he went upon arrival in the city to wash away the dust and dirt of the four-day trip from Vera Cruz. He also visited the clothes-washing establishments in the city as well as a British-owned cotton cloth factory, both of which he described in detail. He commented unfavorably on the Mexican internal tariff on imported raw cotton as well as cotton cloth.[8] He favorably contrasted the fresh and bracing air with that of the seashore. Jalapa, the capital of the state of Vera Cruz, had "a large and commodious stone" palace as the residence of the governor; it was, however, now occupied by General Scott as both his residence and his army headquarters.

Semmes, on the night of his arrival, visited the general and presented his letter of credence from Commodore Perry. The general "did not appear at all pleased" with the navy officer's mission. He told Semmes that Perry had no need to send an officer on such a mission, that a letter would have sufficed to arouse the general's interest in the passed midshipman, that he did not want to establish more than one line of communication with the Mexican government, and that he intended personally to be that channel. Semmes replied that he had his orders from his own superior and could not very well return to Vera Cruz without having fulfilled those orders. Although Scott declined for the present to give Semmes an escort so the navy officer could fulfill his navy instructions, the general did suggest that Semmes might remain with the army and that when Scott should advance nearer to Mexico City "it might be convenient for him to put me in communication with the minister to whom my despatches were directed." This suggestion opened the door for Semmes's army career during the Mexican War.

At about the same time, N. P. Trist, chief clerk of the U.S. State Department, arrived at Scott's headquarters "with full powers, as commissioner, to negotiate a treaty of peace whenever the Mexican government might be so inclined." Scott overreacted to this second official desiring to establish communication with the enemy, and the famous Scott-Trist controversy developed. Indeed, Scott reacted more strongly to Trist than he did to Semmes.[9] Although Scott and Trist shortly reconciled their differences, Scott and Semmes did not do so. Both men were stubborn. Semmes's attitude toward Scott as expressed in his memoirs is one of consistent criticism. The navy officer was not a forgiving antagonist.

The Scott-Semmes antagonism grew as the Scott-Trist antagonism developed. Scott sent an aide-de-camp to inform Semmes that he "might return to the squadron" as Scott "was resolved not to permit me to hold any communication with the Mexican government, as he was the only proper channel through which any negotiation for the exchange of prisoners should pass." Semmes was probably more articulate than the general. He first applied for an interview with him but was denied it. So he wrote a letter on May 8, 1847, in response to the verbal communication from Scott. It was reasonable, respectful, and forceful. He reviewed their conversation, stated that the president had charged Perry with a mission, and Perry had chosen him, Semmes, to fulfill the president's order. By denying him the means to do so, Semmes implied, Scott was negating a directive of the president of the United States.

The next day Semmes received a long and conciliatory response from Scott. The general for the first time informed Semmes that Rogers was no longer being held as a spy but as a simple prisoner of war and that he was free on parole to move about in Mexico City. He did not state when he learned these facts concerning Rogers, but he did cite Mexican officers captured at the battle of Cerro Gordo, thus he probably had known them when he had talked with Semmes. Scott also mentioned that Trist would soon be in Jalapa and also would ask Scott to place him in communication with the Mexican government. He would not forward any communication to the Mexican government until he was nearer to Mexico City; at that time he would forward any communication that Semmes or Trist might deem proper. "In the meantime, you can remain here, return to Commodore Perry's squadron, or advance with the army, as may seem to you best."

Semmes, of course, did not want to return to the boring blockade duty. Soon after arriving in Jalapa, he had taken living quarters with two officers of Scott's quartermaster department, a wise choice of a man who loved good food and good wines. Captains Erwin and Wayne were living in the customhouse, "a commodious but unfurnished stone building." The two captains, of equal army rank to Semmes's navy lieutenancy, did all in their power to make him comfortable: "I soon paid them the compliment of feeling very much at home." He continued for three months to share their mess (i.e., quarters and food). Louis A. Hargous, an American merchant from Vera Cruz, joined them in the customhouse and contributed to their "pleasure and instruction" by his fund of information related to the country and by his intimate acquaintance with the Mexican character. Monsieur Auguste, formerly with Hargous's kitchen in Vera Cruz, had accompanied Hargous to Jalapa and had charge of the men's commissariat. Auguste, who dressed like a dandy, wore his saber, and twirled his mustache at all the pretty girls he met, was offended to be called a cook—he was an *artiste gastronomique.* "We found him a very important man in the campaign." Semmes and Seymour remained with Erwin and Wayne for three months.

Semmes criticized Scott for remaining in Jalapa too long. He maintained that Scott should have moved to Puebla in late April when Santa Anna had no force to oppose him. As it was, Scott did not reach Puebla until May 15, 1847, twenty-seven days after the battle of Cerro Gordo. Scott maintained that he had lost soldiers who had enlisted for one year and who returned to the United States and that he had to await reinforcements from Vera Cruz. Semmes's point was that had Scott moved before the volunteers left, he would have had the same number of troops as he finally took to Puebla. As it was, Scott was unable to increase the size of his army and finally fought his way to Mexico City with the same number of men he had at Jalapa and Puebla. In this matter, Semmes seems to have been right and Scott wrong.

Before leaving Jalapa, Scott issued a proclamation offensive to the Mexican people. In an effort to rally the "people," Scott criticized the Mexican government for the army leaders trying to create an atmosphere for peace throughout the population of Mexico. But, as Semmes wrote, five-sixths of the Mexicans could not read, had no vote, and thus had no influence over the political leaders of the country. Scott's proclamation, aimed at the masses of Mexicans, reached only those he was criticizing. Napoleon, Semmes maintained, "was the only modern general whose proclamations will bear reading. His never exceeded a half dozen lines." Scott's proclamation, Semmes argued, was "egotistical in tone, and in its want of tact simply re-opened the sores of the Mexican body-politic [the one-sixth of the population]." Then Semmes created a political axiom: "Nations, like individuals, do not like to be told of their faults, and least of all, do they like to be told of them by their enemies."[10]

On May 14, General Scott finally received the additional troops and supplies for which he had been waiting. Semmes and Seymour, by virtue of their mess arrangements, belonged to the general's staff and therefore were to move "in his shadow." The caterer of their mess relieved them of all trouble "on the score of subsistence"; so Seymour had no duties but to pack "the tin pots and forked sticks" they had used on the road from Vera Cruz. He had only "to buy himself an extra plug of tobacco, reeve a new lanyard for his jack-knife, and take leave of his washer woman, and we were ready for the road."

It was Sunday, and as they left Jalapa the church bells calling the good people to mass, the army bugles, and the ironclad hooves of the army horses over the paved streets "presented, in strange contrast, the sounds of war with those of 'peace and good-will among men.' " Once out of the city, the long line of soldiers marched through a beautiful but rugged countryside. At first it was only hilly, then it became mountainous, at times even dangerous. On the second day of the march, they passed the mountain peak called the Cofre of Perote. Semmes greeted it "as an old friend," for he "had often gazed upon it from the deck of the *Somers*" when he had been blockading Vera Cruz. They spent the second night of the march in the town of Perote. The group was quartered in a home where only the old housekeeper greeted them, the family being absent. At first she was frightened by the American soldiers, but they soon put her at ease. "Seymour, who was not sure but the old beldam might have a pretty daughter, was the principal agent in this process of dulcification." Auguste was happy to find a well-ordered kitchen, and he prepared a fine evening meal. After describing the fortress of Perote, and deciding it was used more to intimidate the populace than to protect it, Semmes concluded that "the sooner the plowshare is passed over it, and all similar structures in Mexico, the better it will be for the people."

The travelers were less fortunate the next forty-eight hours in their marches and overnight accommodations. The scenery was boring by day and the facilities uncomfortable by night. Finally, they approached the city of Puebla, anticipated by sight of the 17,700-foot mountain known as Popocatapetl. But first they stopped at the village of Amosoque, with about two thousand inhabitants, most of whom worked in the manufacture of spurs. Semmes and Seymour, among others, purchased new spurs in this village. Seymour chose the biggest he could find; Semmes was not sure but that Seymour was beginning to "ape the air of a dragoon." After traveling through an uninteresting countryside, they caught their first view of Puebla "from a slight eminence, some six miles from the city." It was not an imposing sight, "the city being situated in a plain, and but a small portion of it being visible. Standing in the midst of an almost boundless plain, and at the base, as it appears at first sight, of the giant volcano Popocatapetl, it dwindles to a mere point in the landscape, and becomes comparatively insignificant." The American flag floated proudly from the steeple of "Our Lady of Loretto."

General William J. Worth had taken possession of the church; "the walls were lined with our troops, looking down upon us in an affectionate welcome, as we rode past." Generals Worth and John A. Quitman rode out to greet General Scott and the troops, who then marched down a tree-lined causeway and passed through one of the seven *garitas*, or internal custom-houses, "that serve in Puebla, or elsewhere in Mexico, to harass and destroy the inland commerce of the country." After riding for half a day on dusty roads and beneath a scorching sun, the newcomers welcomed the sight of "tree-lined avenues, green-sward, and the running streams of water." An infantry regiment met them to serve as an honor guard and to greet the commander in chief. "We were now in the heart of the enemy's territory and in secure possession of the second city of the republic." The newcomers were struck by Puebla's "great size, the imposing appearance of its well-built streets, the splendor of its shops, the rattling of its coaches—a thing new to us in Mexico—the general air of business and activity everywhere prevalent; and above all, with the picturesque *coup d'oeil* of both town and people—the balconies and house-tops being crowded with spectators."[11]

Semmes immediately thought of the area as it had been during the days of Cortez: "In a letter to Emperor Charles V, Cortez described the city of Tlascala as being superior to Granada in Spain, in point of size and population, in the style of its houses, and in the abundance of the necessaries of life." The people worked hard, fought off the city of Mexico, and stubbornly maintained their independence while other nations around them were being subdued by the all-powerful Aztecs under the lead of the great Montezuma. "Those once populous cities on the plain of Puebla have long ceased to exist, and the modern Mexican plants his corn and his barley on the graves of the departed generations." As he looked upon the Pueblan plain, the young navy officer mused: "If civilization is to be measured by the aggregate of happiness it produces, we may question whether the new civilization is superior to the old."[12]

Semmes then analyzed the contemporary condition of the cotton worker in Mexico. Using statistics provided by the Mexican government, which gave the wage earned by the worker, he concluded that the average cotton worker in Mexico, through indebtedness to the landowner, was not better off than the slave in the United States. He reported also that in Yucatan he more than once was "applied to by likely young Indians, to buy them . . . for the small sum of thirty or forty dollars." This system of financial dependency is called *mozo*. His figures and argument are convincing, but he presented them to justify slavery in the Southern states of the United States:

This is the boasted freedom of the Mexican soil, about which there has
been so much senseless declamation in our congress, since the conclusion
of the war. The well-fed and well-cared for dependent of the southern
estate, with us, is infinitely superior, in point of both physical and moral
condition to the *mozo* of the Mexican hacienda. The "hewers of wood and
drawers of water" are slaves everywhere, as I have found; and whether the
slave is so, *lege scripta* or *lege necessitatis,* is, as the lawyers say, a distinction
without a difference.[13]

Why did Raphael Semmes, a seaman and a lawyer, and not a landowner,
so desecrate his fine book, published in 1851, by this defense of slavery? At
the time he was writing, he rented a house in Mobile, Alabama, and had no
more than two female household slaves. He had no vested interest in maintaining the institution. Perhaps it was because he had been born to slaveholding parents; perhaps it was because he had been raised by a slaveholding
uncle. Or perhaps it was because he sincerely believed in the states' rights
interpretation of the United States Constitution. Indeed, as the reader will
see, he concluded this book on Mexico with a strong justification of a federal system based on the rights of the individual states in all political and
social activity except international diplomacy and commerce. Finally, he
was writing this section during the sectional crisis concerning the expansion
of slavery in those territories acquired during the Mexican War. Did he add
this material on the Mexican *mozo* system, and compare it unfavorably with
American slavery, in an effort to influence American public opinion? It is a
possibility.

Finally, this part of the book departs from Semmes's stated purpose of
writing about the Mexican War as he experienced it. It speculates on what
Semmes called the "politico-economic light," which he distinguished from
"a social view" of people's experiences, and it does so at a time when historians had not yet divided their concepts of history into such specific areas of
study. To the extent that Semmes made that distinction, he was a historian
ahead of his time.

He was not, however, a "scientific" historian; he did not base his descriptions upon scientific research. Furthermore, his section on the "social views"
of Puebla are more descriptive than analytical. He described the life-style
of each level of society in Puebla: the kinds of houses they lived in, the kinds
of clothes they wore, the sort of work they did.[14] He derived these descriptions from reflections on his observations.

He did have a good sense of humor. The streets of Puebla were wide and
well paved, but they had no names. Each square was independent of the
others and had its own name. Semmes lived at the army's quartermaster

headquarters "in the *Calle del Reboso*," that is, the block or square he lived in was called that name. The adjoining blocks each had different names, each unrelated to the other. "A better system for bewildering a stranger, could not have been devised." The system made it useless to ask directions, he decided, so he

> scoured it in every direction, for the first few days after my arrival, and having mapped it out in my head, sailed after by well-known landmarks, as church steeples, etc. When Seymour was along, I generally made him "take the departure" and "keep the reckoning." He soon became expert in this kind of navigation, and would sometimes say to me as we returned home, "We have passed the steeple of San Jose, sir, and made the *Cruces* on the starboard-bow; we're not far from the *Reboso*."[15]

As usual, Semmes described the cathedral in great detail, using proper architectural and religious terms. He also visited and described the bishop's palace, which had a library of more than 50,000 volumes, chiefly on religion, but with many volumes on "history, law, medicine, the exact sciences, and the *belles lettres*." While an old priest was showing him the books, Semmes tried to "look wise, and like wise men held my peace."

The upper social class of people hardly left their homes for the first few days of the American occupation. Then as their fear of the Americans declined, they gradually began to emerge and to walk the streets, "the women even gaining courage to decorate themselves in their evening costumes, and to look with eyes of evident admiration, upon the comely and manly forms of our younger officers, whom they could not but contrast favorably with their more puny husbands and beaux."

Semmes wrote that "no women are more kindhearted or more full of the amiable sensibilities of the sex than the Mexican. Perfectly feminine in character," he wrote, "they are indeed the vine to cling around the oak, which nature designed the sex to be. They would be shocked at the idea of holding public meetings, or discussing, in open forum, the equal rights of women, as unsexed females sometimes do in other countries."

On the other hand, Semmes considered the women of the lower class to have no virtue. He frequently saw girls at the age of thirteen or fourteen carrying their infants through the streets. He considered these girls "thus early reduced to a life of toil and hardship to be in an infinitely worse condition than the female slaves on our southern plantations, who have masters to feed and take care of their infants." From a purely materialistic point of view, he was probably correct.

Scott and his army stayed in Puebla for three months. During that time

Semmes remained attached to Scott's staff. He sometimes dined with Scott and the various officers the general invited to dinner. On the occasion of one such dinner, Semmes drew word pictures of the general officers present: They all seemed to have positive characteristics of personal and military virtues, especially General Worth, and the young navy officer mellowed somewhat in his views of the army commander, asserting that Scott was fair in his treatment of the officers and men in the army. He averred, also, that Scott's administration of the city was fair and profitable for the natives, and that opinion is affirmed by recent historians. He would later change his opinion of the commanding general.

On July 11, "General Scott at length made a movement in behalf of our unfortunate prisoners."[16] Semmes failed to mention that this act was exactly what Scott had promised he would do. The general wrote to the Mexican president, proposing an exchange of Passed Midshipman Rogers and three army officers, including the future politician and diplomat Captain Cassius M. Clay. Semmes was appointed, along with three army officers, to ride out with an escort of two companies of dragoons, flying a white flag of truce, to present the note to the Mexican president. Despite the excitement aroused by a chance to fulfill his assigned task, Semmes, as was his habit, made notes on the beauty of the countryside. The emissaries rode from Puebla into a beautiful and fertile agricultural area. They passed over a stream that, Semmes noted, emptied into the Pacific Ocean. This was the first stream the American army in central Mexico had crossed that fed into that ocean "whither our empire was so rapidly tending; and many were the reflections to which it gave rise. . . . Our small navy on that side of the continent [the west coast of North America] . . . had already added the Californias to our vast domaine, and our flag would no doubt soon encircle the globe as that of the greatest commercial nation of the earth." That reflection, as Semmes rode across a stone bridge, is the most clear indication in all his writings that he was, indeed, an adherent to the popular notion in the United States of Manifest Destiny. But avid reader that he was, Semmes also had another thought, a historical one: "It was near this stone bridge, that we were crossing, that the renowned Cortez had halted for the night, on his march . . . in 1519, a century before the pioneers of the race which was now overrunning the country, had landed at Jamestown and Plymouth!"

They spent the first night at the Rio Frio, or Cold River, at an elevation of 10,119 feet, where there was an inn, run by an "old German," and a cluster of huts. Because the inn did not have enough space for all the officers, they cast dice to determine who would spend the night in its relative comfort. Although usually an "unlucky dog" at gambling, Semmes won and spent the night in a bed—except that he was aroused by what seemed to be "an infernal shout of demons." He arose and carefully opened the door through which the sounds appeared to come. To his astonishment, he "beheld a long table spread with viands, and covered with bottles and glasses, and our host about 'half-seas-over,' holding a midnight revel with about a dozen of our dragoons," all of them speaking German as well as did the innkeeper. To his astonishment among the gamboling soldiers was Seymour, singing the "exuberant praises of 'Faderland' " and enjoying the good food and drink. Semmes and Seymour would, within a short time, spend another night with their jolly German host.

The next day the American detachment did, finally, overtake a Mexican general. Semmes and the commander of the small force, Captain Philip Kearny, U.S. Army, met with him and were informed that they could not proceed to Mexico City. They gave the Mexican their dispatches and took their leave. In another day they were back in Puebla: "Although we had a very agreeable excursion, like the luckless suitor in court, 'we took nothing by our petition' in the matter of exchanging prisoners—Santa Anna never deigning to give any reply to General Scott's communication, until we had given him another 'licking.' "

Upon his return from the unsuccessful effort to set up an exchange of prisoners, Semmes, in the company of Major General Gideon J. Pillow and a number of other officers, rode out from Puebla about six miles to visit the pyramid of Cholula. The pyramid, he wrote, has

> an appearance of a natural mound . . . covered by a growth of shrubs and forest trees. It is truncated, and its apex is crowned by a picturesque gothic temple, embowered by venerable and fondiferous trees, from all appearance, from two to three centuries old. This small and unpretending gothic temple seated on the top of the pyramid of Cholula was to my mind the most befitting place for the worship of the Most High, I had ever beheld.

But the attraction this place had for Semmes was not only religious; he also related it to Cortez's massacre of the Cholula inhabitants. As Semmes tells the story, the natives pretended to welcome Cortez and his soldiers but in reality planned to lull the conquistador into a sense of false security and then slaughter the Spaniards while they slept. But Cortez was warned by a friendly Mexican and countered the natives' plans by laying a trap for them. Cortez's troops, although outnumbered, carried out their chief's bloody scheme successfully, killing most of the inhabitants. Semmes, for the only time in his memoirs, criticized his hero for this bloody massacre of the Mexicans.[17]

A few days after the excursion to Cholula, Semmes was surprised as well as gratified to learn that "Passed-Midshipman Rogers was at the headquarters of the general-in-chief." Rogers had made his escape from Mexico City two days earlier and with the help of a guide found his way to Puebla. Although Semmes's "mission was, thus, suddenly brought to a close," neither he nor Rogers intended to return to the squadron that was still blockading the port of Vera Cruz. Because General Scott's communication with Vera Cruz had been cut off for some time, he allowed them to remain at the army headquarters "awaiting some opportune moment, [to] seek some proper position for ourselves in the ranks of our military brethren."

Scott slowly but surely increased the size of his army during the four weeks he remained in Puebla. By the second week of August 1847, his forces numbered about 13,000 men. About the same time, Lieutenant Raphael Semmes, U.S. Navy, was attached to the staff of General Worth as an aide-de-camp, and young Rogers was appointed to the same post in the headquarters of General Pillow. Semmes's desire to march to the Halls of the Montezumas now had an official blessing. Still, in his moment of exhilaration, Semmes found time, once again, to criticize Scott: Scott's marching force was only about 11,500 men because he had to leave a garrison in Puebla as well as a large number of invalids in the hospitals. "Thus," Semmes wrote, "after waiting four months, and giving the enemy ample time to recruit and strengthen himself, he was but little, if any, better prepared for offensive operations than he had been before he discharged the volunteers at Jalapa, and by that act, lost the glorious opportunity of seizing by a *coup de main,* the enemy's capital!" It was the same theme he had played when he criticized Scott for remaining in Jalapa instead of immediately joining Worth in Puebla. His argument then had been that, after Cerro Gordo, Santa Anna had no army with which to defend the capital city; now, five months after the battle of Cerro Gordo, Santa Anna had succeeded in assembling a sizable force. Semmes concluded that Scott had gained no numerical advantage by his delays in Jalapa and Puebla.[18] He probably was right.

One of his first duties as an aide to General Worth was to deliver a message to Colonel T. P. Ransom, with whom, years earlier, Semmes had been a shipmate aboard the frigate *Constellation.* "When we confronted each other—we had not met since [serving together aboard ship]—I, with my heavy cavalry sabre and immense Mexican spurs, and he, in the jaunty uniform of a colonel of infantry, which became him so well, we were so amused by the mutual transformation, that our first salutation was a hearty laugh." Fortune, Semmes concluded, had played a strange trick on both of them, transforming both sailors into soldiers "and sending us forth on a campaign in the valley of Mexico, which had, up to this period, been so much of a *terra incognita*, as to be associated in our minds with little else than Cortez and Montezuma." Unfortunately, Semmes's former shipmate would die in the battle of Chapultepec, almost at the gates of Mexico City.[19]

With the assignment to Worth's staff, Semmes became an even more ardent supporter of Worth. In his eyes his new commander could do no wrong. Semmes wrote, just before the advance from Puebla began, that the controversy that later developed between the two generals began with Worth's successful administration of Puebla prior to Scott's arrival in that city. Worth's guarantee of the protection of the Pueblans' life, religion, and property, Semmes maintained, enabled him to govern the city of some 70,000 persons with his "handful of men." He claimed that "Any narrow, military reasoning based upon technicalities, which could be brought in opposition to this liberal and enlightened policy pursued by General Worth, was unworthy of the commander-in-chief of a great army." Indeed, Scott so criticized Worth's actions, some of which were, indeed, bizarre, that the latter requested and received a Court of Inquiry. The court censored Worth despite his strong defense, and no reconciliation occurred between the two generals. "Major-General Scott," Semmes wrote, "seemingly could not realize the fact that his former aide-de-camp, was now fifty-five years of age, and, like himself, a major-general in the army of the United States."[20] Semmes continued his criticisms of Scott throughout the remainder of the war.

Scott finally issued orders for his divisions to begin their move, in twenty-four-hour intervals, toward Mexico City. On August 7, 1847, Brigadier General David E. Twiggs led his division of regulars out of Puebla, on the road to Mexico City, and was followed the next day by General Quitman's 4th Division of Volunteers. Then it was General Worth's turn to move:

> We were astir at an early hour, at "headquarters" where the servants and orderlies, before daylight had been running hither and thither, packing trunks, and stowing baggage-wagons; and very soon the rumbling of artillery in the streets, and the tramp of infantry, showed that our forces were marshalling in front of the general's quarters, to await his commands. We were in the saddle after a hasty breakfast at seven o'clock.

Semmes noted that the huge crowd of Pueblans who gathered, despite the previous departure of two divisions, was "so great that we could scarcely move." He attributed this grand send-off to the fact that Worth's division had been in Puebla two weeks longer than the other ones and the people had that much more time to become acquainted with the soldiers, "and many were the apparently cordial leave-takings between them and the soldiery." Semmes did not mention the possibility that the Pueblans simply were happy to see the Americans leaving their city. Instead, he reveled in the mountain air and the scenery: "The morning was bright; and as we passed out at the *garita de Mexico*, into the open plain, all nature seemed arrayed in the sweetest smiles of summer, presenting to our enchanted view, green waving fields, and richly carpeted meadows, over which were wafted on the morning air, the dewy fragrance of the young grass, and perfume of the shrub and flower."

The division covered only ten miles the first day due to the mountainous terrain; the heat and alternately the rain also slowed it the following day. On the third day, however, the weather was cooler and the scenery even more beautiful: The division made double their previous marches and encamped at the Rio Frio, where Seymour and Semmes had made friends with the "old German" innkeeper during their futile trip to arrange an exchange of prisoners. The soldiers had to sleep in the cold rain, but fires of chopped pine enabled them to pass "a tolerable night," Semmes wrote. "We of the staff quartered ourselves on my old friend the German. . . . He prepared an excellent supper for us, and brought forth from his cellar an extra bottle or two of old Rhenish. His young *Dutch* friend, Seymour, was equally well taken care of."

The next morning, the division marched early "as a second army of conquest, winding its way over the same heights, from which had fluttered the pinnons of Cortez." They crossed the Anahuac ridge of the Cordilleras mountains, "the most magnificent portion of this stupendous range of mountains, from Cape Horn to the frozen oceans of the north." After climbing to a height of 10,400 feet, some five miles from Rio Frio, they stopped on a plateau "to breathe the wearied men and animals." From that vantage point they "caught their first glimpse of the great valley of Mexico. . . . We seemed to be looking upon an immense inland sea, surrounded by ranges of stupendous mountains, crested by snow and clouds." From that summit level they descended about five miles, and when near the foot of the mountain they could see the lake and town of Chalco, beyond which and to the left they could see the encampments of Generals Twiggs and Quitman—"their white tents looking like mere specs in the great valley." General Quitman's division was camped at a hacienda called Buena Vista, and Twiggs's was about three miles closer to Mexico City in the small town of Ayotla, located on the north shore of Lake Chalco, and about fifteen miles from Mexico City. General Scott's headquarters were with Twiggs's division in Ayotla. "There lay our countrymen," Semmes wrote, "numbering in all but about four thousand men, in the presence of all the Mexican hosts, numbering twenty-five thousand!" Santa Anna, he asserted, could easily have destroyed General Scott's and General Twiggs's divisions before either Pillow or Worth could have come to their defense. "If General Santa Anna had been a Napoleon, the history of this campaign might have worn a different aspect."[21]

General Worth's division passed through the encampment of Quitman's division, halting a moment for "hurried enquiry and congratulation." Worth turned southward from Buena Vista; his division encamped along the east coast of Lake Chalco, in the small town of Chalco.

This movement of Scott's army without serious incident or loss was rather remarkable. The three divisions, fully manned and armed, marched across mountains as high as 10,400 feet, taking with them their horse-drawn cannon and mule-drawn supply wagons. The soldiers marched alongside the wagons and cannon with their weapons and full packs on roads that, according to Semmes, at the highest points were little more than foot trails without railings. Men and animals arrived before Mexico City tired and worn, and they encamped within twenty-five miles of their destination without any reported casualties of men or animals.

Perhaps even more remarkable was Santa Anna's failure to oppose the Americans. Semmes noted on several occasions that a particularly steep defile would have been a perfect spot for the Mexicans at least to delay if not destroy the wagon trains or even to impose severe casualties on the American soldiers. But the Mexicans obviously had determined to fight only at the city's walls and gates, trusting perhaps in the American reluctance to inflict harm on the civilian population of the city.

However, before any action against the enemy took place, Scott and Worth became involved in yet another controversy that eventually reached even into the White House in Washington.[22] Of course, Semmes, in his book, sided with Worth. According to the navy officer, the fault lay with Scott, who criticized Worth for taking the initiative in ordering a scouting expedition to determine the best route for the attack on Mexico City. As it turned out, Scott did follow the recommendations of Worth's scout, and later the two generals exchanged bitter letters that led Scott to imprison Worth for a short period of time. Worth appealed to the president of the United States. In this incident Semmes was correct in supporting General Worth because the secretary of the army, obeying a White House directive, eventually reprimanded Scott. The incident certainly did not enhance

Scott's chances of fulfilling his ambition to win a nomination for the presidency of the United States!

Scott at Ayotla first intended to attack directly along the Ayotla–Mexico City route (see map 1), but his scouts reported a strong Mexican force across the route at Peñón. Even in the midst of his controversy with Worth, Scott faced the military realities; he changed his mind and accepted Worth's recommended route of attack.

In the account of the battle of Mexico City, Semmes described primarily the role of Worth's division. But he also gave shorter accounts of the actions of the other divisions and of Scott's orders. His is a firsthand, eyewitness description of battles in which he participated, coupled with overviews of the strategy and tactics of the American army.

Semmes's first participation was as an observer in the Duncan reconnaissance that was the basic cause of the later Scott-Worth controversy. In his book, written during the period 1848–51, Semmes was careful to stress that he deserved no credit for the survey because he accompanied Colonel James Duncan merely as a guest. The road from Chalco moved southward, first to the small village of Chimalpa, thence to Ayocingo, "a small village containing some 1200 inhabitants . . . [lying] picturesquely at the base of a mountain range that circumscribes the western portion of the valley, and near the borders of the lake." The lake itself was no longer "the magnificent sheet of water surrounded by villages," as Cortez had seen it; "it was little else than an extensive marsh, intercepted in various directions by grass-grown canals, and natural channels, sufficient only for the passage of small boats." Three miles past Ayocingo, the terrain changed into a richly cultivated meadow, containing haciendas "with their extensive fields of corn, and rich pasture grounds, on which were quietly grazing numerous herds of cattle." The estates were "separated from each other, and crossed and recrossed, not by roads, but by canals." Along the banks of the canals was a complicated network of dikes constructed to guard against the overflow of the waters. "Rows of the willow and of the Lombardy poplar, with its tall and graceful cone, were planted on the dikes, forming avenues of great extent." The survey team also passed through a large olive grove, "the trees of which . . . grew to an immense size, and interlaced their wide-spreading branches, so as to exclude almost entirely the rays of the sun." Although the road was very rough in places, the engineers deemed it quite suitable for military use. The survey team did not travel the whole road: They had marched but twelve miles out of Chalco. Nonetheless, they returned to make a most favorable report. Hence it was on the report of twelve miles of roadway that the Scott-Worth controversy rested. And the navy lieutenant had seen and been a part of it all.

Except for a small force left to occupy the Mexican army at Peñón, the four divisions under Scott's command commenced the campaign against Mexico City by marching to the south of Lakes Chalco and Xochimilco, toward San Agustin, where Scott intended to make his headquarters. (See map 1.) Worth's division led the way; the first day they made only twelve miles from Chalco to the village of Tetelco. The general and his staff slept in the small town hall, "which had nothing to offer us in the way of accommodation, except good stabling for our horses, and walls and a dry roof for ourselves." After an hour's march the next morning they halted, climbed a small hill, "and had our first distinct view of the domes and steeples of Mexico [City], of the villages of San Augustin and Tacubaya, and of the intervening valley, teeming with beauty and luxuriance." They could even see the top of Peñón where "still fluttered the Mexican ensign, as if unaware of the great game of strategy which was being played."

They stopped for the night in a small village situated under a grove of olive trees, where they parked their wagons and bivouacked the men under the interlaced branches of the trees. The general and his staff, including Semmes, quartered themselves with the padre, who was also the village mayor. Many women and children lived with the mayor in his house; the women called him "Father"; but the children called him "by the more significant" appellation of "Uncle!" After spending a comfortable night, the division moved out at an early hour. About two miles short of San Agustin, their destination, they "had a full view of Mexico, at about the distance of eight miles." They moved on into San Agustin, meeting no opposition. Because the Mexican high command knew nothing about the road Worth and the others traveled on that day, the enemy was "astonished to find that we had passed over a route, with artillery and baggage, which he had deemed scarcely practicable for infantry." By that march, the Americans had solved the problems of facing the Mexican strong points of Peñón and Mexicalcingo, which had given them "so much anxiety in the beginning of the campaign."

Santa Anna learned of Scott's movements and countered them by sending his forces to Churubusco and San Antonio. The Americans at San Agustin were just nine miles from Mexico City, but Santa Anna's forces in San Antonio, about two miles north of San Agustin, and two miles further on toward the city in the village of Churubusco, effectively blocked an American move from San Agustin directly to Mexico City. General Worth ordered his engineers to reconnoiter Santa Anna's position at San Antonio, and General Scott ordered a survey of the road from San Agustin westward to determine the possibility of flanking Santa Anna's forces situated on the San Agustin causeway. Worth learned that "the enemy was posted in great strength at San Antonio, in our front, his defenses consisting of an extensive field work well supplied with heavy artillery. His right rested on the village and on an extensive field of lava." This lava field, according to Semmes, "had been poured down upon the plain in ages long past, by volcanoes now extinct, and which extended all the way to the mountains, thus occupying the space between the two roads, and forming a barrier against the approach of cavalry and artillery." Santa Anna's left flank extended to the marshy ground that was partially inundated, near the head of Lake Xochimilco. Thus it seemed that the enemy's left flank would be impossible to turn.

Captain Robert E. Lee, in the meantime, had surveyed the lava field, known as the Pedregal.[23] His report indicated that infantry could maneuver through the lava, but no artillery could possibly be transported through it. Semmes thought very highly of Captain Lee: "Endowed with a mind which has no superior in his corps, and possessing great energy of character, he examined, counseled, and advised, with a judgment, tact, and discretion worthy of all praise. His talent for topography was peculiar, and he seemed to receive impressions intuitively, which it cost other men labor to acquire." Captain James L. Mason, Worth's engineer officer, "though a very young man, was scarcely, if at all, Lee's inferior in this respect, and he early acquired the esteem and regard of General Worth."

The two engineer officers made their reports. Lee favored attacking the capital by the road diverging to the left. The only barrier there, he maintained, was the fortified post of Padierna, which he claimed could be carried with but little loss. Mason, however, preferred to open the main road to Mexico City by attacking Santa Anna's position at San Antonio, "with the bayonet, by a flank movement over the pedregal," directed against the Mexican right flank. Both opinions were well received by the generals, and both were partially acted upon.

The battle against the Mexicans occupying the strong position at Padierna began August 19. Scott used elements from the divisions of Quitman, Pillow, and Twiggs. The Mexican commander there, General Valencia, believing his position at Padierna to be invincible, refused to obey Santa Anna's order to fall back to San Angel. The Americans outflanked him and the next day routed Valencia's troops. The general fled the scene of warfare, never again to be heard from during the war. The road northward through San Angel to Churubusco was then opened to the Americans.

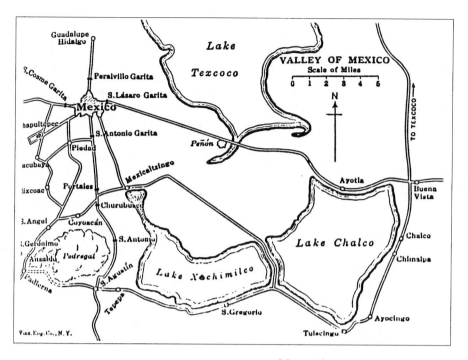

Map 1. Area around Mexico City

Meanwhile, Worth's troops began to probe the Mexicans in San Antonio. Scott, now at Coyoacan, sent Pillow on the road that bypassed Churubusco (see map 1) toward San Antonio, where he arrived at about the time Worth initiated a flanking movement through the Pedregal. Santa Anna, also at about the same time, ordered his troops at San Antonio to fall back to Churubusco.

Lieutenant Semmes participated in the rout of the Mexican army at San Antonio and described it in detail. Ever the seaman, he used naval imagery to describe the lava field:

> Passing through a small thicket of thorn and briers, that skirted the road, we soon entered upon the field of lava, over which it was impossible for any one but a footman to pass. I cannot better describe this pedregal, than by comparing it to the sea, which having been lashed into a fury by a tempest, had been suddenly transformed by the wand of an enchanter into stone. We picked our way . . . over and between these stony billows, and leaped from crest to crest, as a fissure would present itself. . . . We hurried forward and made a dash for the road in time to cut the enemy's retreating

column in two, driving General Bravo over the meadows in the direction
of Dolores, while the remainder made the best of its way to Churubusco.

"Nothing," he wrote, "could exceed the scene of confusion, which was here
witnessed. The magnificent causeway, lined on both sides by stately shade
trees, was filled as far as the eye could reach, by masses of the flying enemy."
He happened to see an amusing scene just as he came out onto the road:

> I saw lying prostrate, under one of the shade trees, a remarkably bulky-
> looking figure, in the uniform of a Mexican general, and a soldier of one
> of our companies standing by him. Supposing the officer to have been
> killed, I inquired of the soldier if this were the fact. "Oh, no sir," said he,
> "he is only a little out of wind, being a fat man; I have just run him down."
> The general afterward informed me, that in the hurry of the retreat, his
> aide-de-camp had run off with his horse, and that this was the cause of
> his being captured! A thing which, I suppose, could only occur in Mexico.

As soon as General Worth saw that the flanking movement had made
contact with the enemy, he ordered his remaining forces to make a frontal
attack on San Antonio; the two American forces linked together and entered the town only to find that the enemy had fled on the road to Churubusco: The battle of San Antonio was over, and the battle of Churubusco
was about to begin.

Scott, meanwhile, had initiated his army's march from Padierna to the
village of Churubusco, a distance of slightly less than five miles, and reached
it just as Worth's forces arrived after their victory at San Antonio. (See map
2.) Santa Anna then faced attacks from both north and south. Despite his
desperate situation, Santa Anna's army forced the Americans into one of
the most difficult battles of the Mexican valley. Semmes referred to it as
"the great battle of this eventful day in which all the forces on both sides
were engaged . . . the battles of Contreras [Padierna] and San Antonio being mere preludes." Both of the American approaches to the village were
strongly defended, "the greatest attention . . . being paid to the principal
route [because it led directly to Mexico City] which . . . was the one taken
by Worth." Semmes set the scene for his reader:

> Just in the rear of the scattering hamlets, known as the village of Chu-
> rubusco, there was a wide and deep canal [Rió de Churubusco] cutting the
> causeway and continuing over the plain perpendicularly to the road, a long
> distance to the [enemy's] left. This canal was bridged at the intersection
> with the causeway, and at the hither end, or head of the bridge, there was
> constructed a field work, known in military nomenclature, as a *tête de pont*.

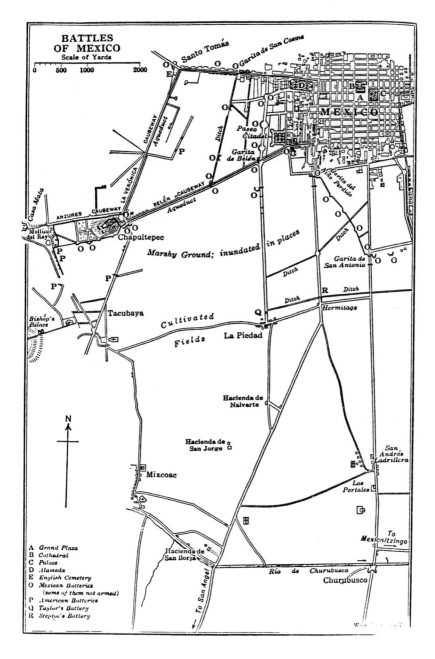

BATTLES
OF MEXICO
Scale of Yards

A Grand Plaza
B Cathedral
C Palace
D Alameda
E English Cemetery
O Mexican Batteries
   (some of them not armed)
P American Batteries
Q Taylor's Battery
R Steptoe's Battery

Map 2

> This work . . . was regularly bastioned and curtained, and surrounded in
> every part, except at the gorge, by a formidable wet ditch.[24]

The field work was armed by four cannon and protected on either side by
"dense masses of infantry" who were sheltered by dikes "extending along the
banks of the canal." Because the American troops were maneuvering on a
dead-level in front of the formidable defenses, "the bloody work which General Worth had before him" was readily obvious.

About three hundred yards to the Mexican right of the *tête de pont* was
the fortification of San Pablo that guarded the approach of General Scott's
troops. This fortification "consisted of a stone church that served as a sort
of citadel and two walls, one within the other." Three pieces of artillery
were situated in embrasures of the outer wall. "The flat roof of the church
and the steeple afforded excellent positions for marksmen, who could see
everyone who approached while they themselves were covered by parapets
and walls." The protective walls, however, were unfinished and left open
to the north and east sides of the complex; the cannon of the *tête de pont*,
however, protected the vulnerable sides of the San Pablo complex.

The key for the Americans to win the battle, therefore, was to capture
the *tête de pont*. Semmes wrote several pages to prove this rather obvious
point.

General Worth's troops undertook the fight for control of the bridge. It
was not easy; the dangers described above, while recognized by the troops,
were not readily overcome. Semmes was among Worth's attacking troops
and described the battle of the bridge:

> As we advanced, first the enemy's artillery from the *tête de pont*, which
> enfiladed the road, and then his musketry opened upon us. General Scott
> had got into action on the enemy's right a short time before us, owing to
> our delay at San Antonio; and now a tremendous roar of artillery and
> small arms was heard from one end to the other of the enemy's line, ex-
> tending more than a mile. Like old Bernal Diaz, I seem to hear this crash
> of battle still.

The explosions of cannon at quick fire and the rapid and vivid flashes of
the rifles created not only the sound but the smoke of battle. Although the
day was clear, there was no breeze, and smoke from the guns settled low
"and reflected back, as is sometimes seen with regard to lightning in a thunder storm, the quick and vivid flashes of the various fire-arms." Semmes
continued, "The scene was grand beyond description; there was now
scarcely a breath of air stirring; and while the stillness of the valley was

broken by the dire thunders above described, nature in striking contrast to the bloody work which was going on, seemed only to smile; and presented to the eye of the beholder, her green fruit trees, and tall grain bowing low with refreshing plenty."

Worth ordered several units to advance on his right flank, while one unit of infantry moved up the road directly toward the bridge. The units on the flanks suffered terrible losses; after the battle, one hundred dead were counted. The troops moving up the road directly to the bridge were forced back. However, one of the flanking units survived the enemy fire and "dashed past at 'double quick' the deep wet ditch that surrounded the work, and carried it with the bayonet, men and officers rushing pell mell into the embrasures and over the walls, without the help of ladders." The enemy was shocked and gave way. In a moment, "the cheers of our brave fellows announced that we had possession of the *tête de pont.*" The key to the battle had been turned.

The victorious soldiers on the bridge turned the enemy's captured cannon to the unprotected sides of San Pablo. Up to that time Scott's troops had suffered terrible losses and had gained nothing; even Semmes's navy friend, Captain Ransom, with whom he had laughed at their navy uniforms in army service, had been unsuccessful. But now the Mexican defenders of San Pablo fled the fire of the captured cannon, and the Americans attacked the retreating enemy. The battle of Churubusco was over; the American army was within four miles of the city of Mexico. With the bloody battle ending in victory, several army officers testified to the valor of their staff members. General Pillow specifically cited the "fearless and gallant conduct" of Passed Midshipman R. C. Rogers, the one responsible for Semmes's U.S. Army service. Apparently feeling relief from the tension of writing about the battle in 1849, as he must have felt at the moment of victory in 1847, Semmes turned to humor to express that relief.

And now, in imitation of other chiefs, I must not forget to bring to the notice of the reader, *my* "personal staff." Seymour, arrayed in his tarpaulin hat, with about three yards of ribbon around it, and with his pea-jacket buttoned up to the chin . . . and girded taut around his waist, by a flaming red sash, and mounted on a rough-looking Mexican pony, which was in the habit of having a fight with him and throwing him every twenty-four hours, was sometimes visible and sometimes invisible. . . . He swears he killed two Mexicans with his own hand. . . . I can testify, with more certainty, to his having pryed my horse out of a ditch, into which I had fallen chin-deep in water while attempting to leap it, with a fence rail, which he called a capstan-bar; and to his having gotten hold . . . of a pocket full of cigars and a flask of *aquardiente;* and that the *aquardiente* was not bad to take after a hard day's ride.

They pitched their tent that night "on the very spot [Ladrillera, known formerly as Xoloc] on which Cortez had established his headquarters, some three centuries and a quarter before, while prosecuting the siege of the city, which we were now attempting, in our turn, to enter."

After celebrating the victory with Seymour's *aquardiente,* Semmes began to reflect upon the battle and the men lost in it, and he asked himself: Was it necessary to fight the battle? The total American losses were eleven hundred, of whom eighty-four were officers.

As was his habit, Semmes undoubtedly made notes on his observations and personal experiences. From those notes, a little over a year later while writing his book, he asked: "What was to be gained by the capture of Churubusco?" "Nothing," he answered, "since the enemy would himself have abandoned it, the moment we had taken up a position at Tacubaya, or any point in its rear, as he had done the Peñon and Mexicacingo, when we took the route around Lake Chalco." Santa Anna, he maintained, would have done so "because of the necessity of withdrawing his troops to oppose a new front to us." He recalled also "that this was not a battle offered to us by the enemy on the open field, and which we were not at liberty to decline, but a terrible and bloody assault upon strong works, in front, which we wrested from the enemy at a sacrifice of eleven hundred men, in order that we might have command of a road, into which we could have entered peaceably, in the rear, and of which we made no use, when we obtained possession of it."[25]

He acknowledged that Churubusco had weakened the enemy's army, which is the argument used in supporting Scott's decision to enter the battle. But, he countered, the Americans were in no condition to play such a game, "being in the heart of the enemy's country, beyond the reach of reinforcements, and having but 10,000 men to his 30,000." Where the Americans would lose one man, the Mexicans could lose ten "and gain by the operation" because in "his eight millions of population, he had plenty of recruits to step into the shoes of his dead soldiers—we had none." Semmes returned to this argument several times in the remainder of the book.

N. P. Trist of the U.S. State Department, it will be recalled, was still traveling with Scott's headquarters. He saw the Churubusco victory as the perfect time to call a truce and to enter into negotiations for peace. General Scott, in the circumstances, almost had to accede to Trist's demands, so a truce was declared in order to establish the terms for an armistice. After Churubusco, General Scott established his headquarters at Tacubaya, to the south and slightly west of Mexico City, where General Worth joined him. Semmes, an aide to Worth, was frequently in the company of the two generals. They undoubtedly were reminded that the navy officer was fluent in the Spanish language as well as trained in the intricacies of international law. Scott appointed Semmes as the American secretary and interpreter for the negotiations to establish an armistice, and he had an intimate knowledge of the negotiations to arrive at the terms of peace. His views concerning the negotiations both for the terms of an armistice and for the establishment of peace between the two American republics, then, must carry the weight not only of an eyewitness but also of an intelligent and trained participant.[26]

Semmes opposed an armistice so soon after the costly victory of Churubusco. Indeed, in order to negotiate the terms of an armistice, Scott had recalled cavalry units from Worth's and Quitman's divisions from the almost undefended gates of Mexico City. Why not enter the city, Semmes wondered, and then impose an armistice or, better yet, a treaty of peace? Semmes quoted from a Santa Anna letter in which the Mexican justified the armistice. The general-president wrote that while he was "preparing to renew the conflict the enemy *solicited* an armistice in order that Mr. Trist might be heard, which I granted because the suspension of hostilities would give my troops rest, reestablish their morale, and enable me to collect the dispersed, and adopt other measures to insure a reaction." Semmes was incensed that the action of Trist and Scott allowed Santa Anna to turn the armistice into an American request, as if the American army had lost the battles of the Valley of Mexico! "Where were the wits of Mr. Commissioner Trist and of General Scott, that they did not see that this was not the mood in which a negotiator, desirous of peace, enters upon his duties?"[27]

Nevertheless, Semmes served as interpreter and took notes as the diplomats negotiated the terms of the armistice. "We sat up the whole night, disputing with our opponents, about the *wording* of a few articles, to the precise phraseology of which, Senor Mora, who did all the talking on the Mexican side, attached great importance." The ratification of the armistice terms were exchanged on August 23, "three days after the battle." The negotiations had taken place within the city, at the home of Edward Mackintosh, the British consul in Mexico City, whom Semmes considered to be very pro-Mexican. The terms were promulgated to both armies on August 24 as the Armistice of Tacubaya. The peace negotiations failed miserably, as Semmes had anticipated, and the Mexicans violated some of the armistice provisions. General Scott, now exasperated with the peace proceedings, wrote Santa Anna accusing him of those violations and declaring that if Santa Anna "had not rendered a satisfactory excuse for such violations by noon the next day," then he, Scott, at that time would declare the armistice to be at an end. Santa Anna did not do so; Scott then declared the armistice to be ended at noon on September 7. Negotiations had failed, and for the weary soldiers it was back to war.

As Semmes had anticipated from his experience as interpreter during the meetings that drew up the ground rules for the armistice, the peace negotiations failed for the Americans but had given Santa Anna "a respite of seventeen days to rest his troops, re-establish their morale, collect the dispersed, and adopt other measures to insure a reaction." Furthermore, some of the armistice provisions—such as allowing the American army to purchase food and other supplies in Mexico City—had led to fighting between citizens and American soldiers; one soldier was killed. Semmes characterized the whole armistice episode in these words: "Thus was terminated, in ill-humor, on both sides, an act which was begun in folly on ours, and treachery on that of the enemy."

Anticipating with his reader the return to battles, Semmes paused to recapitulate the American situation

> after having been now thirty days in the great valley of Mexico, in which events of such vast moment, as I have described, followed each other in such rapid succession: We had made the masterful movement around Lake Chalco, had fought the battles of Contreras, San Antonio, and Churubusco, and had reached a new base of operations at Tacubaya. But with the exception of turning the Peñon and Mexicalcingo, and forcing the pass of Contreras, what had we accomplished? Nothing. We had turned aside from our road, to fight the battles of San Antonio and Churubusco, without results; nay, more, with bad results, as we had lost eleven hundred men, more than one tenth of our force.[28]

And the most costly and useless battle was yet to be fought.

On September 7, 1847, the day Scott informed Santa Anna that he was ending the armistice at noon on September 8, General Scott received reports of Mexican troops in sizable force in and around the castle-fortress of Chapultepec and Molino del Rey, located on the western slope of the Chapultepec hill. (See map 3.) Scott and Worth, each with several of his staff, mounted the roof of the bishop's palace in Tacubaya. From that height they easily could see enemy troop movements in and around the fortress. General Worth advised Scott to attack Chapultepec with all his forces, but the commanding general refused, saying that the Molino del Rey (King's Factory) was "a foundry in active operation, busily engaged in casting guns and shot, boring cannon, etc., and stated that no doubt this display of force was intended to protect these operations." Semmes and the others could see no indication that the *molino* was acting as a munitions factory: no smoke and, indeed, no chimney; no noise; and no indication of workers present. General Scott rejected the objections and "in a careless, off-hand manner" ordered General Worth to "brush away the enemy, under cover of the coming night, cripple the machinery, spike or destroy the guns, and then withdraw his troops to Tacubaya." It was to be a useless and costly battle. Scott later maintained that his information concerning the gun factory had been provided to Trist by one of his "Mexican sources."

General Worth ordered two reconnaissances, requested permission to delay the attack until daylight the next morning, and asked for additional troops from another division. General Scott granted all of these requests, but he rejected Worth's plan to leave a battalion at the base of the Chapultepec hill. These requests and plans were not made directly to Scott by Worth but by messenger-officers; this method of communication between the two generals reflected the growth of their estrangement from one another, an estrangement that had begun after the battle at Cerro Gordo and especially during their stay in Puebla. Scott's reason for refusing to allow the battalion to remain at the base of the Chapultepec hill was that "his line of attack would be the right of Chapultepec, and that once in the city, Chapultepec would fall by its own weight." The inability of the two generals to communicate directly with one another resulted in the most bloody and costly battle of the campaign of the Valley of Mexico. Semmes blamed Scott for the useless and deadly battle of Molino del Rey. Once the battle began, it became obvious that the Mexicans overwhelmingly outnumbered Worth's troops, were well entrenched, and intended to protect Chapultepec. It also was obvious that the rumor of a gun factory was a fiction, designed to induce the Americans to attack a strongly fortified position. (See map 3.) During the battle Semmes served Worth in a number of ways. He scouted the enemy positions, he took orders from Worth to the various officers, and—as always—he observed and took notes.

Semmes set the battle-stage for his reader. The Americans moved out of Tacubaya before daylight: "The night was perfectly clear, but without moon, and the sun afterwards rose in all its glory, over the battlefield, to light up the work of carnage and death."

The Mexican army was well entrenched in two buildings, the Molino del Rey to Worth's right and the Casa Mata to his left. Cannons were placed in the area between the two buildings, defended by a large number of in-

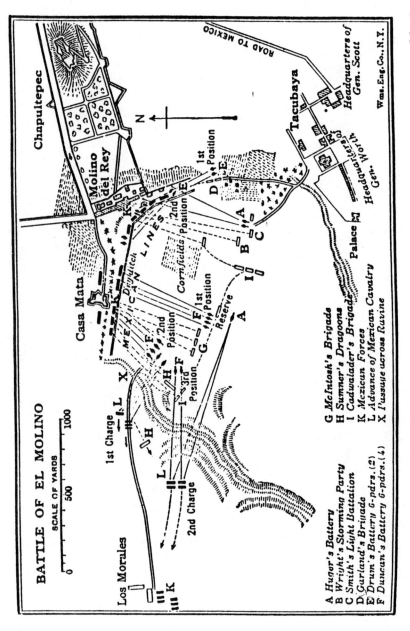

BATTLE OF EL MOLINO

SCALE OF YARDS

0   500   1000

A Huger's Battery
B Wright's Storming Party
C Smith's Light Battalion
D Garland's Brigade
E Drum's Battery 6-pdrs.(2)
F Duncan's Battery 6-pdrs.(4)
G McIntosh's Brigade
H Sumner's Dragoons
I Cadwalader's Brigade
K Mexican Forces
L Advance of Mexican Cavalry
X Passage across Ravine

Wm. Eng. Co.·N.Y.

Map 3

fantry. On one occasion a few American soldiers drove the Mexicans from their cannon but were almost immediately driven back when the Mexicans realized "they had been dispossessed of this strong position, by a mere handful of men." Regaining their cannon, the Mexicans then proceeded to bayonet the wounded American soldiers "with a savage delight." It was a critical moment for the Americans. "The fine military face of our chief, now compressed in sternness, exhibited more anxiety than I had ever seen before upon it." Worth ordered a battalion and a portion of a brigade to attack the Mexicans, and the gun was captured a second time. Meanwhile, some American cavalrymen had ridden too close to the Casa Mata, and some were shot from their saddles "and the affrighted and wounded horses [were] careening wildly over the field." The Mexicans, though outnumbering the Americans, soon fled from the field, and the battle of Molino del Rey was over. According to his orders, Worth withdrew his battered troops to Tacubaya.

What had they won and at what cost? They had won nothing because the Mexicans were still in the castle of Chapultepec that guarded the two city gates of San Cosme and Belen. What had been the cost? Nine officers were killed and 49 wounded, and 729 rank-and-file soldiers were killed and wounded, for a total casualty count of 787, or "one fourth of the whole command!" And for what? Nothing. There was no gun factory in the Molino del Rey; all of the Americans, upon Scott's orders, withdrew from the battlefield. Mexicans killed "could not have been short of one thousand five hundred," plus eight hundred taken prisoner. And at the end of the carnage, the battlefield remained as it had been before the killings—a useless piece of land lying between the two armies.

The American dead were buried "on the heights of Tacubaya." As the end of the service approached, at the words of "dust to dust" the sappers' spades "covered up from view of their brethren, forever, another holocaust to the angry passions of mankind." The battlements of Chapultepec "were crowded with spectators, looking forth upon the solemn scene, which a bright sunlight rendered quite distinct to them, and our minute guns, as they were fired from time to time, were echoed by the rocky heights on which the formidable old castle was seated."

In his evaluation of the battle of Molino del Rey, Semmes wrote that it had served one important function that the Americans at the time did not apprehend: It had destroyed the high morale of the Mexican army that had been created by the armistice and failed negotiations for peace. The night after the *molino* battle, two thousand Mexican soldiers deserted, and the Mexican general in charge of Chapultepec had to place armed guards over his garrison to prevent more men from deserting. "In short, the *morale* of the enemy (or three-fifths of his power) was broken and gone."

Meanwhile, Scott had examined the various other gates into the city of Mexico and decided that, after all, the best approach would be along the causeway of San Cosme and, just south of that, the Belen Causeway, which led to the gates of the same name. These causeways, and thus the gates, were guarded by the castle-fortress of Chapultepec. Semmes described the battle for the fortress of Chapultepec in some detail but not as a participant. The relatively easy capture of the fortress was made possible "for the want of morale, on the part of the defense" after the battle of Molino del Rey, he claimed.

After the fall of the castle, Worth and Quitman moved forward along the causeways toward the city gates. (See map 2.) Worth's troops, including U.S. Navy Lieutenant Raphael Semmes, moved rapidly against light resistance on the La Veronica Causeway to the settlement of Santo Thomas, turned a sharp right, and entered the San Cosme Causeway. It was a broad avenue, "flanked by deep ditches and marshy grounds, on either side, and an aqueduct, supported by arches of heavy masonry, running along the middle." There were, then, two roads on the causeway, one on either side of the aqueduct. A short distance on the San Cosme Causeway, Worth and Semmes met their first serious resistance. The roadway from Campo Santo to the city gate was occupied "by a straggling village, the stone walls and flat roofs of the houses of which, afforded the enemy great advantages for defense." Worth ordered one unit of his division to advance along the roadway, using the structures of the aqueduct for protection, and other units, "by use of bars and picks to burrow through from house to house." At the same time, two mountain-howitzers were placed on the roof of the church of San Cosme. A young army lieutenant, Ulysses S. Grant, was on the right side of the church roof, while Lieutenant Raphael Semmes commanded the gun on the left side of the church roof.

Semmes, writing long before the American Civil War, made no comment about his counterpart on the other side of the church roof, but modern historians of the Mexican War have noted it as an oddity of that war, which was a proving ground for many high-ranking officers of the later one. Semmes did not mention Grant by name, nor Grant Semmes. Nor did Semmes realize that his companion gunner thought the Mexican War to be unnecessary, as did Semmes, nor that Grant agreed that the battles of Churubusco and Molino del Rey were unnecessary.[29] Odd coincidence that these future leaders in another war, with so many similar opinions, would be com-

manding guns from the same church roof on the way to the capture of
Mexico City.

The "house borers" finally arrived at their destination and with a volley
of rifle fire drove the Mexican defenders from their cannon: Worth had
captured the Gate of San Cosme, and his troops entered the city—the first
Americans to do so. Semmes was proud to have been a part of the final military operation of the war with Mexico, and rightly so. His exhilaration led
him to write that "a merciful Providence had conducted us in safety, through
many hard-fought battles to the ancient and renowned city of Mexico, and
we had written a page in its annals, which will connect, in all time to come,
the romantic and chivalrous deeds of Cortez, Alvarado, and Sandoval with
those of the glorious little army of our republic, under Scott, Worth, Quitman, Twiggs, Pillow, Smith."

The Spanish conquistadors, he wrote, had come "to supplant a semi-civi-
lization, with the newer and more vivifying civilization of the cross"; the
Americans "had come not to sweep away, indeed, the civilization of the
cross, but to revivify it." Semmes and his fellow officers and men "were
agitated by strange and indescribable feelings as we lay down to rest that
night; waking we were in a land of poetry and romance; sleeping in a land
of dreams." Semmes remained only a short while with General Worth in
Mexico City, and his activities and observations were not unique. He was
chagrined that General Scott ordered Quitman's division, not Worth's, to
penetrate into the heart of the city to the Grand Plaza onto which faced the
great cathedral and the Grand Palace, the seat of Mexican government. He
thought that Worth's division, in his mind the first to breach the city gates,
should have had that honor. Instead, it was ordered to stop at the Alameda.
Scott, Semmes argued, had actually changed the facts when he credited
Quitman as being the first to enter the city.

During his short stay in Mexico City, Semmes acted more as a tourist
than as a member of a conquering army. He described the buildings, especially the great cathedral and the Grand Palace, the plan of the city, and of
course the beautiful Mexican women. He analyzed the early problems of the
American occupation and noted the many criminal acts of the common
prisoners who had been released by Santa Anna just prior to his fall; he
described the currency problems that arose from the decline in the value of
the peso. But he took no active role in the administration of the city or in
the occupying forces. In effect, his duty with the American army was over,
and he soon returned to a navy assignment. But he had experienced the
excitement and romance of conquering the "Halls of the Montezumas!"

4

Light House Keeping

Semmes in his book on the Mexican War leaves the reader only with his description of the people and problems in Mexico City. He does not inform us of when or how he and Seymour returned to the fleet off Vera Cruz. Furthermore, the American occupation of Mexico City (September 14, 1847) did not end the fighting in the country. Small Mexican units lay siege to Puebla and to several smaller cities, some of which were on the American supply route between Vera Cruz and Puebla and some to the north. Larger American forces drove the Mexicans from the walls of Puebla and other cities; however, Mexican renegade soldiers continued for some time to harass American supply trains during the negotiations for the Treaty of Guadalupe Hidalgo, which was signed only on February 2, 1848. The United States Senate ratified the treaty on March 10, 1848, and the Mexican Congress did so only on May 25, 1848. Until this latter date, the war technically continued, and the U.S. Navy was busy supplying the American forces in Mexico.

Somehow Semmes had found his way back to the navy off Vera Cruz, then to the Pensacola Navy Yard. He was relieved from active duty and went to his home across the Perdido River, where he arrived in early December 1847. He undoubtedly received a warm welcome from Anne Elizabeth and their five children. He must have been especially happy to see and to hold the youngest, Anna Elizabeth, whom he had never seen because she was born in December 1847 before he returned from Mexico.

After a leave of some three and a half months, about which he has left no written record, Semmes became restless. On January 15, 1848, he applied to the Navy Department for command of the USS *Electra*, a navy supply ship, which he described as "a fine little barque of 340 tons burthen."[1] Before his orders arrived, however, the ship had sailed for Mexican waters, and he had to take passage on another navy vessel. He took with him his brother-in-law, F. W. Spencer, to be his clerk aboard the *Electra*.

Semmes was officially the commander of the *Electra* for six months, January 28 to June 28, 1848, but he actually assumed command of her only on March 3, 1848. Commodore Conner had sailed on the first of the month for Campeche, on the Yucatan coast, so Semmes had several days to become acquainted with his vessel and to take inventory of the goods on the *Electra* prior to reporting officially to the commander of the fleet at Vera Cruz. However, a norther, the kind of storm to which he had lost the *Somers* on December 8, 1846, began to blow. Determined to avoid another such disaster, Semmes maneuvered his ship to a safer and more secure anchorage. He was lucky this time because, as he noted, the winds were not blowing with the same intensity he had experienced aboard the *Somers*. The second day of the storm, March 4, he recorded its effect upon the vessel and noted also that this day was his eldest son's tenth birthday. The norther lasted only three more days, but his son survived another sixty-four years. Duty aboard the *Electra* was dull. Semmes tried to relieve that boredom by recording the slightest noteworthy activity. On March 9 he noted that it was the anniversary of the amphibious troop landing just south of Vera Cruz; on March 11, he spent the day fishing and shooting: "we killed some plover with our muskets." On March 13, he wrote that he heard that day of the death of John Quincy Adams, who had died in Washington on February 23, 1848. Then, in the same breath, as it were, he recorded that the peace treaty had been submitted to the U.S. Senate for ratification. "There is every prospect for its being ratified, and the war being brought to a speedy close—God grant!"

His navy duties were at best tedious. He supplied other navy vessels from the *Electra* but on March 19 commented: "Another dull day—we have not serviced a boat nor has anyone been on board of us." Two days later, however, he was happier: "a couple of our fair countrywomen" had come on a boat to visit the island of Salmadina. "I spent a couple of hours most agreeably in their society." The next day, March 22, undoubtedly thinking of the end of the war and of his home, he recorded that "the Mexican Congress has not yet met [to consider ratification of the treaty]! Truly these people seem bent on self-destruction!" He had received no letters from his home although he "had been away for a month, today." On March 23, he wrote simply: "Another lonely day." His notes indicate, obviously, that he was bored with this tour of duty and that he was becoming more and more homesick for his family. In an attempt to relieve the monotony, Semmes read extensively: "I read and read, and get tired of reading—then walk until I tire myself, and then in desperation, go to reading again. By the way . . . one of the best novels that has fallen into my hands for a long time—perhaps because I read but few—is *Fortesque*, by Sheridan Knowles."

On March 29 he realized that "This is the anniversary of the surrender of Vera Cruz. The war has continued much longer than my expectations—when I first saw our flag floating over the battlements of San Juan de Ulloa. I little thought that it would continue to wave there for twelve months! It is easier to begin a war than to end it!" This boredom led him on April 1 to reflect in an even darker mood on his navy career and on politics in general:

> The month has been the longest I have ever passed. Each of the thirty-one days seemed to be a week at least, so drearily did they pass. Every day I am becoming more and more sick of the sea and its privations—one of the chief of which is the banishment from one's family. This is an anniversary with me, and one which as it returns on each succeeding year, brings less and less cause for jubilation. It is twenty-two years, today, since I entered the navy—eleven of which I have served as midshipman and passed midshipman and eleven as lieutenant! Patriotism needs to be pure indeed, which can stand such tests undiminished. I love my country as a sort of ideality, while I despise its hordes of demagogues who yearly struggle for office, and with no other thoughts than how they may best provide for themselves.

On April 5, 1848, he wrote in an offhanded manner of the February Revolution in Paris, France. Little did he know that at least some of his future experiences would be affected by the policies of the president of the Second French Republic, the future Napoleon III. He was more concerned about Santa Anna, whom he described as the "fallen ex-president of Mexico and the able but unfortunate generalissimo of her armies, in the present war, [who] embarked at Antigua yesterday, it is said, for Jamaica." April 15 proved to be a happy day for the languishing navy officer; the steamer *Iris* arrived with letters from his wife, Anne Elizabeth. One of her letters enclosed "a copy of a joint resolution passed by my native state, complimenting me for my poor services in Mexico, during the present war. I felt honored of this token of regard from my fellow citizens of Maryland."

Semmes's dull supply duties off Vera Cruz seemed on April 23 soon to be over: He received orders from Commodore Conner to prepare for a trip to Pensacola—"very welcome intelligence!" But five days later those orders were countermanded: "It was a great disappointment to me as I had anticipated much pleasure from . . . reunion with my family." That longed-for reunion with his family and the honor bestowed upon him by his native state had lifted his morale, only now to have the countermand dash it into the Gulf waters off Vera Cruz.

But Semmes was a trained navy officer, and that training and his strong intellect sustained him. On May 2 he again received orders from the commodore "to prepare for sea." He wrote: "The intelligence excited me so much, that I became quite nervous, and could not sleep any more during the remainder of the night. I turned out at daylight, and commenced my preparations. In the course of the forenoon [on May 5] the steamer *Flirt* . . . arrived to assist me off." He got the *Electra* underway on May 6 at 2:00 P.M. "and stood out of the middle channel passing seaward." He had a fresh wind from east-northeast, and the ship's bow was directed toward Pensacola!

The homeward voyage, however, was a difficult one: It seemed that the only winds he could get were head winds, and he fought strong currents throughout the voyage. Still, he arrived within sight of Pensacola late on Sunday, May 14, 1848. But the fog was heavy; he had to stand off until the next day, and still the fog persisted. It was only on May 16 that a pilot could come aboard and take the ship into the harbor.

Semmes immediately got a small boat to go to his home on the Perdido River, where he arrived early in the afternoon of May 16. His entries in his journal are brief for the two days he was at home; the one for "Wednesday, May 17th" contains two words only: "At Home!" Those two words say more, perhaps, than a full page could have. One can imagine the navy officer with his children, holding the youngest, advising the eldest, and through it all maintaining eye contact with his still young wife, Anne Elizabeth Spencer Semmes.

But his visit with his family was short; four days after arriving at his home on the Perdido River, he was back at sea, returning to his unchallenging duty off Vera Cruz. Three days out of Pensacola he spoke a New Orleans tour boat and learned that the Mexican Congress had at last assembled a quorum. His hopes were raised for an early ratification and, finally, the end of the war. He arrived at Vera Cruz on June 1, 1848, and heard that his hopes for an end of the war had become a reality with the Mexican ratification of the Treaty of Guadalupe Hidalgo on May 25; the two countries exchanged the ratified treaty on May 30, and the war was officially ended.

With the war over, the navy had the duty to begin returning soldiers and marines to the United States. Semmes and the *Electra* were ordered to Anton Lizardo to take on board "Surgeon Spotswood and such persons, stores, furniture, etc., as may not [already] have been sent to Pensacola" and transport them to that base in Florida. He had to visit several ports where he took on various officers and men. An army colonel presented a horse to Semmes, which he took on board along with the soldiers. On Sunday, July 2, 1848, the *Electra* sailed for Pensacola. The sea became rough and the passengers became seasick, but "the horses having had stalls made for them, stood it very well." Semmes, however, was not as fortunate as the horses. On July 4, he noted: "Having taken cold, I am quite miserable today, with its usual accompanying fever." The voyage was a quick one; *Electra* arrived at Pensacola on July 7, 1848. Semmes did not mind the fever; he had performed his last duty related to the Mexican War.

Semmes learned with great delight that he had been detached from the *Electra* and assigned to the Pensacola Navy Yard as inspector of provisions and clothing, a task he held from July 9, 1848, to October 12, 1849, and a task he could perform while living at home with Anne Elizabeth and their five children. His new duties were not particularly taxing. The fever and the cold suddenly left him; he quickly regained his strength and energy. For fifteen months he enjoyed both his family and his navy duties.

The Mexican War had been good to Semmes—if that is possible. He had experienced both navy and army duties; he had become acquainted with navy captains and army generals; he had learned the Mexican way of life; and he had taken notes from which, in 1851, he would publish a book that would become a best-seller in 1852 and would be used by twentieth-century historians as an original source for their studies on the Mexican War. His future navy duties, to which he would be assigned from time to time, would continue to be exercises in learning. Between such assignments, he would practice law in Mobile, Alabama, and see to the education of his older children. Even during the long periods of time when he was not on active navy duty, he would profit from his navy experiences. But the mature Raphael Semmes was still in the making.

The good life of living at home and performing his duties at the Pensacola Navy Base was interrupted only once when he relieved the commander of the schooner *Flirt* from July 9, 1848, until April 6, 1849. During his tour aboard the *Flirt*, he sailed once again to the Mexican waters, to Yucatan where he observed the Indian War. He reported that the Americans there were not molested in any way and indicated that the war if "not originally instigated by the British inhabitants of Belize, has been favored and kept in activity by them."[2]

The *Flirt* interlude satisfied Semmes's love for the sea, and he was happy to return home and resume his duty as inspector of provisions. Soon, however, he began to feel that he had higher duties than those of his navy assignment: those of a husband and father. His older children, Samuel Spencer and Oliver John, were near eleven and ten years old; their education had been provided mostly by their mother. Capable as Anne Elizabeth was, Lieutenant Semmes knew that they needed a more formal education where their intellects would be challenged by professional teachers and by boys their own ages. The Mobile, Alabama, private schools were reportedly challenging ones, and Semmes decided to move there from the Perdido River residence. On October 4, 1849, he requested a three-month leave in order to move his family to "the vicinity of Mobile, Alabama, where I design establishing it for the convenience of educating my children." In the same year, he was admitted to the Alabama bar and he established his law office in Mobile. The navy, with an excess of officers, more than satisfied his request: On October 12, 1849, it detached him from duty to await orders. It was the beginning for Semmes of almost six years without navy duty.

The move to Mobile and the nearly six years of civilian life proved to be a time of passing for Semmes. He ever afterwards considered himself a citizen of the state of Alabama. His law practice provided him with sufficient income to support his family and to supplement it further he occasionally participated as defense counsel in navy court-martial cases. One case in particular influenced his future as well as that of his client, Passed Midshipman John McIntosh Kell of the USS *Albany*.

Kell was from a well-known Georgia family that had many important ties to influential people, both in the navy and in state and national government.[3] Some fourteen years younger than Semmes, Kell was born on January 23, 1823. He entered the navy in 1841, had sailed as a midshipman on a cruise to the Pacific Ocean and to the East Indies, and then was appointed as a student to the newly founded navy academy at Annapolis, Maryland, in November 1847. He and other midshipmen considered themselves to be seasoned sailors, some having served in the Mexican War. They resented being treated as novices and presented the superintendent with many discipline problems. Nonetheless, Kell passed his final examinations in June 1848 and was appointed to the officer rank of passed midshipman. He requested assignment to the Mediterranean Squadron, "as my former cruising have been [*sic*] long and tedious in the Pacific and Gulf of Mexico." The navy, however, had already ordered him to the *Albany*, to cruise in the Gulf of Mexico.

It was during the *Albany* cruise in the West Indies that Kell and three of his Annapolis classmates were treated, in their minds, as mere midshipmen and not as passed midshipmen. They were ordered to awaken the lieutenants for their duty tours and, worst of all, to carry candles to them—duties usually performed only by midshipmen. Kell and his classmates refused to do so, giving the ship's commander their reasons for refusing the orders of their superiors. The four were accused of insubordination and taken to the Pensacola Navy Base for a general court-martial. One of Kell's fellow-accused passed midshipmen was Francis G. Clarke, who had served as a midshipman on the *Somers* under Semmes's command. Indeed, it was Clarke who had saved the life of Semmes just after that ill-fated ship had sunk off Vera Cruz.

Semmes had been appointed to serve on the board of the court-martial, that is, to act as one of the judges. But the lawyer-officer could hardly deny Clarke's request to become his defense counsel. The other three accused young officers, including Kell, asked Semmes to defend them also. Despite Semmes's knowledge of law and of naval regulations, he was unable to overcome the argument that they had, indeed, refused to obey a superior's orders. The four passed midshipmen were dismissed from the service.[4]

At the trial, young Kell favorably impressed the navy lawyer. Semmes saw in him a man not only of great personal pride but also of honor, loyalty, and high intelligence. During the next war, Semmes would turn to Kell to serve as his first lieutenant on board both the CSS *Sumter* and the CSS *Alabama*. In his Civil War memoirs, Semmes credited Kell for the efficiency with which those two ships prosecuted the war against Union merchant ships. That great joint adventure began with Kell's insubordination aboard the *Albany*.

During the remainder of Semmes's long leave from the navy he served on courts-martial several times, either as a judge or as a defense counsel. His law practice in Mobile did not occupy his full time, so during 1849–51 he devoted much of his time to the task of converting his Mexican journal into a book. By March 1851 he was ready to submit the manuscript to a publisher; he requested and received permission from the navy to travel to Cincinnati to consult with William H. Moore and Company, Publishers. His timing, as it turned out, was almost perfect. Nomination conventions for the 1852 presidential election were about to convene, and the publishers saw possibilities for large sales in Semmes's anti-Scott manuscript, should the now retired general be nominated for the country's highest office. The journal was published in 1851 as *Service Afloat and Ashore during the Mexican War*. The widow of General Worth, who had died in 1849, thanked Semmes for the kind way he treated her husband in the book when recounting the Scott-Worth conflicts.

In June 1852 the Whig Party nominated General Scott as its candidate in the upcoming presidential elections, and William H. Moore and Company immediately published a condensed version of Semmes's book under the title *The Campaign of General Scott in the Valley of Mexico*. Almost needless to say, it became a best-seller as the year's campaign progressed. Semmes supported Franklin Pierce, the nominee of the Democratic Party, but did not campaign for him, possibly because professional military officers were supposed to be neutral in politics and because of Pierce's anti-Catholic views. Pierce's aggressive foreign policy, including the annexation of Cuba, which Semmes had advocated in his *Electra* journal, undoubtedly appealed to the navy officer.

Semmes appears to have tried to benefit from his book's contribution to Pierce's election. Discouraged that he had received no promotion and feeling that he was forgotten by the navy, he undertook a letter campaign to rectify his situation. Before President Millard Fillmore left office, Semmes in vain had written to the secretary of the navy seeking support for an appointment for his eldest son, Samuel Spencer, to the U.S. Military Academy at West Point and strongly expressing his own disappointment with his navy career. After Pierce's inauguration, Semmes, through new Secretary of the Navy J. C. Dobbin, repeated his earlier requests to President Fillmore, apparently hoping his book's influence on the new president's election would elicit a favorable response.

He seized the moment also to express his satisfaction with navy reforms advocated by Dobbin, adding his own suggestions. Seeking room for promotion of middle-grade officers, Semmes recommended that "all officers over a certain age shall be retired as a matter of course" and that a bureau of personnel should be established to oversee such policies. The slow promotion of younger officers, he wrote, had discouraged many of them for years and had led others to resign from the navy. Brazenly referring to his own service career, he wrote that such a policy administered by a bureau of personnel would benefit the navy by encouraging experienced middle-grade officers to remain in the service.

Drawing upon his experiences in court-martial cases, he also recommended—and this appears to have been a disinterested issue—that an office of judge advocate general be created. His purpose was to place the legal work of the navy into legally competent hands. Again referring to his own experiences in court-martial cases, he further recommended that the judge advocate general be empowered to summon civilian witnesses in order to assure that justice be done. But the navy did not immediately see fit to follow this suggestion; not until 1880 was the Office of Judge Advocate General established.[5] A bureau of personnel was established even later.

By his strong and basically sound suggestions, Semmes had attracted the attention of Dobbin. Even though his request in 1855 for an active duty assignment went unheeded, on September 15, 1855, the Navy Department notified him of his promotion to the rank of commander, the third highest rank in the navy. For some unexplained reason, the navy recommissioned him to the rank of commander on August 29, 1856, and then on November

25 recalled him to active duty as lighthouse inspector of the Eighth Light-house District, which included the Caribbean and Gulf coasts. The fact that earlier in his career he had served as a surveyor for more than four years (September 1840 to April 1845) along the same coasts possibly led to this new assignment. Semmes undoubtedly was thrilled both with his promotion and with the new assignment: He was again at sea and still close to his home; it was almost an ideal assignment for the family man and navy officer.

The United States lighthouse system had been allowed to fall into disarray during the decades of the 1830s and 1840s. In 1851 the government ordered a thorough investigation under the direction of the secretary of the treasury. The members of the investigative board were prominent navy officers and civilians. The board issued its recommendations in early 1852 and in October of that year, following the report, the president created a nine-member Lighthouse Board and placed it in the Department of the Treasury. The new board members were high-ranking army and navy officers plus two civilian scientists.[6]

Two years after his appointment as a lighthouse inspector, Commander Semmes was detached from that assignment and appointed on September 24, 1858, to the position of secretary of the Lighthouse Board. At about the same time his second son, Oliver John, received an appointment to West Point from President Pierce. Both of the appointments undoubtedly were a recognition of Semmes's expertise, as well as his persistence. Because his new position involved no sea duty, Semmes moved his family from Mobile to a house in Maryland, near the city of Washington, D.C. Maryland was a slave state, so he undoubtedly moved the house slaves along with his family to help Anne Elizabeth with the children and to perform the normal household chores. The move did nothing to destroy Semmes's Southern and Alabama mind-set.

Indeed, his attention throughout the decade of the 1850s was so concentrated on his and his family's well-being that in none of his writings did he ever mention the changes—social, demographic, economic, technological—that occurred in the United States between 1850 and 1860. He failed to note the 35 percent population increase—mostly through immigration from western and northern Europe—or the decline of the proportion of slaves from 16 percent of the population in 1850 to 14 percent in 1860, or the demographic changes with the movement of people to the upper Midwest. The technological changes that produced new products from the factories in the Northern states and the Great Lakes area apparently did not attract his interest. Nor did he mention the growing production and export of corn and wheat, especially from the lake port of Milwaukee (from 317,000 bushels in 1850 to 13,000,000 bushels in 1861), nor the invention of the McCormick reaper that made that growth possible. He even failed to acknowledge the growth of manufacturing in the South, especially the 101 percent increase in agricultural implements, the 387 percent increase in engines and machinery, or the 80 percent increase in the manufacturing of shoes and boots in the South.

Perhaps more important, he failed to acknowledge the various inventions that were working to change the way Americans traveled, heated their homes, plowed their fields, wove their cloth. Railway mileage, for instance, increased from 8,500 miles in 1850 to more than 30,000 miles in 1860. And the man who had described in detail the Mexican cities did not mention the improvements in American cities: the "subterranean railways," street and sidewalk pavements, water and sanitation systems. He even overlooked the dramatic increase in shipbuilding: In 1854–55 more than a million tons of shipping was built, much of it in the South.[7] To his credit, he did not defend slavery.

In *Service Afloat* he devoted six chapters to the coming of the war, overlooking the specific changes that had occurred in the 1850s. Writing after the Civil War and after emancipation, he treated that issue merely as a Northern excuse for war; the basic and immediate cause he considered to be economic, not moral. Ever the lawyer as well as the seaman, he based his argument primarily on constitutional grounds: "The judgment which posterity will form upon our actions will depend, mainly, upon the answers which we will be able to give to two questions: first, had the South the right to dissolve the compact of government under which it had lived with the North? and secondly, was there sufficient reason for such dissolution?"

In his argument for the right of any state to secede from the Union, he first distinguished the right of secession from the right of revolution, which he considered to be "inherent in all peoples, whatever may be their form of government." The thirteen original colonies, he wrote, had "exercised the right of revolution when they withdrew from" Great Britain. But "not so with the Southern States when they withdrew from their copartnership with the Northern States. *They exercised a higher right.*" He claimed that the Southern states had not formed "a part of a consolidated government [with the Northern states] as the colonies had with the British Government." The Southern states, he argued, "were sovereign, equally, with the Northern States, from which they withdrew, and exercised, as they believed, a peaceful right, instead of a right to revolution."

He then asked the question: "Had, then, the Southern States the peaceful right to dissolve the compact of government under which they had lived with the North?" In a tightly reasoned argument of some fifteen pages, he began with the 1777 Articles of Confederation, which recognized the sovereignty of each member state; and he cited Daniel Webster and Justice Joseph Story, both of whom were strong Unionists but who admitted that if "the [1789] Constitution were a compact between the States, the States would have the right to withdraw from the compact." He then set out to prove that the Constitution was, indeed, such "a compact between the States."

Citing the debates as reported in the "Journal and Debates of the Philadelphia Convention," which convention drew up the 1789 Constitution, Semmes wrote that one is "struck with the scrupulous care with which all the states guarded their sovereignty." The Northern states, he claimed, were "quite as jealous, in this respect, as the Southern States," and he cited particularly Massachusetts and New Hampshire. He also detailed similar positions taken by the states of Virginia, North Carolina, and Pennsylvania. And finally he quoted the Tenth Amendment to the U.S. Constitution: "The powers not delegated to the United States, by the Constitution, nor prohibited by it to the States, are reserved to the States, or to the people." This provision, he wrote, makes "it clear beyond doubt, that the States not only had no intention of merging their sovereignty in the new government they were forming, but that they took special pains to notify each other, as well as their common agent, of the fact."

He also quoted the words of various statesmen, such as James Madison, who in reference to the wording of the preamble to the Constitution—"We the people . . . "—said that the phrase referred not to "the people as composing one great society, but the people as composing thirteen sovereignties." Alexander Hamilton, Semmes maintained, also spoke "only of States and of compacts made or to be made by States." This "compact view," he held, prevailed to about 1830. Change resulted from a growing difference in the economies of the Northern and Southern states. The tariff laws of 1824 and 1828, he maintained, were enacted to protect New England manufacturers, and their "effect was to shut out all foreign competition, and to compel the Southern consumer to pay two prices for all the textile fabrics he consumed." When South Carolina in 1830 nullified the tariffs, "all New England was arrayed against" it. "New England orators and jurists rose up to proclaim that the Constitution was not a compact between the States."

Having satisfied himself that the sectional differences and constitutional interpretations resulted from the tariffs of 1828 and 1830, Semmes turned to his final question as to the causes of the war: "Was Secession treason?" To answer this question Semmes quoted from the eighteenth-century Swiss philosopher, Emerich de Vattel, whose *Law of Nations* (1760) seemed to justify liberal revolutions:

> Several sovereign and independent States may unite themselves together by a perpetual confederacy, without ceasing to be, each individually, a perfect state. They will, together, constitute a federal republic; their joint deliberations will not impair the sovereignty of each member, though they may in certain respects, put some restraint upon the exercise of it, in virtue of *voluntary* engagements.

Semmes did not use Vattel's words to justify liberal revolutions but rather to refute Daniel Webster's interpretation of the U.S. Constitution, namely that "the people of the United States have chosen to impose control on State sovereignty." Semmes called Webster's ideas "the germ of a monstrous heresy that have riven the United States asunder in our day!"

He next asked the question: "In what part of the Constitution is the doctrine of secession found?" He answered that such a provision was unnecessary "because the States who formed the instrument, delegated certain powers to the Federal Government, retaining all others." The states had seceded from the Articles of Confederation not all together but one by one. Furthermore, those articles were stipulated to be *perpetual.* Such an article of perpetuity does not appear in the Constitution; why?

> It could not have been an accidental omission, and the motive probably was, that the Convention of 1787 were ashamed to attempt, a second time, to bind the sovereign States which they were in the act of pulling asunder. It was in accordance with this understanding that both New York and Virginia in their ratifications of the new Constitution expressly reserved to themselves the right of secession; and no objection was made to the right of such conditional ratifications.

Having satisfied himself on the right of secession, Semmes turned to the question: "Was there sufficient ground for this dissolution?" To answer it he turned to European history. "The American Constitution died of a disease inherent in it." It was framed on false principles because it attempted to bind "together, in a republican form of government, two dissimilar peoples, with widely dissimilar interests." Monarchical governments in Europe, such as the Austrian and Russian Empires, could succeed through force. But "if a republic should make the attempt, that moment, it must, of necessity, cease to be a republic, since the very foundation of such a government is the consent of the governed." The American Revolution was fought on that principle "in favor of three millions of the subjects of Great Britain." But "in those

States of the Southern Confederacy, there were eight millions!" When a government must use force against its people and against their will, Semmes wrote, at that moment it ceases to be a republic.

Alexis de Tocqueville in his *Democracy in America,* Semmes maintained, realized this point thirty years prior to the Civil War when he saw "looming up in the distance, the horrible and hideous form of that unbridled and antagonistic majority which has since rent the country in twain." Semmes agreed: "Liberty is always destroyed by the multitude, in the name of liberty." And when this multitude becomes a majority of a people "in a free government it becomes a faction" representing "certain classes and interests to the detriment of other classes and interests." At that moment, Semmes wrote, "then farewell to public liberty; the people must either become enslaved, or there must be a disruption of government." Already in the 1830s de Tocqueville had seen this disruption: The states, he wrote, are "more like hostile nations, than rival parties, under one government."

Semmes elaborated upon de Tocqueville's "hostile nations" theme. It could not be otherwise because "the origin of the two sections has been diverse." Virginia and Massachusetts "were the two original germs, from which the great majority of the American populations has sprung; and no two peoples, speaking the same language and coming from the same country, could have been more dissimilar in education, taste and habits, and even in natural instincts, than were the adventurers who settled those two colonies." Those who chose the more congenial climate of the Chesapeake "were the gay and dashing cavaliers, who, as a class, adhered to the fortunes of the Charleses, whilst the first settlers of Massachusetts were composed of the same materials, that formed the 'Praise-God-Barebones' parliament of Cromwell." The two peoples had an instinctive repugnance of one another. The Puritan was "a seedling of the English race, which had been unknown to it before." Puritans were "gloomy, saturnine, and fanatical in disposition" and seemed to "repel all the more kindly and generous impulses of our Nature, and took pleasure in pulling down everything that other men had built up" only "because it had not been done by their own hands." Furthermore, they hated tyranny "only when they themselves were not the tyrants; they hated religious intolerance, but it was only when not practised by themselves." Semmes's Roman Catholicism was speaking out.

The two germs of differences between the Puritans and the Cavaliers, he wrote, "grew step by step into two distinct nations." The "cold and inhospitable climate and the rugged soil" of New England drove the Puritan to "the ocean and the mechanic arts," while Virginia's "soft climate and generous soil" led the Cavalier to agricultural pursuits. Thus with such ease, and perhaps accuracy, did the native Marylander and adopted Alabamian paint the origins of the social and economic differences between North and South.

Only in the context of those differences between Puritan and Cavalier did Semmes treat the "peculiar institution" as a factor in the coming of the Civil War; he never mentioned morality in relation to slavery. All the colonies, he wrote, at first were slaveholding, but as the economic factor became more and more apparent to the New England Puritans, "one by one the Northern States got rid of their slaves." In the South, he claimed, "the superior fertility of the soil and the geniality of the climate enabled the planter to employ the African to advantage; and thus slave labor was engrafted on our system of civilization as one of its permanent features." These factors—climate, fertility of soil, and wealth—led inevitably to the differences between the two sections. "In the North, almost every young man was under the necessity . . . of laboring with his own hands for the means of subsistence," while the Southern planter with his "hundreds of vassals" developed a "luxurious style of living."

As soon as the Constitution was established and the new government went into effect, "parties began to be formed, on sectional interests and sectional prejudices." The North needed protection for its shipping "in the way of discriminating tonnage dues, and the South was opposed to such protection; the North wanted a bank, to facilitate their commercial operations; the South was opposed to it." Most important, the North wanted protection for its manufacturers, and the South opposed such protection. The tariff laws enriched the North, and the South gained nothing from them. The tariff law of 1842, Semmes maintained, was more oppressive for the South than anything that preceded it. In taxes, also, the South provided three-fourths of the federal revenue and "received nothing in return." The result was an economic gain for the North and a loss for the South.

> Whilst [the South's] abundant crops supplied all the exchanges of the country, and put in motion throughout the North, every species of manufacturing industry, from the cut nail, which the planter put in the weatherboarding of his house, to the coach in which his wife and daughters took an airing, it was found that from year to year, mortgages were increasing on her plantations, and that the planter was fast becoming little better than the overseer of the Northern manufacturer and the Northern merchant.[8]

Semmes cited South Carolina's 1832 nullification of the tariff, the compromise tariff of 1833, and the "more oppressive tariff of 1842, from which time onward no attempt was made to conciliate the South . . . and [it] sank, hopelessly, into the condition of a tributary province to her more powerful rival."

Finally, as a cause for the war, Semmes treated the question of slavery. He reiterated that originally all the colonies were slaveholding, but as the economic differences developed, Northerners found slaves to be uneconomical while Southerners found them to be an economic asset. The expansion into the western territories led to further controversies over slavery. The North opposed expansion of slavery into the new lands because it feared, Semmes claimed, that those states too would prosper to the detriment of the Northern economy. This opposition led to new controversies that would not be settled until the Kansas-Nebraska Act of 1854. Although the Fugitive Slave Act of 1850 provided for the return of such slaves to their owners, it was not, Semmes noted, executed by the antislavery settlers in the new lands. Northern opposition to the expansion of slavery was based on Northern economic needs. It was all-important, Semmes claimed, that the North acquire a *means* to appeal to the people of the new lands, and to this end "they enlisted the clergy in their crusade against the South." The pulpit, he claimed, became a rostrum "from which to inflame the Northern mind against the un-Godly slave holder." Furthermore, "religious papers were established which fulminated their weekly diatribes against the institution; magazine literature, fiction, lectures by paid itinerants, were all employed with powerful effect in a community where every man sets himself up as a teacher, and considers himself responsible for the morals of his neighbor." Thus, he maintained, were the minds of the North turned against the South. And so easily, then, did Semmes reject any moral element in the antislavery movement of the North.

Most Southerners, Semmes continued, rejected the notion that differences on the slavery issue could divide the country into two separate parts. Thus Semmes saw the slavery issue as an instrument of the economic and political ones. While it is true that he did not dodge the existence of slavery as a factor in the coming of the Civil War, he did ignore the moral issue of slavery, basing his arguments entirely on sectionalism and economics.[9]

As all these issues grew more and more intense during the 1850s, Southern voices, and even some Northern ones, were raised in behalf of moderation and understanding. Semmes referred to two earlier American statesmen to illustrate the ties that bound Northerner and Southerner. Daniel Webster, a Northerner, had warned his constituents that "A bargain broken on one side is broken on all sides." And he let the words of James Madison of Virginia illustrate his point that the South did not *want* to secede from the Union: "The kindred blood which flows in the veins of American citizens, the mingled blood which they have shed in defence of their sacred rights, consecrate their union, and excite horror at the idea of their becoming aliens, rivals, enemies." Much of this feeling, Semmes maintained, still lingered in the bosoms of Southerners despite the North's "rough handed" treatment of the South:

> Like an unhappy bride, upon whose brow the orange wreath had been placed, by hands that promised tenderness, and protection, the South had been rudely scorned, and repelled, and forced, in tears, and bitter lamentation, to retract the faith she had plighted. . . . Like the deceived and betrayed bride, the least show of relenting, and tenderness was sufficient to induce the South to forgive, and endeavor to forget.

The history of the relations between the South and the North, Semmes stated, was "full of compromises and apparent reconciliations," such as the compromises of 1833 and 1850. "The South, like the too credulous bride, accepted these evidences of returning tenderness, in good faith; the North, like the coarse and brutal husband, whose selfishness was superior to his sense of justice, withdrew them, almost as soon as made."

The election of 1860 for the United States presidency proved to be the decisive factor that led to the temporary destruction of the Union and to war. The Democratic Party was unable to agree on a single candidate, and finally, in a kind of death wish, chose two different ones: Stephen A. Douglas and John C. Breckenridge. The new Constitutional Union Party nominated John Bell. Thus those who opposed the Republican Party candidate, Abraham Lincoln, divided among themselves their 2,815,617 votes, while Lincoln received only 1,866,452. Lincoln's votes were concentrated and he earned 180 electoral votes to his opponents' combined 123. The South, by its inability to settle upon a single candidate, had opened the door for a midwestern abolitionist to enter the White House.

During the interval between the election and the inauguration of Lincoln, the incumbent president, James Buchanan, made strong efforts to prevent a general secession of the Southern states. His peaceful efforts failed, and South Carolina seceded from the Union on December 20, 1860, and was followed by Mississippi on January 9, 1861, Florida January 10, 1861, and Commander Raphael Semmes's adopted state, Alabama, the next day.

The U.S. Navy commander had observed these events with great consternation. What should be *his* course of action? Should he remain in the U.S. Navy? Should he await the action of his native state, Maryland, where he then resided, or join his adoptive state, Alabama? Indeed, had he yet formed any opinion on the political and social questions that had led to this potential disruption of the Union? His two or three domestic slaves did not qualify him as a "slaveholder"; he could easily convert their subsistence into weekly wages. But what of Anne Elizabeth, who was a native of a nonslave state, Ohio—what would be her reaction to any decision he might make? Semmes pondered these events and his own reactions to them: What should he do? Would Anne Elizabeth follow him permanently into the citizenship of a slave state? What would be the reaction of his second son, Oliver John Semmes, then a cadet at West Point? Commander Semmes undoubtedly was not alone; thousands of Americans, North and South, were pondering similar questions. How many Southern states would secede? Would war follow? How will my life change?

5

Secession, War, and the CSS *Sumter*

As Commander Raphael Semmes, member of the U.S. Lighthouse Board, pondered the question of his future and that of his family, events began to overtake him. The state of South Carolina reacted to the election of Abraham Lincoln in November 1860 by seceding from the United States on December 20, 1860. The southern tier of states followed suit the next month: Mississippi on January 9, 1861, Florida the next day, and Alabama on January 11, 1861.[1]

Even before South Carolina's secession, Semmes took it upon himself, while still a U.S. Navy officer, to seek advice from Alexander H. Stephens, a longtime leading political figure in Georgia and in the Congress. Stephens had made a speech in Georgia in which he opposed secession, insisting that the moderates in the North would compromise and accommodate the South.[2] Semmes's letter, dated December 11, 1860, reveals his indecision. Apparently, even at that late date, he was still struggling to reach a final decision.

He began the letter by congratulating Stephens on the speech. He had "devoured the great speech with acolyte enthusiasm," convinced that whatever befell this great country Stephens's name would be forever linked with this struggle for human liberty. To characterize himself as having the enthusiasm of an acolyte and as being "in the presence of a great high Priest" was most unlike Raphael Semmes. It is the only instance in all of his writings that he placed himself in a position of such sycophancy. Why in the earliest stages of the secession crisis did he resort to it? Perhaps the answer is the depth of his concern over the future of his country and of his proper place in that future.

The Southern voters by failing to unite against the election of Abraham Lincoln, Semmes continued, have raised a question, in the presence of which all other questions sink into insignificance: "How shall the union of these states be preserved, and if this be impossible, how shall we unite the

South in a confederacy of its own?" It is a question, he continued, "that every patriot and citizen is called upon to answer, it matters not to what party he may heretofore have belonged."

Despite his stated concern about "preserving the union of these states," he predicted that "by the middle of January next, South Carolina, Georgia, Alabama, Florida, and Mississippi, if not Louisiana and Texas, will be out of the Union." The officers of the navy, he wrote, "will probably resign, as their respective states withdraw from the Union." He then referred to his own dilemma: Suppose his native state of Maryland should not secede. Navy officers of the seceded states would have a right to be received by the new government, but

> Maryland is my native State . . . and suppose she lags . . . and in the meantime the more remote Southern States form themselves into a confederacy, and organize their government, including their Army and Navy, would the door be open for the admission of officers circumstanced like myself? . . . Now, my judgement, my inclinations, and my affections all incline me to link myself with the first movement of the South, in any and all events, but I should be unwilling, unless invited, to appear to thrust myself upon the new government, until my own state had moved. Can you open the door at the proper time, for my admission into the Navy of the Southern Republic, and may I regard myself as your client, in the Roman signification of the term, and rely upon you to notify me when the proper time has arrived for my action?
>
> I am still at my post at the Light-House Board, performing my routine duties, but listening with an aching ear, and a beating heart for the first sounds of the great disruption which is at hand.[3]

At least some ambiguity occurs in this letter: Would he, despite his "judgement, . . . inclinations, and . . . affections," remain in the U.S. Navy if Maryland remained in the Union and if he received no invitation to join the navy of the Southern Confederacy? Had he already given himself over to an inevitable separation of the Southern states from the Union? Or was he simply playing the two sides against each other, thus leaving his options open? Had he yet made plans for his family in the event of separation of South from North or even in the event of war? His later decisions concerning his family and his own course of action incline one to believe that this letter to Stephens was less than candid; he probably was seeking information on which to base his future decisions concerning career and family.

Stephens did not reply to Semmes until he "could see the result of the political issue in my state [Georgia], then pending, involving the question of

longer remaining in the Union or not. That question was finally settled yesterday," January 19, 1861. "She is again a free, sovereign, and independent
republic. . . . I did all I could to induce the people not to take the step they
have taken." Despite having voted against the ordinance of secession, he
continued, "I shall with all my energies and heart stand by her fortunes."
He added, in answer to Semmes's plea: "Should a Southern Confederacy be
formed, as I suppose it will be, very soon, I will take great pleasure in presenting your name, to those who may be in authority, as one capable and
willing to render efficient service, in her Navy." But, dwelling on the fact
that his native state, Maryland, might lag in its decision to join the Confederacy, Semmes inquired of Stephens about admission for latecomers such as
himself who held public office, as he did on the Lighthouse Board.

The correspondence with Stephens appears to have been Semmes's back-
up plan. His adopted state, Alabama, had seceded from the Union on January 11 at a convention that also issued an invitation to the other seceded
states to send delegates to Montgomery for the purpose of forming a provisional government of the seceded states. The Provisional Government of
the Confederate States of America was formed on February 4, 1861, with
Jefferson Davis as provisional president and Alexander H. Stephens as provisional vice president. Later the two men were elected to the same offices
under the permanent Constitution of the Confederate States of America.[4] Jabez Lamar Monroe Curry, perhaps at the request of Vice President
Stephens, wrote to Semmes, acknowledging the latter's letter of January 24,
and assuring him that it would be a pleasure to bring his name before "the
powers that be." "To all who appreciate skill, courage, intelligence, science,
the disclosure of your willingness to unite your destiny with ours, will bring
much gratification," he wrote. "Your joining the Alabama cause will lessen
very much the embarrassments of our initial position, to be able to secure so
early, the matured experience and ability, which are, ordinarily, the result
of years of mortifying failures, and disappointments. As an Alabamian, I
thank you for the tender of your services, and while presenting your name,
will be happy to remember that of your son [a cadet at West Point] also."[5]

Semmes soon determined his course of action: He would leave the U.S.
Navy and cast his lot with the South. The ambiguity had been solved with
the secession of Alabama on January 11, 1861. His offer to join with Alabama in opposing the incoming administration of Abraham Lincoln reflects
his moment of decision. Still, he did not immediately resign from the U.S.
Navy; Curry had requested Semmes to advise him on "the organization of
the Navy, Light House Establishment," and so forth "under the new government."

On February 6, about the length of time Curry's letter would have been in transit from Mobile, Semmes wrote an eight-page evaluation of the South's navy yards and of the need to protect coastal trade as well as to establish proper administrative offices of the new navy. These recommendations were based primarily on the assumption that war was not an immediate threat. He dealt at some length on coastal shipping, an activity that Northern ships had provided in the past. He wrote that coastal trade was not profitable enough to attract foreign participation because of the added costs to foreign bottoms, such as obtaining supplies and needed ship repairs, providing for the families of the crew, and even recruiting new crew members as the original crew, as in all ship crews, would leave the ship at some port, or become ill, or even die. Coastal trade, then, would be much cheaper if carried by ships of the South:

> The Southern coasting trade in Southern bottoms is already very considerable, particularly along the coasts of Alabama, Mississippi, Louisiana, and Texas, and from the many fine specimens of home built craft to be found in these waters, I have no doubt whatever that in the course of a few years, we shall see Gulf ships manned by Gulf seamen successfully competing with foreign ships for our overseas carrying trade.

This point led into Semmes's major advice to the new government: "You will need, of course, a naval force to look after and protect this commerce and to display your flag abroad as well as to guard the numerous inlets and harbors along your extended line of coast."

For coastal defense, he wrote, "heavy batteries on cheap bottoms will be sufficient." Such "cheap bottoms" would be vessels powered by steam, such as the heavy tugboats that plied off the mouths of the Mississippi River, which soon could be transformed into formidable floating batteries and moved hither and thither at will, and which by reason of their light draft could take shelter at pleasure against a superior force. Semmes then turned to the necessary undergirth of any naval force: shipyards and ship construction.

> You have at Pensacola an extensive and well improved Navy Yard with dry dock and (floating) wharves, timber sheds, and other conveniences and appliances for ship building, and within the last twelve months, two very credible specimens of naval architecture have been turned out at that yard—the Pensacola of 2158 tons, and the Seminole of 801 tons. . . . Owing to superior facilities . . . these two ships were built at cheaper rates than similar ships in the Northern dock yards.

He recommended also the navy yard at Brunswick, Georgia, as an excellent
yard for the South.

These two yards, he continued, would be sufficient for the South's needs.
Skilled mechanics could be maintained in them "so as to concentrate a corps
of artisans and laborers . . . who could be kept . . . in the employment of the
government." He also claimed that with "all the various processes of manufacture being concentrated at a single point, the division of labor ensues and
each man in consequence becomes more perfect in his art."

Semmes did not think war would occur, but he nonetheless recommended that the president of the new government should collect a "commission of officers at the Capital to arrange a program of coast defence." As for
naval officer personnel, he recommended "eight or ten captains, as many
commanders, and a proportionate number of lieutenants, say thirty-five or
forty." Such a number of officers would allow the new government a sufficient number for bureau work and to command a couple of navy yards as
well as to have commanding officers for each of the ports of Charleston,
Savannah, Key West, Mobile, New Orleans, and Galveston, each of whom
should have under him two or three good vessels, to be purchased and prop-
erly armed for coastal and harbor defenses. Turning to the organization of
the new navy, he recommended the establishment of bureaus for the administration of naval affairs "in aid of the Secretary of the Navy." These
bureaus, he felt, could be modeled after those of the U.S. Navy, except reduced in number. Two, he thought, would be sufficient: one for the yards and
docks and construction and equipment; the other for all other branches,
such as ordnance and hydrography, clothing and provisions. Two captains in
the office of the secretary of the navy, he continued, "would enable that
officer to conduct understandingly all the affairs of the Navy." He recommended also that a bureau be established instead of a Lighthouse Board, a
recommendation that was later acted upon.

Early in the Mexican War, it will be recalled, Semmes had criticized
Mexico for using privateers. Now he advised Curry to do just that. He de-
fined the term for the Alabama congressman: "a well organized system of
private armed ships, known as privateers." He further explained that if war
should come it would be by a commercial people whose ability to do harm
to the South would consist chiefly in ships and shipping. To balance such a
force, he recommended the use of privateers, who would be motivated by
"private cupidity." The new government must, however, place such cupidity
under sufficient restraint to prevent it from degenerating into piracy. Thus
"you could have a large irregular sea-force, to act as an aid to the regular
naval force, so long as the war lasted, and which could be disbanded without

further care or expense at the end of the war." The most striking of these recommendations to the Confederate provisional government is that of the use of privateers. A trained lawyer and a seaman, Semmes knew better than anyone else that privateering had been outlawed by the Declaration of Paris in 1856. True, the United States had not signed that declaration but had adhered to its other provisions even though the nation had not, since its adoption, been at war. Technically the Confederacy as an heir to United States policies therefore could adopt privateering as a legitimate act of war. When Semmes himself was accused during the Civil War of being a privateer, he heatedly denied it, and rightly so. It is, perhaps, too much to hold a public figure over a long period of time to absolute consistency. At any rate, during the Civil War the South's privateers were thoroughly suppressed by the United States Navy.[6]

One final note on these recommendations for the organization of a Confederate navy: Semmes was writing before South Carolina's firing upon Fort Sumter and before Lincoln's inauguration as president of the United States. While the times were tense, while both Northerners and Southerners were concerned about the possibility of war, President Buchanan's policy was pacific. He hoped still to preserve the Union by inducing the seceded states to reverse their position. President-elect Lincoln also was willing to compromise in order to save the Union: "He reiterated his fundamental belief in the right of the states to maintain slavery in their midst and explained that he intended no interference with that right. He favored enforcement of the fugitive slave law." He even went so far as to indicate his willingness "to accept a constitutional amendment protecting existing state slavery."[7] No wonder Semmes made his recommendation for a peacetime Southern navy!

The strange interlude between secession and the outbreak of war was a time of stress and strain on Raphael Semmes, affecting both his career decision and his family relationships. While the commander was advising the provisional government of the South on the establishment of a peacetime navy, events had moved faster and faster. He was promoted from secretary of the Lighthouse Board to full membership on the board. He soon would have to make a decision:

> I was looking upon these momentous events with a strained eye, and a beating heart. I was soon called upon in honor to make a choice, leading God knew where. It might be independence under the Constitution, placed in new hands, where it would be safe from the spoiler. It might be to subjugation and death! How was the question of allegiance to be affected by any step that I might take?[8]

Anne Elizabeth, realizing his tendency to follow his adopted state, urged him to remain in the U.S. Navy. She insisted that to resign would be both "rash and improvident." She probably was thinking of her responsibilities to the children still at home. Her three daughters and the youngest child, Raphael, Jr., were still dependent upon their parents for their education and subsistence. How could Anne Elizabeth fulfill those responsibilities if her husband left the secure income the U.S. Navy provided the family? Also, having been raised in Ohio, despite her two or three household slaves, she was basically antislavery. Indeed, her husband felt that she was too much influenced by her Ohio relatives who were strong Unionists.[9] More likely it was her rearing rather than their sudden influence. At any rate, Semmes resented her attitude and her effort to impose her will upon him. Despite his strong family feelings, he would not allow her to influence him. Also a strong person, she followed her convictions and soon took their three daughters and young Raphael to Cincinnati, where they spent the first years of the war.

During those stressful weeks, Semmes later wrote, "I had made up my mind to retire from the Federal service, at the proper moment, and was only waiting for that moment to arrive." The moment came on February 14, 1861; "while I was sitting quietly with my family, after the labors of the day, a messenger brought me the following telegram":

Montgomery, Feb. 14, 1861

Sir: On behalf of the Committee on Naval Affairs, I beg leave to request that you will repair to this place, at your earliest convenience.

Your obedient servant,
C. M. Conrad, Chairman.

Commander Raphael Semmes
Washington, D.C.

Although he and Anne Elizabeth had not resolved their differences, he replied the same day: "Despatch received; I will be with you immediately." The die was cast.

The next day he wrote a short note to the U.S. secretary of the navy. It was in typical nineteenth-century style:

Washington, D.C., Feb. 15, 1861

Sir: I respectfully tender through you, to the President of the United States, this, the resignation of the commission which I have the honor to hold as a Commander in the Navy of the United States. In severing my connection with the Government of the United States, and with the Department over which you preside, I pray you to accept my thanks for the kindness which has characterized your official deportment towards me.

I have the honor to be very respectfully your obedient servant,

Raphael Semmes,
Commander U.S. Navy

Hon. Isaac Toucey, Secretary of the Navy
Washington, D.C.

Toucey accepted the letter in a note of the same date. The following day, Semmes wrote to the secretary of the Lighthouse Board informing him of his resignation and of its acceptance, adding: "I desire to say to the members, individually, and collectively, that I shall carry with me to my home in the South, a grateful recollection of the amenities, and courtesies, which have characterized, on their part, our official intercourse." Semmes for some reason expected recognition for his service with the Lighthouse Board and was disappointed that his letter of resignation "was not even honored with an acknowledgment of its receipt."[10]

In his book, published in 1869 as *Memoirs of Service Afloat during the War Between the States,* Semmes emphasized that during these early months of 1861 there was "no talk about traitor and treason." Again, that strange interlude between secession and war permitted members of Congress as well as military officers to resign their positions without prejudice and to freely travel to the South or even throughout the North.

As Semmes prepared for his journey south, Anne Elizabeth, their three daughters, and Raphael, Jr., prepared for their journey to join the Spencer family in Cincinnati. Just as the states were separated, so too were many families and friends. It was a sad war for many reasons.

Travel as well as mail and telegraphic service between North and South continued unabated until mid-April 1861, when the state of South Carolina fired upon United States troops stationed at Fort Sumter in Charleston harbor. Semmes was violating no law or any restriction when he took the train from Washington to Montgomery, Alabama, the seat of the Provisional Government of the Confederate States.

The day after his resignation from the U.S. Navy was accepted, Semmes bid farewell to his family. He boarded a train for Montgomery, going through Virginia and North Carolina, two of the Southern states that had not yet seceded. Semmes recorded in *Service Afloat* his feelings as the train rolled through the "level tract of pine lands between West Point and Montgomery. The pine woods were on fire as we passed through them, the flames now and then running up a lightwood tree, and throwing a weird and fitful glare upon the passing train."

> The scene was particularly Southern, and reminded me that I was drawing near my home, and my people, and I mechanically repeated the words of the poet:
>
>> Breathes there a man with a soul so dead,
>> Who never to himself hath said,
>> This my own, my native land!

And his heart, which until then had felt "as if a heavy weight were pressing upon it," at that moment began to send "a more pressing current through my veins." That night ride through the flaming pine woods "stood as a great gulf in my memory, forming an impassable barrier, as it were, between my past and my future life." Elsewhere he was to write that "Civil War is a terrible crucible through which to pass character." That night in the fiery pine forest of eastern Alabama he passed through that crucible; it was his second rite of passage. The doubts about leaving Anne Elizabeth and the children, the fears of an uncertain future, seem to have evaporated now that he was in his "own, his native land." He fell into a deep sleep and arrived in Montgomery in the morning of February 19, relieved and refreshed.

He immediately contacted C. M. Conrad, chairman of the Congressional Committee on Naval Affairs. That day he attended the meeting of the unicameral Provisional Congress of the Confederate States and was impressed by its outstanding members. The next day, February 20, 1861, he met with all the military men who had preceded him to Montgomery, among them navy officers, some of whom he had served with in the "Old Navy": Captains Lawrence Rousseau, Josiah Tattnall, Duncan N. Ingraham, and Victor M. Randolph, and Commanders Eben Ferrand, Thomas W. Brent, and Henry J. Hartstene—all men with whom he would serve in the C.S. Navy. Little did those men realize that they were in the company of the man who would become the most famous officer of the C.S. Navy.

The following day he met with Jefferson Davis, then the president of the provisional government. Davis had arrived in Montgomery only a day before Semmes. The two men were not strangers, for they had met in Washington when Davis was a U.S. senator from Mississippi. The newly arrived Davis had not yet a secretary or a residence: He was "living in a very simple and unpretending style in the Exchange Hotel." He spoke to Semmes first on the "subject of the want of preparation for defence, in which he found

our states, and the great labor that lay before us, to prepare for emergencies."
Although Congress had not yet had time to organize a navy, he designed
"to make immediate use of me, if I had no objections."

Davis presented a letter to Semmes, dated February 21, 1861, in which
he directed the former navy officer to go on a "shopping trip" to the North
"to make contracts for machinery and munitions for the manufacture of
arms and munitions of war."[11] The letter reflected Davis's knowledge of the
munitions industry in the North, learned no doubt while he had served as
secretary of war under President Franklin Pierce. The instructions were
quite specific, indicating individuals as well as factories for Semmes to contact. Davis even expected the removal of factories from the North to the
South. The next day Semmes was again on the train, headed north on his
"shopping trip."

He stopped in Richmond and examined the state arsenal and the Tredegar Iron Works. He was especially impressed with the latter, which he found
active in the casting of cannon, shot, and shells, and which "was capable of
almost indefinite enlargement." Indeed, those works would serve the South
almost to the last day of the Civil War. He continued to Washington, where
he consulted with "the artifer Wright, at the U.S. Arsenal . . . on the subject
of his percussion-cap machine." In this first interview Wright appeared to
Semmes to be ready to enter into a contract with the Confederate States
to make such a machine for the South. Semmes, however, thought Wright
to be "unreasonable in his demands for compensation," because he demanded $3,000 "for the use of his patent and for his personal superinten-
dence of the manufacture of the machine." Wright also wanted to confer
with his superior at the U.S. arsenal "as otherwise he might lose his place,
which was valuable to him." Semmes had no objection to the request because he "claimed the right not only to contract with any artisan in the
employment of the Government of the United States on any subject of private concern . . . but to induce him by an offer of higher pay to leave his
employment and accept service under our Government." Semmes then returned to Richmond to meet with a certain Major Barbour, who was superintendent of Harper's Ferry Armory. He left it to a trusted friend to offer
Wright $3,000 for the delivery of one of his machines to the South and a
salary of $1,500 a year to work in a Southern arsenal. He was not optimistic
that Wright would accept those terms.

In Richmond, Major Barbour informed Semmes that the machinery he
was seeking belonged to a certain Mr. Ames of Springfield, Massachusetts.
While in Richmond Semmes also conferred with a Captain Dimmock, the
superintendent of the state arsenal, who promised to aid Semmes "in any

manner in his power." He offered to accept delivery of powder and munitions and then forward them to Semmes in the South. He also learned that a partner in the Tredegar works was in Montgomery to sign a contract for guns and munitions for delivery to the South.[12]

How strange that citizens in states still in the Union were so willing to make contracts for the Confederacy. But we see it with hindsight; they, at that time, did not know that within six weeks the two sections of the country would be at war with one another.

Back in Washington, Semmes experienced some of the confusion inevitable in the early days of organizing a new country and a new government. A certain George W. Morse, Semmes learned, was there trying to make contacts with mechanics and to buy arms-producing machinery, in conflict with his own efforts. Morse wrote in complaint to Davis that Semmes "had been sent here fully authorized to transact the same business . . . and was going to the East to see Mr. Ames." So Morse did not send his report to Davis "as, no doubt, Captain Semmes has kept you well informed on the subject."[13] Such misunderstanding and overlapping of assignments was, perhaps, inevitable.

Meanwhile, Semmes, who had been staying with his family while in Washington, took final leave from Anne Elizabeth and their children. He would not see Anne Elizabeth again for almost four and a half years. As he was leaving Washington by train for New York, he saw the preparations for President Lincoln's inauguration on March 4. He was especially resentful of the troops that General Winfield Scott, his old Mexican War antagonist, had gathered for that occasion. Scott, he wrote, "was then verging toward senility and second childhood." He had gathered "together troops for some days, in the Federal capital, for the purpose of inaugurating, amid bayonets, a President of the United States!" Semmes had no desire to witness Lincoln's inauguration, so he hurried away from "the desecration" of the capital city. He arrived in New York on March 5, 1861.

His first act in New York was to leave the city and visit his second son, Oliver John, a cadet at West Point. No other record remains of that visit, but he was careful in his memoirs to identify the son, not by name, but as one who was to become a major of light artillery in the Confederate army. It is well he saw his son then, because he would not see him again until late 1864; even so that was earlier than he would see Anne Elizabeth, his daughters, and his namesake.

He made tours of the various workshops in New York, Connecticut, and Massachusetts. He found people not only willing but "anxious to contract with me." He purchased large quantities of percussion caps in the city of

New York and sent them without disguise to Montgomery. He made a contract for the removal to the Southern states of a complete set of machinery for rifling cannon, "with the requisite skilled workers to put it into operation." Some of these men, he wrote, who "thus would have sold body and soul to me for a sufficient consideration occupied high social positions, and were men of wealth." He could not refrain from suggesting that these New England businessmen were amoral, willing to sign contracts with any government if the profits were sufficiently large.

Semmes was instructed by Stephen R. Mallory, newly appointed Confederate secretary of the navy, to buy several ships suitable for coastal service, strong enough to carry at least one heavy gun. Such ships could be used, obviously, as privateers. The navy commander searched the harbors of New York and Boston but could find no ships fitting the requirements.

March was now drawing to a close. "The war-cloud was assuming darker and more portentous hues, and it soon became evident that my usefulness in the North was about to end. Men were becoming more shy of making engagements with me, and the Federal Government was becoming more watchful." Semmes decided to avoid the railway running through the Federal capital city—his family was no longer there—and through two states that had not yet seceded. Instead, he boarded a steamer, plying between New York City and Savannah, Georgia. He noted with amusement that it flew two flags, "the Federal flag at the peak, and the Confederate flag at the fore." He arrived at Montgomery on April 4, just eight days before the firing on Fort Sumter. During his absence from Montgomery, the Confederate Congress had established a Light-House Bureau, with a navy officer in charge, as Semmes had earlier recommended. He was appointed to head that bureau but had time only to appoint clerks and to open a set of books before the firing on Fort Sumter "and the tocsin of war was sounded."

Semmes immediately informed Secretary Mallory of his desire to go to sea. A board of navy officers in New Orleans was assigned the task of selecting light and fast steamers to sail against the Northern commercial fleets. Their search mostly had been in vain, but Mallory showed him the report on one ship that had been condemned by the board. Semmes saw possibilities in her: "Give me that ship; I think I can make her answer the purpose." Mallory consented, and Semmes knew that "it was time to leave the things of peace to the future." It was the beginning of almost four years of duty constantly at sea; Semmes could not have been happier.

Immediately, on April 18, 1861, Mallory detached Semmes from the Light-House Bureau duty and appointed him commander of the steamer *Sumter*, named after the fort in Charleston harbor.[14] The secretary of the navy appointed several officers to the ship, most of whom would serve with Semmes also on the CSS *Alabama:* Lieutenants John M. Kell, whom Semmes knew well and whom he undoubtedly requested, R. T. Chapman, who accompanied Semmes to New Orleans, John M. Stribling, and William E. Evans; Paymaster Henry Myers; Surgeon Francis L. Galt; Midshipmen William A. Hicks, Richard F. Armstrong, Albert G. Hudgins, John F. Holden, and Joseph D. Wilson. This "family of officers" would serve Semmes on both the *Sumter* and the *Alabama.*

Semmes traveled by steamer from Montgomery to Mobile, where he met Lieutenant Chapman. He found the city where he and his family had lived for many years to be "like the rest of the Confederacy, in a great state of excitement." From Mobile, the two officers took a steamer to New Orleans, arriving there on Monday, April 22. Semmes immediately reported to the commanding naval officer, Captain Lawrence Rousseau, who supported Semmes in preparing the *Sumter* for sea. On the same day, Semmes and Chapman "inspected and took possession of his new ship." He found her to be "as unlike a ship of war as possible." Still, he wrote, he was pleased with her appearance: "Her lines were easy, and graceful, and she had a sort of saucy air about her." But it would take the navy officer two months to convert the peaceful, even if saucy, packet vessel into a ship of war.

His first report from New Orleans reassured Mallory that "with proper alterations" he would be able "to make her a very suitable vessel for our purposes." Her sole duty would be to capture Northern commercial ships, ships that would be unarmed but nonetheless carrying valuable cargoes that would be legitimate prizes of war. Semmes would not be fighting other men, only other ships, like his own, made for peaceful purposes but now serving wartime needs.

Semmes entered into his varied duties with enthusiasm and competency. He stayed in a hotel in New Orleans and, to supervise the ship's refitment, daily crossed the river to Algiers where the *Sumter* lay. He corresponded regularly with Secretary Mallory, who worked to fill the remaining officer slots, to provide the ship's battery and munitions, and to coordinate the arrival of the matériel as it was needed in New Orleans. The two men thus developed a close relationship and a mutual respect, a relationship that would last throughout the war.

Semmes set mechanics to work on the day of his arrival in New Orleans. They had to remove the top deck housing, strengthen the deck to hold cannon, change the masts and sails, provide sleeping quarters for the crew and officers, take aboard large water tanks, order and place the cannon. After recruiting the crew members, Semmes had to become closely acquainted

with the officers and noncommissioned officers so as to make proper assignments. He early on appointed Lieutenant John Kell as his first officer, that
is, the one to actually run the ship on a daily basis. He had first met Kell, it
will be recalled, when he unsuccessfully defended him for insubordination
in a court-martial. During the preparation of the *Sumter* for sea, the two
men developed a mutual confidence and understanding that was to last the
rest of their lives, long after the war. Semmes also came to know the other
officers and assigned them to duties best suited to their personalities and
abilities. Indeed, his success as a raider upon the high seas can be traced to
the relationships he established with the officers during the fitting-out of
the *Sumter.*

Semmes faced unexpected delays in procuring cannon and ammunition.
Some cannon had been sent from the Norfolk, Virginia, Navy Yard, which
had been taken over by the Confederate navy just after the firing on Fort
Sumter. When they did not arrive in New Orleans in due time, he then sent
an officer to locate them. The officer had to pick them up one by one "as
they had been thrown out on the road-side to make room for other freight."
Semmes also faced undue delays in the manufacturing of the water tanks;
they were almost the last item installed on the ship.

Semmes's chief criticism of the vessel was that her propeller could not be
lifted when the ship was under sail and acted as a drag in the water. He
could never get more than nine knots out of her, even under sail and steam.

Finally, just as Semmes was ready to take the *Sumter* downriver he inad-
vertently became engaged in a heated correspondence with the governor of
Louisiana. Semmes had stored some gunpowder in a state facility, and when
he sent men to transfer it to the ship, they found it was not there. Semmes,
feeling the pressure to get to sea, wrote a sharply critical letter to the governor, who protested and responded in kind. Eventually, the two men reconciled their differences. But such an incident was characteristic of Semmes's
problems in preparing the *Sumter* for sea. Delays occurred in delivery of
materials, in recruiting seamen, in making the changes in the ship's interior,
and these delays cost Semmes dearly in getting to sea. When he first saw the
Sumter he had anticipated having her to sea in perhaps three to four weeks;
the time actually was two months, lacking four days. Semmes, despite all
his efforts, was frustrated by these delays in the conversion of the ship into
a ship of war.

Once he was satisfied with the ship, he had to recruit the enlisted personnel—the sailors who would have to carry out the orders of both commissioned and noncommissioned officers. He needed men familiar with
shipboard life and duties. He found them where most ships, warships or

freighters, found them: on the docks and in the cheap hotels and bars of the seaport. They were men who had jumped their ships or who merely were between sailings, men who made their livelihood on board any ship that would pay them—the human flotsam and jetsam of every seaport in the mid-nineteenth century. They did not have to be Americans. The crew consisted of Americans, of course, but also of Englishmen, Irishmen, some Germans, and other Europeans. In some cases language difficulty actually occurred, but because the technique of handling sailing vessels was common experience among all sailors and because the petty officers were all Americans, mostly Southerners, Semmes had little difficulty in handling the vessel.

The crew included the four lieutenants (Kell, Chapman, Stribling, and Evans), Paymaster Myers, Surgeon Galt, and Midshipmen Hicks, Hudgins, Armstrong, and Wilson, and First Engineer Miles J. Freeman, who had three assistant engineers. There were also those of the lower specialist ranks: boatswain, gunner, sailmaker, and carpenter. Perhaps the crew member closest to Semmes next only to Kell was W. Breedlove Smith, the captain's clerk. And then there was the black slave who served as Semmes's valet and cook and who was perhaps the least loyal of the crew. He would later jump ship while it was in a South American port.

Semmes's chief concern was the long delay in getting to sea. The duration of almost two months that it took him to be able even to test the vessel in the waters of the river was a great disappointment to him. Much had occurred during that time: President Lincoln had proclaimed a blockade of all Southern ports, and the U.S. Navy had established a blockade of the Mississippi's three channels that flow into the Gulf of Mexico; and Jefferson Davis had proclaimed that he would issue letters of marque for privateers to prey upon Northern shipping, and indeed several privateers were already active in the Gulf and coastal waters.

The two presidential acts had been made in "pursuance . . . of the laws of nations." Of necessity, then, other seafaring nations had to respond in order to protect and guide their own subjects. On May 14, 1861, a British government proclamation forbade the belligerents to recruit British subjects, equip or arm warships on British territory or in British territorial waters, or in any way to enhance the war-making power of such vessels. The French proclamation, issued on June 10, 1861, included the same prohibitions and further restricted belligerent use of its ports except to make repairs resulting from "acts of God." Both proclamations also forbade their subjects from participating in any belligerent activities and referred them to domestic laws that gave the governments the powers to enforce neutrality.

Even before the *Sumter* was on the high waters, then, the American Civil
War had become an international event; its impact would be felt, literally,
around the world, and Commander Raphael Semmes on board both the
Sumter and the *Alabama* was the chief agent of that worldwide impact of
the American conflict.[15]

A more immediate concern that Semmes faced, however, was the U.S.
Navy blockade where the three mouths of the Mississippi River flow into
the Gulf of Mexico. After the successful test run upriver, Semmes dropped
the ship downriver, feeling at best gloomy about his chances of getting the
Sumter through the blockade and to sea. Furthermore, the test run upriver
had been too short to acquaint the sailors fully with their duties at sea. He
faced the real possibility, after all the hard work of two months, of having
his ship sunk below him before he could put her in operation or, perhaps
even worse, of having her captured and put into Northern service.

As *Sumter* dropped down from New Orleans on the Mississippi River,
Semmes mused on his chances of getting safely through the blockade and of
actually capturing Northern merchantmen. Not only was he disappointed
with *Sumter*'s speed—no more than nine knots—he also worried that he
could carry coal enough only for eight days' fuel. Without coal he would
have difficulty overtaking even an enemy merchant ship because "the propeller would remain a drag in the water, there being no means to hoist it."
He mused: "It was with such drawbacks that I was to take to the sea, alone,
against a vindictive and relentless enemy, whose Navy already swarmed our
coasts, and whose means of increasing it were inexhaustible. But the sailor
has a saying that 'Luck is a Lord,' and we trusted to luck."[16]

His successful escape through the Union blockade, however, was to result
more from Semmes's superior seamanship than luck. He had received from
the Confederate government, now in Richmond, Virginia, his sailing orders, confirming the *Sumter* to be a regular vessel of the Confederate States
Navy. In response to that letter he wrote: "I have an excellent set of men on
board, though they are nearly all green, and will require some little practice,
and drilling, at the guns, to enable them to handle them creditably. Should
I be fortunate enough to reach the high seas, you may rely upon my implicit
obedience of your instructions, 'to do the enemy's commerce the greatest
injury in the shortest time.' "

He dropped down to Confederate Forts Jackson and Saint Philip and
communicated with the Confederate officers, both army and navy, who
were in charge of the forts, from whom he received additional ammunition
and a howitzer, which he placed on *Sumter*'s taffrail "to guard against boat

attacks by night." He remained three days at anchor, drilling his crew "before venturing into the presence of the enemy."

The enemy was the U.S. Navy ships on blockade duty. Semmes needed a river pilot to guide his ship through a pass, but all pilots refused to cooperate. Captain Semmes knew how to handle insubordination; he sent an armed guard to bring several of the pilots to his ship and he ordered them to remain on board so that at least one could be on duty at all times. Only in this way could he get "the native northerners" to perform their duty. While *Sumter* was awaiting an opportunity to slip past the Union ships, Governor Thomas Overton Moore of Louisiana and John Slidell, soon to be sent to France as the Confederate diplomatic agent, came to the forts on an inspection tour. Semmes went ashore to invite them aboard *Sumter;* the captain was proud of his ship and of his men, who reflected the drilling and training that his young officers had imposed upon them during the past seven to ten days. He was happy to show those statesmen "how much a little discipline could accomplish in the course of a few weeks." While Semmes was proud to show off his ship to Slidell, he little anticipated that in another two years, on another ship, he would, in a French port, appeal to Slidell to aid his sailors and officers, victims of his greatest disaster.

But Semmes seldom tried to anticipate the future; the present too much demanded his attention. The pilots held aboard the *Sumter* ultimately provided the service the ship needed. Early on Sunday morning, June 30, 1861, an oysterman came aboard the *Sumter* and informed Semmes that the USS *Brooklyn,* on blockade duty, "had sailed off in chase of a sail, and was no longer in sight." This was the moment Semmes and his men had been awaiting. With a pilot aboard, *Sumter's* steam pressure was increased, and she "bounded off like a thing of life." But Semmes was not yet in the clear; the pilot informed him that he did not know the waters or the bar of Pass à L'Outree; he "was a S. W. bar pilot." Semmes drew upon his past experiences: He decided "to attempt the passage of the bar, from my own slight acquaintance with it when I had been a light-house inspector." However, he did not have to draw upon that past experience; the pilot house, seeing *Sumter's* difficulty, sent a qualified pilot to her. As *Sumter* approached the bar, Semmes discovered that the *Brooklyn* had chased a ship only seven or eight miles "and probably had had her telescopes on the *Sumter* all the while." *Sumter* was now in danger of destruction or capture; what to do?

Against the advice of a lieutenant who had served aboard the Union vessel and reported her speed at thirteen knots as opposed to *Sumter's* maximum nine knots, Semmes decided to make a run for it. The two ships were nearly equal distance from the bar, but *Sumter* had the advantage of a five-knot current. As he cleared the bar, Semmes realized that the Union vessel was three and a half to four miles distant, and therefore *Sumter* was just out of range of the Union guns. The two ships loosed and set their sails; the chase was on!

> As I knew I could lay nearer the wind than she, being able to brace my yards sharper, and had besides, the advantage of larger fore and aft sails . . . I resolved at once to hold my wind, so closely, as to compel her to furl her sails, though this would carry me a little athwart her bows, and bring me perhaps a little nearer to her, for the next half hour or so. A rain squall now came up, and enveloped the two ships, hiding each from the other. As the wind blew off to leeward, and the *Brooklyn* reappeared, she seemed fearfully near to us, and I began to fear I should realize the foreboding of my lieutenant. I could not but admire the majesty of her appearance, with her broad flaring bows, and clean, and beautiful run, and her masts and yards, as taut and square, as those of an old time sailing frigate. . . . I knew of course that as soon as she fell into my wake, she would be compelled to furl her sails. This she did in half an hour or so, and I at once began to breathe more freely, for I could still hold on to my canvas.

"I have witnessed many beautiful sights at sea," Semmes wrote, but none more so than when the *Brooklyn* "clewed up and furled . . . all her sails."[17] Semmes had outsailed the enemy; he sent his crew aloft to man the rigging, and three cheers were sent up for the ship, her flag, and especially her captain. Semmes had won more than freedom by his seamanship; he had won the devotion and admiration of his crew. The *Sumter* was free to enter upon a voyage of destruction, and Semmes was free to enter upon the most successful career of any sea raider in maritime history.

Freedom, however, was not on his mind as he sailed into the Gulf of Mexico. As evening set in, Semmes leaned on the carriage of a howitzer and reflected on the past few months:

> How hurried and confused they had been! It seemed as I had dreamed a dream, and found it difficult, upon awaking, to unite the discordant parts. A great government had been broken up, family ties had been severed, and war—grim, ghastly war—was arraying a household against itself. A little while back, and I served under the very flag which I had that day defied. Strange revolution of feeling, how I now hated that flag! It had been to me as a mistress to a lover; I had looked upon it with admiring eyes, had dallied with it in hours of ease, and had had recourse to it in hours of trouble, and now I found it false!

But like other seamen who had changed flags, Semmes put these thoughts behind him. And like other former U.S. Navy and Army officers now serving the Confederacy, Semmes drew upon his experiences and knowledge gained in the "Old Service" to fight for freedom as he understood it.

He had sailed extensively in the Gulf and Caribbean waters, in the Atlantic Ocean, and in the European waters, especially those of the Mediterranean Sea. In the "Old Navy" he had also learned the prevailing winds and currents of those waters, which were the "crossroads" used by both commercial and military ships. And during the Mexican War he had commanded different types of ships. All of this knowledge he put to good use in fulfilling his new duty: destroy as many Northern merchantmen as possible in the least possible time.

As a lawyer in Mobile, between active-duty tours, he had specialized in maritime law. He knew the value of various cargoes and the methods of labeling them. Thus it was easy for him to identify ownership, value, intended use, and destination of the cargo in any U.S. merchant ship he hailed. Equally important, despite his knowledge of international law as it applied to the sea and to the ships that sailed on it, he had taken with him aboard the ship a copy of Phillimore's *Commentaries upon International Law,* which he used more to justify his decisions than to arrive at them. Captured cargo, he knew, had to be adjudicated as to ownership and value. But he did not yet know, as he sailed the *Sumter* into international waters, the best method of adjudicating captured U.S. merchant ships or how to dispose of them and their cargoes. His experiences during the early weeks of the *Sumter* cruise were to be a learning process for the lawyer/sea captain.

Free at last from the USS *Brooklyn,* he set course for one of the "highways" of the sea and entered into his career as a commerce raider. His first destination was Cape Saint Roque, Brazil, which he referred to as "the turning point of the commerce of the world." He intended to "make a dash of a few days at the enemy's ships on the south side of Cuba, coal at some convenient point, stretch over to Barbados, coal again, and then strike for the Brazilian coast."

The *Sumter* exited from the Gulf of Mexico as it sailed between Cape Antonio on the southwest tip of Cuba and the opposite coast of Yucatan, then into Caribbean waters. As the *Sumter* was running between the coast of Cuba and the Isle of Pines, flying English colors, the lookout shouted "Sail ho!" and said he sighted two sails dead ahead. Semmes hailed the first one, sent a boarding party aboard her, and verified that she was an English vessel and allowed her to continue her voyage. The second ship refused to show her colors until Semmes lowered the English flag and raised the Confederate one and then fired a shot across her bow; she then showed the stars and stripes of the United States. She was the first of his many captures on the high seas.

Semmes, despite his previously expressed feelings as he had fled from the *Brooklyn,* had mixed emotions about destroying a ship flying the American flag. Later he wrote in his *Memoirs of Service Afloat and Ashore during the War Between the States:* "Here was our first prize, and a most welcome sight it was; but I well recollect the mingled impressions of joy and sadness, that were made upon me by the event." The ship, flying the American flag, "was my relative, and erst had been my friend—how could I fail to feel some pity for him, along with indignation, which his crime had excited?"

Semmes sent a boarding party to the ship under a lieutenant who returned "bringing with him the master and his papers." When the captain of the ship was brought aboard the *Sumter,* he said to Semmes: "Nothing could have surprised me more than the appearance of the Confederate flag in these seas." Semmes, feeling compassion for the captain from Maine, replied: "My duty is a painful one to destroy such noble a ship as yours, but I must discharge it without vain regrets; and as for yourself, you will only have to do what many thousands have done before you, submit to the fortunes of war—yourself and your crew will be well treated on board my ship." The ship was bark rigged and nearly new; she was sailing in ballast, seeking a cargo of sugar in some Cuban port.

Having verified the captured ship's Northern ownership, and having transferred to the *Sumter* provisions—cordage, sails, and paints—Semmes ordered his boarding party "to torch her." Thus Semmes's first capture and destruction of an American merchant vessel took place just off Cuba on July 3, 1861; her name was the *Golden Rocket.* As the torches were applied, Semmes described the spectacular event: "The forked tongues of the devouring element, leaping into the rigging, newly tarred, ran rapidly up the shrouds, first to the tops, then to the top mastheads. At one time the intricate network of the cordage of the burning ship was traced, as with a pencil of fire, upon the black sky beyond, the many threads of flame twisting and writhing, like so many serpents that had received their death wounds." The ship's main mast fell over her side, into the sea, "making a noise like that of the sturdy oak of the forests when it falls by the stroke of the axman."

As the ship burned in the waters, Semmes and his men fell silent; seeing the flag under which they had previously served burn with the rigging brought lumps to their throats. Indeed, the officers of *Sumter* took a collection to present to the captain of the *Golden Rocket* because they had learned that he had no insurance to cover the loss of his new ship.

Commander Semmes had handled his first experience of destruction rather well. Confirming the status of the ship had been easy. She was obviously and admittedly an enemy ship and had no cargo, so Semmes had no adjudication to make in determining the ownership of either ship or cargo. The importance of the capture and destruction of the *Golden Rocket* is that she was the first victim of Semmes's two-ship, three-year career as a raider on the high seas. Furthermore, the friendliness that developed between the officers and crew of the *Sumter* and those of the *Golden Rocket* was unique in Semmes's career as a sea raider. But this first experience did set certain precedents that Semmes and his crew would follow throughout the war.

The first precedent that Semmes would follow for the next thirty-six months was the treatment of prisoners, both seamen and officers. Semmes was proud that he had treated all the prisoners he took aboard both raiders in accordance with the laws of war: "We were making war upon the enemy's commerce, but not upon his unarmed seamen." The captain of the *Golden Rocket* dined with *Sumter*'s officers, and the crew was put into a mess with its own cook; their rations were the same as those of *Sumter*'s crew. Unless Semmes had more prisoners on board than he could safely handle, he treated all the prisoners from his various captures in the same fashion.

Finally, prior to burning the ship, Semmes had his boarding officer bring to the *Sumter* the "excellent chronometer" belonging to the captain of the *Golden Rocket*. It was only the first of many chronometers that Semmes acquired in the same fashion during both of his cruises. The chronometers were not just mementos of his victims. Rather, Semmes prided himself as a navigator, and every night while at sea he checked his navigator's calculations, partly perhaps to safeguard his ship but also because he enjoyed navigation. His collection at the end of *Alabama*'s cruise must have been as many as seventy or more chronometers.

Although Semmes and his crew, all seasoned seamen, were saddened by the sight of the burning *Golden Rocket,* that feeling did not deter Semmes from actively seeking other U.S. merchantmen with the intent to destroy them. Moreover, he always scrupulously abided by the international laws of the sea. The next day was the Fourth of July, the first one since secession, and he refused to celebrate it. In the late afternoon of the Fourth he sighted two ships, hailed them, and sent a boarding party to each. Their papers showed them to be U.S. ships but with neutral cargoes. Following the laws of the sea, he decided to take them into a neutral port for adjudication of the cargoes. He ordered the boarding officers to follow *Sumter* into the Cuban port of Cienfuegos. Just as he approached the lighthouse, the lookout sighted two more sails to the southeast. Semmes immediately ordered his two victims to await his return and set out for the newly sighted vessels. He gave his orders and the crew quickly responded: "*Sumter,* feeling the renewed impulse of her engines, sprang forward in pursuit of the doomed craft ahead, as if she knew what was going on." Semmes came upon the two crafts quickly and "hove them to, by hail, and brought the masters on board." They were both New England ships and had just left the harbor of Cienfuegos, laden with sugar. Their cargoes were certified as Spanish property. The master of one of the ships appealed to Semmes in behalf of his wife and a female companion of hers, both of whom were just recovering from the effects of yellow fever. Semmes assured him they would be treated "with tenderness and respect" but that he could not release the vessel on their account. Semmes now had four ships, as well as two recuperating women, to take into the Cuban port.

However, the crew of one of the first two ships captured, the *Cuba,* overpowered the small boarding party under Midshipman Albert G. Hudgins and sailed away during the night. On its voyage to New York, Hudgins attempted to retake the vessel but failed when he was shot in the arm. Later in the war, the young midshipman was paroled and served under Semmes in the James River Fleet. Commander Semmes never repeated the mistake of sending such a small boarding party aboard a captured ship.

Semmes had taken his captures into a Cuban port because it was convenient and also because he wanted to test the reactions of the local administrators. But officials in Cienfuegos had no instructions from their government as to the correct procedures they should follow. Accordingly, they at first refused to allow him to take the vessels up the small river and into the harbor. The *Sumter* stayed at the mouth of the river that night, Semmes intending, nonetheless, the next morning to convoy the captures upriver and into the harbor. Much to his surprise, however, at sunrise three other ships—all American ones—approached from the harbor. He made sure to follow them into international waters, then he captured them. That made six ships that Semmes, like an old hen gathering her brood of chicks, had to escort some miles upriver to the harbor of Cienfuegos. All were American ships with neutral cargoes.

Spain had not yet followed the lead of Great Britain and France in declaring neutrality. Thus the officials in Spanish America had no instructions from Madrid as to their proper reactions to the situation in which Semmes placed them. Semmes hoped to influence them to leave the prizes in their care until they could be "adjudicated by a Court of Admiralty of the Confederate States." He appointed a local citizen as "prize agent" for the six U.S. ships and instructed him to take measures to protect the ships and their cargoes. The prize agent was instructed also to have the ships and their cargoes certified by a notary and to send the certified papers to the judge of the Confederate States District Court in New Orleans. Semmes hoped "that some of the nations, at least, would give an asylum for my prizes, so that I might have them formally condemned by the Confederate States Prize Courts, instead of being obliged to destroy them." It was a vain hope that was never fulfilled, but it reflected the power of his vision of the flames devouring the *Golden Rocket*. At least he had placed six Northern merchant vessels temporarily out of commission, for as soon as Spain issued its proclamation of neutrality, the Cuban commandant released the six vessels to the United States.

The Cuban officials allowed Semmes to take on board a hundred tons of coal and fresh provisions for the crew as well as to fill his water tanks. In the evening of his last day at Cienfuegos, as the sun was sinking, Semmes in the company of a junior lieutenant took a walk along the banks of the river. They strolled for an hour and more "amid the rich tropical vegetation of this queen of islands, now passing under the flowering acacia, and now under the deep foliage of the orange tree, which charmed two senses at once—that of smell, by the fragrance of its young flowers, and that of sight by the golden hue of its luscious and golden fruit." As he had done during the Mexican War, he continued to describe in detail the beauties of nature. Such experiences always relaxed and refreshed him. With *Sumter* better provided than when she sailed from New Orleans, and with Semmes's soul revived by his short stroll on the lush Cuban riverbank, the ship and the captain resumed their cruise against Northern merchantmen.

In two short days Semmes had burned one vessel and captured six others; never again during his two cruises would he experience such success.

In the early evening of July 7, 1861, Semmes directed *Sumter*'s bow southeasterly, headed ultimately to the island of Curacao, off the coast of Venezuela. Ever the navigator, he noted as *Sumter* passed the Cayman Islands that his charts placed the islands some "fifteen or sixteen miles too far to the westward," a fact he recorded "to put navigators on their guard." A strong head wind forced him to use so much coal that he abandoned his plan to recoal in the Barbados Islands; changing course, he headed under sail only for the Dutch island of Curacao where he arrived off the town of Saint Anne on July 17, 1861.

The governor of the island sent a message to him, forbidding him to take the *Sumter* into the harbor, which Semmes maintained was a "foretaste of the trouble that the Federal Consuls were to give us in the future." Semmes responded by sending Lieutenant Chapman into Saint Anne with Semmes's reply. In it, the Confederate navy officer reminded the Dutch governor that the great powers of England and France through their declarations of neutrality both admitted Confederate navy vessels into their harbors. "Am I to understand from your Excellency that Holland has adopted a different rule, and that she not only excludes the prizes, but the ships of war themselves, of the Confederate States? And this at the same time that she admits the cruisers of the United States, thus departing from her neutrality in this war, ignoring the Confederate States as belligerents, and aiding and assisting their enemy?" For two hours the elders of the town debated the issue while Lieutenant Chapman sat and waited. Semmes sent a note to Chapman informing him that because *Sumter*'s guns had not been used recently, Semmes had decided to practice the men at the guns. After three or four shells landed on the small mountain just above the building in which the council was meeting and burst with precision "like a clap of rather sharp ragged thunder," Chapman was seen returning to the ship with a smile of victory on his lips. He informed Semmes that permission had, after all, been granted for *Sumter* to enter the harbor.

Semmes's strong-armed tactic to force the weak Dutch colonial government to permit the *Sumter* into its harbor was unique, and he never again had to resort to such tactics. He had established his rights as a belligerent power, and that is exactly what he intended to do. He blamed the colonial officials' attempt to refuse his ship's entry into the harbor on the resident U.S. consul. It is, however, quite likely that the Kingdom of Holland had not yet sent instructions to all its colonial officials. After all, *Sumter* was not only the first Confederate warship to enforce Southern belligerent rights; it was the only Confederate navy vessel cruising the high seas. All the other Southern ships were privateers, and since the Declaration of Paris of 1856, privateering had been outlawed and neutrals had the right to refuse such ships from entering their harbors.

Having established his right to the Dutch colonial port facilities, Semmes steamed the *Sumter* through the town into the landlocked harbor. Immediately the ship was surrounded by a fleet of bumboats "laden with a profusion of tropical fruits, and filled with men and women, indifferently—the women rather preponderating." He had last been in Curacao when he was a green midshipman, but now "it seemed as though I was looking upon the same faces, listening to the same confusion of voices as before." The crew took full advantage of the women's services: washing their clothes and selling fresh vegetables and tropical fruits, such as bananas, and blood-red oranges, and even tobacco. "As Jack is a gallant fellow, a little flirtation was going on, too, with the purchasing, and I was occasionally amused at these joint efforts at trade and love-making."

Semmes unconsciously revealed a sympathetic understanding of his common sailors, most of whom were not Americans, much less Southerners. "Jack has a great fondness for pets," he wrote, "and no wonder, poor fellow, debarred, as he is, from all family ties, and with no place he can call his home, but his ship." The captain allowed them to bring aboard various pets, such as monkeys and parrots. "Monkeys were now gamboling about the rigging" and "parrots were waking the echoes of the harbor with their squalling." The crew appreciated the captain's occasional leniency and repaid it with loyalty and quick responses to the officers' orders. At sea for only about six weeks, Semmes had created a tight ship that was effective in fulfilling its sometimes unglamorous role in the American Civil War.

One day Semmes went ashore and was surprised to find "Yankees" ensconced in the small town. One was proprietor of the best hotel, and another, a New Yorker, was the owner of a photography shop, who offered to take a photograph of the *Sumter*. But Semmes experienced an even greater surprise when the private secretary to former President Cipriano Castro of Venezuela came aboard to visit him. His object "was to propose to me to reinstate the exiled President, in his lost position, by engaging in a military expedition, with him, to the mainland." In a flash, Semmes with his quick intellect saw himself facetiously as the "Warwick of Venezuela," who could put "the crown on another's head, if I might not wear it myself." Another quick vision flashed before him: "I might hoist my admiral's flag, on board the *Sumter*, and take charge of all the pirogues, and canoes, that composed the Venezuelan navy." But, he continued, "I was like one of those damsels who had already plighted her faith to another, before the new wooer appeared." Even while these images flashed through his mind, he politely rejected the offer because of his obligations to his own country.

The *Sumter* remained exactly one week in Saint Anne's harbor. Semmes had the ship repainted and refitted, including a new main mast and an overhaul of the engine. The washerwomen's laundry service resulted in a neater looking crew with their shirts now sparkling white. The crew appeared more healthy as a result of the use of antiscorbutic acids. And during the stay in Saint Anne, Semmes also relaxed and refreshed himself by taking a solitary walk in the town. He found it to be a "quaint, picturesque old place, with some few modern houses." The general air, however, was "one of dilapidation, and a decay of trade."

Several ships sailed from Saint Anne to Saint Thomas on the Virgin Islands. Knowing the U.S. consul would send word of *Sumter*'s presence in Saint Anne to the U.S. Navy ships at Saint Thomas, Semmes let it be known that he intended to go back to Cuba, to cruise along its coast. This technique of giving out false information of his intentions worked very well for Semmes during both of his cruises.

As Semmes was preparing the ship to leave Saint Anne, one of his men, "a simple lad named Orr," was seduced away by a Yankee skipper, aided, Semmes did not doubt, "by the Boston hotel keeper, and our particular friend, the consul." Semmes did not consider the loss to be great, and he was especially gratified that no other crewman, despite similar tampering by the same persons, chose to desert the *Sumter*.

From Saint Anne, Semmes headed the ship for Venezuela, specifically toward the coastal city of Puerto Cabello. At about 6:00 A.M. on July 26, 1861, *Sumter* captured the schooner *Abby Bradford*, bound from New York to Puerto Cabello and laden with provisions. Both ship and cargo were American owned, a legitimate prize. The image of the burning of the *Golden Rocket* still bright in his mind's eye, Semmes decided, instead of burning her, to take the ship into Puerto Cabello. Later in the morning of July 26, the two ships entered the port and Semmes, in a long letter cast in the same frame as the one he had presented to the Cuban officials in Cienfuegos, reported to the Puerto Cabello authorities. The American consul, Semmes felt sure, was consulted; the local official, frightened at the prospect of losing Northern shipping in his port, denied Semmes the right to bring his prize into his harbor and, in effect, told him to leave immediately. Of course Semmes refused; but at the same time he was frustrated by the Venezuelan's refusal to treat the Confederate ship as a legitimate belligerent with all the rights appertaining to that designation. Semmes was furious with the mild and proper language used by the city official; it reminded him of the poet's line: "As mild a mannered man, as ever cut a throat."

Instead of leaving immediately, Semmes sent his paymaster ashore to purchase fresh provisions and fruits for the crew, and he gave liberty to such officers as wanted it. Despite this rather childish bravado, Semmes decided to send the *Abby Bradford* to New Orleans to be adjudicated by the judge of the prize court there. As the prize approached the passes of the Mississippi River, she was captured by a Union ship of the blockade fleet and returned to her owner. Semmes's men aboard the ship were made prisoners of war. Although they were soon exchanged, they never rejoined Semmes in his three-year odyssey against Northern shipping.

Abby Bradford was at least the third, and possibly the ninth, of Semmes's captures that he lost. In his memoirs he justified his action:

> I am . . . particular in giving the reader an account of these, my first trans-
> actions, for the purpose of showing him, that I made every effort to avoid
> the necessity of destroying my prizes at sea; and that I resorted to this
> practice, when it became evident that there was nothing else to be done.
> Not that I had not the right to burn them, under the laws of war, when
> there was no dispute about the property—as was the case with the *Golden
> Rocket*, she having had no cargo aboard—but because I desired to avoid all
> possible complications with neutrals.

There is much that is self-serving in this statement. He never did burn a
ship, aboard the *Sumter* or the *Alabama*, that contained confirmed neutral
property; he bonded the cargo and released the ship. Furthermore, he had
no need to apologize or to explain to anyone. His wartime career was a
remarkable one; it set the world record for one captain's career with a cruiser.
Rather, his apologia was a reflection in his mind's eye of the flames envel-
oping the *Golden Rocket*. It reflected, also, the psychological impact of destroying a ship that was flying the flag under which he and his officers had
so long served—and served with a devotion that reflected their love and
respect for the country of which that flag was a symbol. Semmes's first capture on the high seas—not his train ride through the flaming Alabama pine
forest—was his intellectual act of passage, not his spiritual act of passage.

There is more. Semmes, a good Roman Catholic who could see his
church's flaws, nevertheless remained loyal to it because he could also find
comfort and peace in that church. He never revolted against the church. His
revolt against his country's flag, however real on the surface, was a soul-
wrenching pain that, despite his apologia in his memoirs, he could never
ease. So he subconsciously allowed those captive ships flying the flag, ships
he could have destroyed, to return to the flag. The burning *Golden Rocket*
remained in his mind's eye and in his soul a constant reminder of his revolt
against that very flag. It was a spiritual rendering of his devotion to the
United States and to the flag representing his beloved country. He never did
fully recover, psychologically or spiritually, from the sight of the burning
Golden Rocket.

The psychological and spiritual conflicts within Semmes were once
again put to the test. Shortly after he had sent the *Abby Bradford* off to New
Orleans, on July 27 he hailed the *Joseph Maxwell* of Philadelphia. The ship's
cargo was mixed, one half of it belonging to a citizen of the United States
and the other half to a neutral merchant doing business in Puerto Cabello.
Semmes attempted to land the neutral half of the cargo in Puerto Cabello,
but the officials there refused to allow it. Then, rather creatively, he placed
the ship under a prize crew with Midshipman William A. Hicks in com-

mand, with orders to attempt to land the neutral cargo at a Cuban port in charge of a prize agent and then to take the vessel's papers to the Confederate prize court in New Orleans. Hicks found the officials in Cienfuegos to be uncooperative, refusing to allow him to enter the port. Back at sea, he mistakenly identified a Spanish vessel to be an American warship and, in his haste to flee, ran the *Joseph Maxwell* aground. Hicks and his prize crew managed to escape in an open boat and returned to Cienfuegos. The young midshipman had at least rendered the *Joseph Maxwell* unseaworthy; it could be counted among *Sumter's* victims.

Meanwhile, Semmes and the *Sumter* were moving to new hunting grounds. Unknown to Semmes, an old comrade in the U.S. Navy during the Mexican War, David D. Porter, future admiral of the U.S. Navy and now lieutenant in command of the USS *Powhatan,* was beginning his search for the *Sumter* near Saint Thomas on the northern edge of the Caribbean Sea. At about the same time, another U.S. Navy officer and future naval historian and strategist, young Midshipman Alfred T. Mahan, devised a plan to capture Semmes and the *Sumter.* He recommended to the U.S. secretary of the navy that a sailing ship with cannon hidden in false deck housing be fitted out and manned in order to entice the *Sumter* to hail her and attempt to board her. The false housing, young Mahan claimed, could be removed quickly and the cannon could destroy the Confederate ship. He even volunteered to command such a vessel.[18] But Porter and Mahan were searching in the wrong places for Semmes, thanks to the misinformation he had disseminated.

While Porter was at Saint Thomas, Semmes was cruising eastward along the coast of Venezuela. On July 30, the *Sumter* entered the gulf of Para, between the island of Trinidad and the northeast coast of Venezuela. As he anchored the ship off the town of Port of Spain, he realized that "thirty-five years ago I was here as a midshipman! A generation has since passed away. So brief is thy life, O Man!" He ordered coal for the ship upon arrival, but two days passed before it was loaded; the excuse was that the coal vender depended upon free black labor, "which is difficult to procure." Semmes added his own thought about free black labor: "This is another of those fine islands that Great Britain has destroyed by her act of emancipation."

One day as the *Sumter* sat in the harbor, Semmes had a visit from a British navy captain. Their talk turned to the causes of the Civil War, and Semmes freely told his visitor about the tariffs that were so unfavorable to the South and briefly mentioned the constitutional questions involved in the coming of war. "All of this is new to me, I assure you," the Englishman replied. "I thought your war had arisen out of the slavery question." Semmes calmly commented: "That is a common mistake of foreigners," and he entered into a detailed account of how the North had robbed the South by means of the tariffs. "When a burglar designs to enter a dwelling, for the purposes of robbery, he provides himself with the necessary implements. The slavery question was one of the implements employed, to help on the robbery of the South."

After five days in port, on August 5 he got up steam and sailed from Port of Spain through the Dragon's Mouth, turned eastward, and passed between the islands of Trinidad and Tobago. He then sailed southward, down the coast of South America, to the maritime crossroads of the sea, just off the coast of Brazil.

Noting the ease by which blacks maintained themselves with the food crops grown so easily in the luxuriant climate, Semmes pondered upon the future of whites in this garden of Eden: All the West Indies "will lapse into luxuriant wilderness." Racial amalgamation among the islanders "will corrupt what little of European blood remains in them, until every trace of the white man shall disappear." His thoughts then turned to the Southern states in North America: "If we are beaten in this war, what will be our fate in the Southern States? Shall we, too, become mongrelized, and disappear from the face of the earth? Can this be the ultimate design of the Yankee?" These thoughts reflected Semmes's most extreme expression of racism. Despite his explanation to the British captain of the causes of the war, basically Semmes was fighting the war to preserve the white race. Before the war he had held mild views concerning slavery, but the war and his experiences in free societies had changed his racial attitude.

He could switch his thoughts quickly: From his morose racist expressions, the seaman in him immediately turned to the weather. Without changing the paragraph, he continued: "The night was quite light, and taking a fresh departure, at about ten P.M., from the east end of Trinidad, we passed through the strait between it and the island of Tobago . . . and emerged from the Caribbean Sea, upon the broad bosom of the South Atlantic." Winds and strong currents deterred the little ship, so that *Sumter's* coal soon ran out. There was no hope now of chasing possible victims; *Sumter* had to await favorable winds, which were fickle at best. Finally on August 15, 1861, Semmes picked up a pilot off the coast of French Guiana and entered the port of the famous penal colony at Cayenne. Shortly after entering the harbor, Semmes and his men heard cannon firing. At first they thought the firing was saluting the *Sumter,* but they soon realized it was in honor of French Emperor Napoleon III's birthday. The voyage had been difficult, at best, and at worst had cost Semmes many days without sight of an enemy vessel.

Semmes and *Sumter* were ill-received by the French commander. They were not allowed to receive coal or to go ashore. Semmes attributed the French attitude to the American consul's presence at Cayenne. Within an hour after *Sumter*'s boat returned, Semmes was under way, out of the French harbor. He would much later receive a warmer welcome at another French harbor, in another ship.

In need of coal, Semmes doubled back up the coast toward Surinam, the Dutch colony. He had difficulty finding the mouth of the Surinam River, "such is the sameness of the coast," and anchored for the night of August 18. Another ship approached and anchored about four miles from the *Sumter;* Semmes felt sure that if the ship were Dutch, or a mail ship, it would not have waited out the night, as Semmes was doing, but would have continued up the river to the capital city of Paramaribo. He concluded, therefore, that the ship must be a warship and might be an American one. He took the precaution of calling his crew to quarters and cleared for action. Because nothing developed that evening, he left orders for the crew to be called to their guns at 4:30 the next morning. Semmes ran the *Sumter,* flying the French flag, toward the strange ship, which answered also with the French flag. Eventually they settled their mutual misunderstandings, secured a pilot, and moved up the river to Paramaribo, arriving there about noon on August 19. Semmes ordered the coal he needed; not until twelve days later was *Sumter* ready to leave. Semmes received news of the South's victory at First Manassas; he was thrilled not only for the victory but also for the effect it would have on neutral nations. When he learned that the Union commander had been assisted by "the poor old, superannuated Winfield Scott," he could not help but comment, in view of their Mexican War relationship: Winfield Scott "that renegade soldier, lending his now feeble intellect to the Northern Vandal, to assist stabbing to the heart his mother state—Virginia."

While the coaling was in progress, Semmes visited the governor, exchanged visits with other ship captains, and lost two men to desertion, one of whom was his cabin boy, the slave named Ned. Semmes particularly regretted losing Ned because his cabin aboard *Sumter* never again would be so clean and well-kept.

On August 31, *Sumter* once again sailed southward along the South American coast. This time she was headed for the town of San Luis in the Brazilian state of Maranhos. Running through some irregular waters,

Sumter ran upon a sand bank that was only two fathoms below the surface and suffered slight damage to her false keel. At 5:00 P.M., she anchored among some fishing vessels in the shallow harbor of San Luis and remained there two days, recoaling and taking on provisions.

Into the open sea once again, *Sumter* ran well before the winds. Semmes reflected on the past weeks: What had he really accomplished? He had lost twenty-three days seeking coal—twenty-three days without a capture! He had shown the flag in the possessions of three different nations and had, he felt, contributed to neutral recognition of the South's belligerent rights. But he had not fulfilled his first duty. On September 4 he was happy to note that *Sumter* had just passed the mouths of the Amazon River and almost simultaneously crossed the equator. He had brought *Sumter* and her crew into the Southern Hemisphere for the first time, and he had brought the Confederate flag with them.

On Friday, September 6, Semmes navigated the *Sumter* through the treacherous waters of the Bay of Saint Luis, on the shore of which was located the port town of Saint Luis. He was congratulated by a Brazilian navy officer who told him that no Brazilian navy captain would dare to sail those waters without a pilot.

On Sunday Semmes went ashore, too late to attend mass but in time to have dinner with a Mr. Olivier, a native of Louisiana who had settled in the town, and he enjoyed the companionship of a fellow Southerner. The next day, "feeling the necessity of some change" after several weeks of feeling feverish and exhausted, Semmes moved into the Hotel Porto, where he was quite comfortable. The move helped restore his usual good health. The hotel owner had followed the sea, spoke half a dozen languages, operated a theater and two "fashionable restaurants, in beautifully laid out pleasure-grounds in the suburbs." He also "drove a couple of fast horses and was on capital terms with all the pretty women in town." No wonder Semmes recovered so quickly; his stay had not been devoted entirely to Confederate business.

On Tuesday, September 10, Commander Semmes, CSN, called upon the president of the state. By presenting his credentials, Semmes convinced him that *Sumter* had every right to buy coal and other necessities as did any ship flying any other flag. He then told the president, despite his earlier comment to the British officer in Port of Spain, that the South was "fighting the first battle in favor of slavery, and that if we were beaten in the contest, Brazil would be the next one to be assailed by Yankee and English propagandists." The Brazilian seemed to be impressed.

Again without funds, Semmes negotiated with another native of Louisiana, temporarily in the city on business, a draft of $2,000 drawn on the Confederate secretary of the navy. This money enabled Semmes to meet the costs of repainting, buying coal, and living in a hotel. A shortage of funds, however, was to hound Semmes and his ship throughout the cruise. The ship, with new paint and newly enlarged coal bins, was soon ready to depart. Semmes, refreshed, boarded *Sumter* in the early evening of September 14 and the next morning, with a pilot, sailed from the Bay of San Luis.

Instead of heading southward to Cape of San Roque as he originally had planned, he directed the *Sumter* to the northeast, into the currents that formed the "highway" of the sea for ships sailing from southern Europe and the Pacific and Indian Oceans to the Caribbean and North American ports. The *Sumter* experienced unusually strong riptides, which Semmes described in detail, but few if any other ships. Finally, on the tenth day from port, the *Sumter* hailed and boarded a ship that was—at last—American owned, the *Joseph Park* of Boston. Semmes brought the ship's crew of seven and one passenger on board *Sumter,* then sent Lieutenant Evans and six crewmen aboard her to act as scouts to seek out other American-registered ships. For three days the two ships sought other Union-owned vessels but to no avail. During the night of September 28, after taking off some supplies the *Sumter* could use, Semmes set the *Joseph Park* afire "and thus offered another sacrifice to the god of war." The flames running through the rigging of the *Golden Rocket* obviously were still in Commander Semmes's eyes.

Almost exactly one month passed before *Sumter* came across another U.S.-registered ship, the *Daniel Trowbridge,* out of Connecticut, with a cargo owned by the captain. The *Sumter* had to chase the victim from 8:30 A.M. until 3:00 P.M. before capturing her. The ship was well supplied with provisions, and Semmes happily transferred beef, pork, hams, flour, and bread to *Sumter.* The captain of the *Trowbridge* was a surly man. When a messenger sent by Semmes asked him for his ship's logs, he replied: "Damn them, I hope they will do them no good, and if they want a shirt, I will send that too!" After that quotation, Semmes wrote in his journal: "I had this man seized and put in double irons. Latitude, 16° 40′; longitude, 58° 16′." Phlegmatic man, that Commander Raphael Semmes, CSN.

Between the capture of the *Trowbridge* and the sighting of the Dominican mountains, Semmes hailed ten ships, mostly English and French, all of them neutral; *Sumter*'s reputation preceded her. Northern merchant ships with Northern cargoes were avoiding *Sumter*'s reported watery paths.

The *Sumter* had been at sea for almost a month and a half when on November 9, 1861, Semmes directed the ship into the bay of Fort-de-France on the island of Martinique, one of the Leeward Islands that form the eastern boundary of the Caribbean Sea. Semmes visited the governor and received permission to land his prisoners if the U.S. consul at Saint Pierre, another city on the island, would assume responsibility for them. The governor also gave permission for Semmes to buy coal on the open market, which also was located at Saint Pierre.

The next day was Sunday, and Semmes went into Saint Pierre to attend the 8:00 A.M. mass, known as the Governor's Mass. As he had done so often in Mexico, he described the interior of the church, which he found to be "very pleasing, with some valuable paintings." He also enjoyed the "fine music from a band." He noticed that blacks and whites occupied the pews indiscriminately, "though there was no social mixture of the races." He explained to a number of men once again the "true" nature of the Civil War. In the evening he visited shore again and heard band music. He described the event as "A gay and beautiful scene, the moon, the shade trees, the statue of Empress Josephine, the throng of well-dressed men and women, the large band and the fine music, the ripple of the sea, and last, though not least, the katydids, so fraught with memories of home, dear home!"

Semmes seldom referred to "home, dear home!" in his ships' logs. Indeed, he even was unsure as to where his home was: Was it where Anne Elizabeth was living? But where was that? Had she gone to Mobile, as he had requested her to do, and rented a small house for herself, their daughters, and young Raphael? Or were they still staying with his brother in Maryland, the brother who had refused to move from Maryland to join the Confederate cause? Or were they in Cincinnati, in the enemy's territory, with her Spencer relatives? And what of his two older sons for whom he had arranged commissions in the Confederate army? Had they faced the enemy in combat? Were they still alive? He had so many questions about his loved ones! But all he could do was accept the fate war had imposed upon him. He could only follow his own advice that he had given his daughter Electra: "Look always on the bright side of every picture, that this ever-changing wheel of fortune presents to us."[19] So he went about the business of preparing his little ship in order better to destroy the enemy's seagoing commerce. Fate had dealt him a difficult role to play in this most difficult war.

Semmes also had to deal with several Union warships that were assigned the task of destroying *Sumter* and her captain. His former shipmate, David D. Porter, captain of the USS *Powhatan*, had just missed him in Paramaribo and then had gone to Surinam to await Semmes's return; G. H. Scott, aboard USS *Keystone State*, was off the coast of Guiana searching for *Sumter*. And finally, James S. Palmer, aboard USS *Iroquois*, searched for Semmes in the Caribbean Sea. Semmes seemed almost to enjoy the game of hide-and-seek that he played with the three U.S. Navy ships, but he also realized that it was a deadly game he had to play out.

Indeed, the site of that game soon centered on the island of Martinique. News had traveled to the captains of the U.S. Navy ships that *Sumter* was in the Fort-de-France harbor, where Palmer on *Iroquois* learned that *Sumter* had transferred to Saint Pierre. Early on the morning of November 15, Semmes was awakened by the officer of the deck; the *Iroquois* was "standing in for us and approaching us very close." Semmes called all hands to quarters and prepared to repulse an attack by the Northern vessel. But Palmer sheered off within 300 yards of the *Sumter,* then repeated the maneuver several times, imposing upon Semmes the necessity of repeatedly calling his men to quarters. Semmes then ordered his men to remain at their posts throughout the night. The people of the small city learned of the Union ship's presence in the harbor, and Semmes noted that "the market square, the quays, and the windows of the houses are thronged by an eager and curious multitude, expecting every moment to see a combat." At one time, the *Iroquois* approached *Sumter* "within a ship's length" then veered off. Palmer was playing a dangerous game with the international laws of belligerency and the rights of neutrality.

Palmer's dangerous game of intimidation ended when a French warship arrived later in the morning of November 15. The French captain visited *Sumter* to assure Semmes that his purpose was to uphold French neutrality. While he was glad to have that assurance, Semmes nonetheless felt that Palmer already had violated that neutrality by sailing in and out of the harbor, and he also knew that if Palmer anchored within the harbor, the twenty-four-hour rule would apply, thus allowing *Sumter* a head start from the port. (The twenty-four-hour rule applies when two enemy ships are in the same harbor; when one sails, the other must wait twenty-four hours before sailing.) Palmer continued the cat-and-mouse game on the morning of November 16, anchoring about half a mile from the *Sumter.* The French offered to escort the *Sumter* to the French navy base at Fort-de-France, but Semmes refused. Palmer later hauled anchor and left the harbor, remaining just outside it, less than the required league distance. No one mentioned the twenty-four-hour rule, probably because *Sumter* was not yet fully coaled and thus was unable to sail.

Raphael Semmes throughout the *Iroquois*'s maneuvering had assumed a countenance of calm and self-assurance. Indeed, in the late afternoon of November 16, as the *Iroquois* was leaving the harbor, Semmes took "a delightful stroll along the beach to the northward." His attitude undoubtedly reassured his men and confused his enemy. The next morning, a Sunday, he again attended mass in the local Roman Catholic church.

Semmes once again refused a French offer to escort *Sumter* to the military port of Fort-de-France because the harbor of Saint Pierre afforded him more facilities for repair of *Sumter*'s engine and because the configuration of the harbor made Saint Pierre "a more convenient harbor from which to escape." But what chance would *Sumter* have of evading *Iroquois*? The U.S. vessel carried more and heavier guns than did *Sumter* and had an advantage of several knots in speed. Also, Palmer had arranged signals to be made by a U.S. schooner lying in the harbor near *Sumter*. How could Semmes escape against such odds? He would use the enemy's signals and turn them to his own advantage. But he had to await a moonless night to put his risky plan to the test.

On November 23 the moon would not "arise until seven minutes past eleven," and that was the night Semmes would make his desperate attempt to escape.

The afternoon of November 23 became cloudy and rain began to fall; the weather seemed to be working in favor of Semmes. But later the clouds began to disappear, the moon came out, and "Venus, too, looked double her usual size, and being three hours before sunset, shed forth a flood of light little less than that of the moon in a northern latitude." Aware of the other Northern warships that could join Palmer any day, Semmes decided that he should make his run regardless of the less-than-perfect circumstances.

The harbor of Saint Pierre was in fact a large roadstead, with rather tall mountains forming the arms of its entrance. A few minutes before 8:00 P.M., Semmes got up steam and directed *Sumter* toward the southern arm of the harbor. Blue signal lights were hoisted on the masts of the Yankee schooner, a signal that Semmes knew indicated to Palmer that *Sumter* was heading southward, and *Iroquois* began moving in that direction. Semmes then hove *Sumter* to the shadows of the large mountain and headed northward. He stopped once or twice to assure himself that Palmer had not turned about. Satisfied, he then ordered full steam ahead: "As we approached [the north end of the island] the fates which before had seemed unpropitious to us, began to smile, and a rain squall . . . began to envelope us in its friendly fold, shutting in our dense clouds of black smoke, which were really the worst tell-tales we had to dread." The first half hour's run provided Semmes the greatest anxiety, but as the lights of the town of Saint Pierre began to fade away, he "knew the enemy had been caught in his own trap."

Palmer may have been caught in his own trap, but it was Semmes who baited that trap and shrewdly exploited the situation and who by careful planning and, perhaps, superior seamanship rather easily freed *Sumter* from *Iroquois*'s blockade; and he did so before any other Union warships assigned to capture *Sumter* could arrive off Saint Pierre. He ordered *Sumter* into the broad Atlantic where U.S. merchant ships still sailed. He set a north-north-west course and "went below and turned in, after . . . an eventful night." Indeed!

The stay in Martinique had been difficult for Semmes. Not only did Palmer and the *Iroquois* create problems for him, his crew, and his ship, but other Northern warships were a threat almost anywhere *Sumter* might sail—except, perhaps, in the open Atlantic Ocean. It was, Semmes wrote, "my intention . . . to cross the Atlantic, and see what can be accomplished in European waters." He thought that he might be able to "exchange the *Sumter* for a better ship." Little could he have dreamed that, indeed, he ultimately would do just that: exchange the *Sumter* for the *Alabama*.

Sumter's transatlantic voyage was fraught both by nature's storms and by the possibility of capture by any one of the six U.S. warships all with the single mission of finding and destroying her. *Sumter* accomplished a part of her mission: to attract Northern warships from blockade duty. But even as *Sumter* sailed to Europe, the Northern blockade of Southern ports became increasingly more effective. Semmes could only perform his duty of destroying Northern commercial shipping.

Two days after his escape from the *Iroquois*, he sighted his first American ship on the "Ocean Seas," the *Montmorency*, out of Bath, Maine. A nine-hour chase occurred before Semmes could stop the large ship (some 1,183 tons). But alas, she had a neutral cargo. Semmes adopted a new tactic to deal with U.S. ships with neutral cargoes. Instead of taking the *Montmorency* into a neutral harbor for adjudication, he simply bonded her for $20,000, took the parole of her master and crew, then released her. He would follow this method many more times during his years at sea. Had the Confederacy been able to maintain its independence, the bond money would have been due to it.

His next four captures, between November 26 and December 8, were all legitimate enemy vessels with enemy cargoes. In each case, he took off the officers and crew, the chronometers, and whatever provisions and sails he might need aboard *Sumter*, then burned the ship. By December 8, he had forty-three prisoners aboard *Sumter*.[20] Semmes hardly felt like celebrating his conquests, however, because December 8 was the anniversary of his loss of the USS *Somers* during the Mexican War and the deaths of so many of her crew.

Semmes feared that the large number of prisoners might overwhelm *Sumter's* crew, so he put half of them in chains, "the prisoners being ironed and released in turns." Among the captured seamen exempted from "being ironed" were the masters of the captured ships and ten former slaves. The latter requested that they be allowed to work on deck rather than be chained. He fed all the prisoners, including the former slaves, from the food taken from their ships, and within the limits of his ability he treated them humanely. Indeed, he was very proud of the fact that no one, crew member or prisoner, died from illness or mistreatment aboard either of his wartime commands.

But the seas and the demands made upon *Sumter* during the chases took a toll on the little ship. The former slaves were set to work on the pumps because *Sumter* was leaking badly. As if the normal high seas did not do enough damage, during the night of December 11–12 a cyclone struck. The captain had partially prepared for the heavy blows by ordering all the sails clewed up except for the topsails and trysails, the latter being sails designed to keep the ship's bow headed into the high winds. After preparing for the storm as best he could, he retired to his quarters with the hope of getting some rest.

It was impossible. Just as he had fallen into an uneasy slumber, an old quartermaster, "looking himself like the deamon [*sic*] of the storm" with his wind-blown beard and hair, dripping with seawater, shook the captain's cot and said, "We've stove in the starboard bowport, sir, and the gun-deck is all afloat with water!" Semmes had feared such a blow and rushed "to the scene of disaster." But First Lieutenant John Kell erected boards in the proper places, thus restricting the damage to a relatively small area. *Sumter* was not in danger of sinking.

The ship was, however, severely damaged, thus proving that a converted packet boat, constructed originally for duty on rivers and in the Caribbean Sea, was unable to meet the challenges of the high seas, much less serve as a cruiser on those seas. Semmes had purposely chosen the parallel he was following across the Atlantic Ocean in order to prevent his "little cock-boat of a ship" from being knocked into pieces by the storms of the North Atlantic Ocean. He hoped to go into the Azores Islands for the men's and the ship's refreshment, but the storms prevented him from doing so. He turned the ship's bow toward the southern coast of Spain, intending to put into the port of Cadiz.

Christmas Day was spent on the high seas. Semmes gave the men an extra glass of grog and allowed them to lay about the deck, recalling other Christmases. Some of them spoke of their loved ones, mentally clasping them to their bosoms "and listening to the little ones they had left behind." The sailors' talk led Semmes to comment on the men's feelings, perhaps revealing more about his own feelings than those of the sailors. Referring to the changes that had occurred since the previous Christmas, he noted that most of them on that Christmas Day were "afloat under the 'old flag.' That flag now looked to them strange and foreign. They had some of their own countrymen on board; not as of yore, welcome visitors, but as prisoners. These, too, wore a changed aspect—enemy, instead of friend, being written upon their faces. The two 'rival nations,' spoken of by De Tocqueville, stood face to face. Nature is stronger than man."

As *Sumter* approached the entrance into the Mediterranean Sea, her crew were amazed to see many idle ships waiting to enter that sea. The sight prompted Semmes to explain to them that strong currents flow through the straits, sometimes eastward, sometimes westward. The sailing vessels, unable to move against the western-flowing current, simply were waiting for it to change direction. His most impressive comment, however, was that no American ships were among the waiting ones, a testimony to the success of *Sumter*'s cruise: Foreign merchants were not shipping their goods under the United States flag.

His explanation of the Strait of Gibraltar currents led Semmes, ever the intellectual, to write a long tribute to Matthew Fontaine Maury, "the Philosopher of the Seas." He recited Maury's contributions to the understanding of the effect of ocean currents, especially the currents of the Gulf of Mexico, on the climate of western Europe as well as on the creation of "shipping roads." His most telling comment about Maury was the Tennessean's loyalty to his native state; like Semmes, when his state withdrew from the Union, Maury went with it and became a leading officer in the Confederate States Navy. Semmes then took the opportunity in his memoirs to condemn those Northerners who had praised Maury's works prior to the Civil War and who during the war castigated him as a fraud. Semmes tended always to praise the loyalty of Southerners, no matter how extreme their feelings might be, and to condemn Northerners for holding the same strong opinions for their side. To Maury he exclaimed: "Philosopher of the Seas! . . . Thou art a citizen of . . . the world." Your Northern detractors "in the course of a few short years, will rot in unknown graves; thy fame will be immortal!"

Semmes had intended to cruise off Cadiz a few days in hope of burning some American merchantmen, if he could find any, but a bad leak through *Sumter*'s propeller sleeve forced him into harbor on January 3, 1862. *Sumter* had been on the high and rough seas of the Atlantic since the morning of November 24, 1861—for forty-one days. The violent storm and the long chases at top speed had put *Sumter* to the extreme test. Semmes had demanded a performance beyond her design, beyond her capabilities. He knew he had pushed her too far for too long and he must take her into a port where she could receive the attention of trained engineers, steam fitters, sailmakers, and other experts who could heal her wounds. And that is why her captain gently guided her into Cadiz harbor on January 3, 1862, 188 days since her passage through the mouth of the Mississippi River.

As *Sumter* slowly entered the harbor, Semmes could not restrain himself from enjoying the beauty of the city, resting as it did upon the shore of the large harbor: "The city of Cadiz is a perfect picture as you approach it, with domes and towers, and minarets, and Moorish-looking houses of a beautiful white stone. . . . A number of villages lay around the bay and were picturesquely half hidden in the slopes of the surrounding mountains, all speaking of the regenerate old Spain, and of the populousness and thrift of her most famous province of Andalusia." Semmes was especially pleased that several merchant ships in the harbor raised their various national flags in recognition of *Sumter* with her Confederate colors flying at her masthead.

Although *Sumter's* career as a sea raider was not quite over, she remained in Cadiz two weeks, until January 17, 1862. The local harbor authorities were less than cordial to Semmes and his ship. They dared not act on their own because *Sumter* was the first Confederate ship to test Spain's neutrality in the American war. They referred every request from Semmes to the central authorities in Madrid.

His first request was permission to land his prisoners. Much to his surprise, he was informed that Madrid would have to decide whether he would be permitted to do so. The next day he was informed that he must leave within twenty-four hours. Semmes immediately sent a letter to Madrid demanding his right as "a recognized belligerent" first to land his prisoners and second, because of his ship's need for repairs, to remain in the harbor until they could be made. His argument, of course, was perfectly legitimate, and Madrid so informed the Cadiz harbor master. Four days later permission was given to both of his demands.

An examination of *Sumter* revealed a need to put the ship in dry dock, especially to repair the leak around her propeller shaft. The dock admiral was cooperative. Workmen soon found additional repair needs, and *Sumter* remained in dry dock for four days. The captain again faced a shortage of money. With only $1,000 left of his original cruising fund, he tele-

graphed William L. Yancey, Confederate commissioner in London, requesting $20,000, out of which he would pay his repair fees and have a cruis-
ing fund.

While *Sumter* was in dry dock, some fifteen men deserted. Semmes
claimed that they had been "seduced by the agents, spies, and pimps" of the
U.S. consul in Cadiz. In his memoirs, he signified that the deserting sailors
were mostly Irishmen and Englishmen, with a few who came from U.S.
Northern states. About these desertions, he wrote: "With rare exceptions, a
common sailor has no sense of nationality. . . . Although I had sailed out of
a Southern port, I had not half a dozen Southern-born men among the rank
and file of my crew. They were mostly foreigners—English and Irish preponderating." Semmes wrote his usual letter lamenting the role of the U.S.
consul in the desertions and demanding action by the Spanish government
in restoring the men to the *Sumter:* "To deprive me of the power, with the
assistance of the police, to recapture [the deserters] would enable the Consul
to exercise the rights of a belligerent in neutral territory." He concluded this
section of his memoirs: "Our Southern movement, in the eyes of Spain, was
a mere political revolution, and like all absolute governments, she had no
sympathy with revolutionists. It was on this principle that the Czar of Russia
has fraternized so warmly with the Federal President." This was an insight
into the diplomacy of the Civil War that has to date escaped the notice of
authorities on that subject.[21]

Finally, on January 16, her repairs completed, *Sumter* was ordered by
the local officials to go to sea immediately. Semmes refused because he had
not yet received any funds from Commissioner Yancey in London. Semmes
went on shore and met with the local governor, the "blockhead" as Semmes
called him. He found this man to be "contrary to all Spanish rule a large,
thick-set, bull-necked fellow, with whom I saw at the first glance, it would
be of little use to reason." Furious, Semmes returned to his ship having decided to leave Cadiz at once. He had enough coal for the voyage to Gibraltar.
He had learned a hard lesson, once and for all, not to deal with weak neutrals. Hereafter, on both *Sumter* and *Alabama,* he entered harbors only of
strong neutrals, England and France, or their colonial holdings. On January 17, 1862, *Sumter* began her last cruise.

As the ship sailed out of Cadiz harbor, Semmes reflected: "We did enjoy
some good things in the harbor of Cadiz." One was a "superb dinner given
by an English admirer, and another was the market." There he had been able
to purchase "fine beef and mutton from Andalusia, fish from the sea, and
fruits and wines from all parts of Spain." He had been especially impressed
by the fruits: "luscious oranges and bananas that had ripened in the open

air—all produced by the agency of that Mexican Gulf heating-apparatus," which he had explained through the lips of "Professor Maury."

Just before leaving Cadiz he read the "first annual report of the Federal Secretary of the Navy" from which he learned that six Federal warships were "in full hue and cry" after the little *Sumter*. He was proud that he had lured that many vessels from the Union blockade of the Southern coasts.

The short voyage from Cadiz to Gibraltar was marked by the capture of two Northern ships. The first was the five-year-old *Neapolitan* of Kingsport, Massachusetts, en route from Sicily to Boston with a cargo of sulphur. The *Neapolitan* was owned by the famed financial house of Baring Brothers and Company. Knowing that the Boston House of Baring Brothers was a partner of the London company, not a branch of it, and that the ship was registered out of Boston, and that sulphur was a contraband of war, Semmes condemned ship and cargo. He removed food, eighty-six dollars in cash, and other materials that *Sumter* could use, then set the ship afire. The flames could be seen from Gibraltar. Immediately, another ship came within sight. *Sumter* chased her, only to find that her cargo was neutral. He bonded her and let her proceed on her course. The *Neapolitan* was *Sumter*'s last victim.

Struggling against a strong wind, *Sumter* fought her way into Gibraltar harbor and dropped anchor at about 7:30 P.M. on January 18, 1862. It would be her last anchorage as a Confederate ship of war.

Early the next morning Semmes was informed by British authorities that *Sumter* had *pratique*, that is, the right to remain in port as a ship that had passed health regulations. In retrospect, it is rather amazing that the crew was free of disease after the long voyage across the Atlantic and after the crew had received shore passes in Martinique and Cadiz. It was a tribute to Semmes's concern over the diet and the general health of the men.

The reception in Gibraltar in almost every way was opposite that of the Spanish in Cadiz. Semmes went ashore at two o'clock the next afternoon to pay his respect to the commanding navy officer. After a friendly reception, he requested the loan of an anchor because *Sumter* had only one. It was granted. Semmes then walked from the captain's "little oasis, scooped out, as it were, from the surface of the rock, with a nice garden plot and trees and shrubbery," down to the town to visit Lieutenant-General Sir William J. Codrington, governor of Gibraltar. Granting Semmes use of the town's market, the Englishman then informed Semmes that he could not allow him to use Gibraltar as "a station at which to lie at anchor for the purpose of sallying out into the straight and seizing my prey." Semmes responded that this matter "had been settled as contrary to law by his own distinguished judge, Sir William Scott, sixty years ago" and that the governor might rely upon his "taking no step whatever violative of the neutrality of England" so long as "he remained in port." This diplomatic response impressed the governor not only by Semmes's knowledge of international law but also by the compliment Semmes paid him by naming the British judge responsible for the law. Throughout the remainder of his stay in Gibraltar, Semmes had complete cooperation from the English authority.

As his officers made arrangements for supplies and the repairs *Sumter* needed, Semmes devoted himself to an appreciation of the town of Gibraltar, "whose beauty was derived from the fact that the houses are built on the side of the rock, and stand one above the other, presenting the beautiful spectacle every night of a city illuminated." On Saturday, January 25, he received a telegram from Lieutenant James H. North, CSN, who had been sent by Confederate Secretary of the Navy Stephen R. Mallory to buy or arrange for the construction of ironclad ships in France and England. The telegram was succinct: "Do not repair. Important particulars by letter, so do not leave port." The short text of the telegram aroused Semmes's curiosity, but he did not halt the repairs on the boilers and the machinery, nor did he delay in setting up the rigging.

On Sunday, January 26, Semmes attended mass in the Catholic church at Gibraltar. The following Thursday, having not heard further from North, he inspected the famous fortifications of Gibraltar, including the galleries, or huge tunnels, of the Rock. These tunnels, he noted, were from a third to half a mile in length and had embrasures "from space to space for cannon, the solid rock forming the casemates. From these galleries we emerged out upon a narrow footway cut out of the rock, and stood perpendicularly over the sea, breaking at our feet, and had a fine view of the northeast face of the rock, rising in a magnificent mass some fifteen hundred feet." He seemed to be completely intrigued by the Rock of Gibraltar and all that it stood for in naval history.

The next day he received several letters from Commander North informing him that Yancey, still the Confederate commissioner to England, had decided that because *Sumter* was unseaworthy, a new ship built in England would be sent to Gibraltar. Semmes immediately replied by telegraph: "Do not send her. Can come for her. Particulars in mail." The next day, February 3, 1862, he received counterorders from James Mason, the new Confederate commissioner to London, informing him that he could draw on the "house in Liverpool for $16,000" and that he must leave Gibraltar on six days' notice. The "house in Liverpool" was Fraser, Trenholm and Company, which was associated with John Fraser and Company of Charleston,

South Carolina, and with Trenholm Brothers of New York City. The Liverpool house soon came to handle all Confederate finances in Europe.

These contradictory exchanges about the future of *Sumter* and Semmes were followed the next day by the refusal of coal dealers to sell to Semmes; his attempt to buy coal from the English navy supply was also denied. The crescendo of adversity and contradictions grew daily. A Spanish navy officer came aboard *Sumter* to lodge a complaint that Semmes had burned the *Neapolitan* within Spanish waters; but when shown the deposition of the master of the destroyed ship that proved Semmes had not violated Spanish waters, he quietly disappeared from all correspondence. Even so, eleven of *Sumter's* crew had deserted, and Semmes had five men in confinement: "The devil seems to get into my crew. I shall have to tighten the reins a little." On Saturday, February 15, 1862, Semmes noted that it was the "anniversary of the day of my resignation from the Navy of the United States, and what an eventful year it has been!"

Still, the spirit of Raphael Semmes was not broken; the British ironclad, HMS *Warrior*, entered the harbor, and Semmes visited her. He considered the ship to be a "marvel of modern naval architecture. . . . She is a monstrous floating impregnable fortress, and will work a thorough revolution in shipbuilding." He was right. As an afterthought, he added, "With this single ship I could destroy the entire Yankee fleet blockading our coast." As commander of the *Warrior* he might well have done so.

Meanwhile, Semmes still could not purchase coal at Gibraltar. He sent his paymaster to Cadiz to buy it there, of all places. But that proved to be unnecessary, for as soon as *Sumter* built up pressure to twelve pounds, the boilers burst. Semmes's paymaster and another crewman with him were captured en route to Cadiz and taken to Tangiers. *Sumter* was now blockaded by three United States war vessels, one of them the USS *Kearsarge.* Even had the *Sumter's* boilers not blown, the ship could not have sailed from Gibraltar. There was nothing more Semmes, or anyone else, could do to save the ship, even had she been in good condition. Her crew knew this as well as did her captain. He reluctantly decided to abandon the ship and make his way as best he could to England. He did pay one last tribute to *Sumter* after the war, when he wrote in his memoirs:

> When I look back now, I am astonished to find what a struggle it cost me to get my own consent to lay up this old ship. As inexplicable as the feeling is, I had really become attached to her, and felt as if I would be parting forever with a valued friend. She had run me safely through two vigilant

blockades, had weathered many storms, and rolled me to sleep in many calms. Her cabin was my bedroom and my study, both in one, her quarter-deck was my promenade, and her masts, spars, and sails, my playthings. I had handled her in all kinds of weather, watching her every motion in difficult situations, as a man watches the yielding and cracking ice over which he is making a perilous passage. She had fine qualities as a sea-boat, being as buoyant, active, and dry as a duck in the heaving gales, and these are the qualities which a seaman most admires.

The story of the CSS *Sumter* was ended. The ship had not only won over her master but had performed the service her country had demanded of her. Despite being a converted packet boat, under Semmes's tender touch, *Sumter* had lured at various times U.S. warships from that navy's primary duty of blockading the Confederate coasts. *Sumter* had overhauled a total of seventy-eight ships, sixty of which were neutrals; she had burned five ships, the first being the *Golden Rocket* and the last being the *Neapolitan.* When at last her boilers had burned out, *Sumter*'s captain had to abandon her, but he never forgot the ship, and he could never forget her first victim: The image of *Golden Rocket*'s sails and lines burning against the Caribbean night were indelibly etched in his mind's eye. To the very end of the Civil War he regretted every ship he had to burn, and in every case he thought of *Sumter* and that first victim.

As the British steamer on which he and Lieutenant Kell took passage to London moved out of Gibraltar harbor, Semmes took "a last lingering look" at the little *Sumter:* "Her once peopled decks were now almost deserted, only a disconsolate old sailor or two being seen moving about on them, and the little ship herself, with her black hull, and black mastheads and yards, the latter which had been stripped of their sails, looked as if she had clad herself in mourning for our departure." Semmes with a heavy heart bid *Sumter* farewell and turned his thoughts then to his journey to England. What new adventure awaited him there? He could only wonder.

6

Semmes and the CSS *Alabama*

As Semmes sailed from Gibraltar to Southampton, England, he put his feelings for the *Sumter* aside and speculated on his future. Would a ship be awaiting him in England? Both Lieutenant North and Confederate commissioner James Mason had referred to a ship that could be his. But what kind of ship? Would it be another converted packet boat or would it be a real war vessel, designed for the role of a cruiser? He could hardly contain his excitement during the six-day voyage.

Toward the end of April 1862 he arrived in London, "that great Babel," where he and Lieutenant Kell took rooms together overlooking Euston Square. He remained in the city throughout the month of May, "enjoying in a high degree . . . the relaxation and ease consequent to so great a change in my mode of life."

> There were no more enemies or gales of wind to disturb my slumbers; no intrusive officers to come into my bedroom at unseasonable hours, to report sails or land discovered, and no half drowned old quartermasters to poke their midnight lanterns into my face, and tell me, that the bow-ports were stove in, and the ship half full of water! If the storm raged without and the windows rattled, I took no notice of it, unless it was to turn over in my bed, and feel all the more comfortable, for my sense of security.

He and Kell enjoyed the view from their windows, "looking out even in this early season, upon well-grown and fragrant grasses, trees in leaf and flowers in bloom."

Semmes had never before mentioned fear or the lack of a "sense of security" during *Sumter's* voyage. His concept of a ship's captain was always to reflect a strong self-confidence and to instill in his crew the notion of success. That concept is why he had given the order to outrace the Union vessel that tried to prevent *Sumter's* safe exit from the Mississippi River; it is why he had taken a leisurely stroll on shore while Palmer on the *Iroquois* threatened *Sumter* in the harbor of Saint Pierre; it is why he had stood confidently on *Sumter*'s deck during violent storms; and it is why his officers and men trusted their captain to lead them to safety from the enemy and from the sea's violence. Now, in London, he could relax and smell the new-grown grass and look out upon the peaceful daily goings and comings of the Londoners. The month-long stay in England restored tranquillity to his soul and mind.

He went leisurely about his business. Included were "interviews" with Commanders James North and James D. Bulloch. The latter was busy with No. 290, a ship he expected to command that was under construction in the Laird Ship Yards on the Mersey River across from the city of Liverpool.[1] Semmes thus became convinced that no ship was available to him, and he decided to return to the Confederacy.

Before he could find passage on a neutral ship, however, he met an English gentleman who, with his maiden sister, would play an important role in the life of Raphael Semmes and even in that of Anne Elizabeth, both during and after the war. He described the visitor as "being a somewhat portly gentleman, with an unmistakable English face, and dressed in clerical garb." He was the Reverend Francis W. Tremlett, of the Parsonage, in Belsize Park, near Hampstead, London. Upon being introduced to Semmes, the clergyman said, "I have come to take the Captain of the *Sumter* prisoner, and carry him off to my house, to spend a few days with me." Semmes protested that all he needed was quiet and rest. But the rotund Englishman replied, "That is the very thing I propose to give you; you shall come to my house, stay as long as you please, go away when you please, and see nobody at all, unless you please." Semmes could not refuse such an offer of hospitality and spent several days in the Tremlett household, which included Tremlett's mother and his maiden sister, Louisa. Semmes wrote that the Tremlett household became "but little less dear to me than my own home in America." It was the sister, close to the age of Semmes, who solidified the Tremlett-Semmes relationship, a friendly one—and perhaps more. Anne Elizabeth, at least, later found much difficulty with that relationship.

In the latter part of May, Semmes finally found transportation for himself and his small staff on the British ship *Melita*. He was careful to ascertain the legitimacy of the ship's voyage: She was to sail only to Nassau on the Bahama Islands, an English territory, so that he would be sailing from neutral Great Britain to other neutral British soil, safe from Union capture. *Melita* sailed in late May 1862 and arrived at Nassau June 8. There Semmes met several Confederate navy officers, including Captain George T. Sinclair, who had a letter for Semmes from the secretary of the Confederate navy. The meeting was purely happenstance, but it changed Semmes's life forever;

the letter ordered Semmes to assume command of the future CSS *Alabama*. On such delicate threads of chance does history hang: Semmes and *Alabama* have become synonymous in the history of the Civil War.[2]

Before he left Nassau, he wrote a long response to Secretary Mallory's letter. In it he thanked the secretary for the assignment to the *Alabama* and informed him of the officers he intended to take aboard, including Kell as first lieutenant, Surgeon Galt, and Marine Lieutenant Becket K. Howell, brother-in-law to President Jefferson Davis. He also indicated his intent to have the chronometers he had collected on *Sumter* sent to England, along with other nautical instruments and charts. Finally, he thanked Mallory for nominating him to the rank of captain; throughout *Alabama*'s cruise he was referred to as Captain Semmes, the title applying to his rank as well as his position as captain of the ship.

Delayed several "anxious weeks" before he could get passage on a ship back to England, Semmes sent a letter to Bulloch, informing him of his appointment to *Alabama* and requesting him to get the ship to a rendezvous without waiting for Semmes's arrival. In Nassau, Semmes spent his enforced time in the pleasant company of his officers and "some very pretty and musical Confederate ladies whose husbands and brothers were engaged in the business of running the blockade." The weeks, he wrote, "would have passed pleasantly enough" had it not been for his fear that *Alabama* would be put to sea before his return to England and that he would, thereby, lose command of her.

As events materialized, he was right about the ship's departure from Liverpool but wrong about who would command her. Bulloch was an unusual man, sublimating his own ambitions for the good of the cause. By the time Semmes arrived in England (August 8, 1862), Bulloch five days earlier had gotten *Alabama* to sea and arranged for a tender to deliver seamen, arms, rigging, food, uniforms—in short, all that *Alabama* would need for a long cruise against the enemy merchant ships. Despite his own disappointment, Bulloch warmly greeted Semmes, congratulated him upon his promotion, and informed him of the plan to rendezvous with *Alabama* on the ocean seas.

Semmes, busy gathering his officers from *Sumter* to join him on *Alabama* and making the necessary financial arrangements with Fraser, Trenholm and Company, failed to notice Bulloch's disappointment. He did pay a small tribute to Bulloch, though misspelling his name: "Bullock [*sic*] had contracted for, and superintended the building of the *Alabama*, and was now going with me to be present at the christening of his bantling. I am indebted to him, as well as the Messrs. Laird for a very perfect ship of her class."

Perhaps Semmes had not known of Bulloch's dueling with the Union spies, or of his difficulties in getting *Alabama* to sea, or of his hopes to command her. It is true that Bulloch's historical role compelled him to work in secret and that of Semmes to work in the world's spotlight.

Bulloch had sent the ship, empty, as if on a trial run, under command of a British merchant captain to Praya Bay, Terceira Island, one of the Portuguese-owned Azores Islands. He employed another British ship and captain to convey crew, food, clothing, munitions, and cannon—all things *Alabama* would need for an extended cruise against American-owned merchant shipping—and to rendezvous with *Alabama* at Praya Bay. Bulloch and Semmes with his officers were aboard that supply ship.

The arrangement seemed to the Confederates to be a perfect dodge of the existing international law that prohibited a belligerent from acquiring and arming a ship of war from the soil of a neutral country. Both Semmes and Bulloch were satisfied that the plan was foolproof; at least it worked for them at the time. Later, in 1873, after a three-year conference at Geneva, Great Britain was required to pay the United States $15.5 million. That decision, known as the "Alabama Claims," was based on the principle that a sovereign state must enact laws, called "Domestic Laws," sufficiently strong to prohibit its citizens from acting in an unneutral fashion toward any belligerent. The fitting-out of *Alabama* in neutral waters with munitions sent from England did not violate the domestic law of England as of 1862; England was fined because of the "insufficiency of its domestic law," not because of any act committed by Bulloch or Semmes. Nonetheless, *Alabama*'s successful cruise contributed to an interpretation of international law and incidentally established the city of Geneva, Switzerland, as the site for future international negotiations and eventually, after World War I, as the site for the headquarters of the first organization established for the purpose of preventing war—the League of Nations. *Alabama*, Bulloch, and Semmes, then, had become the instruments through which Western nations first attempted to outlaw war.

Such future events, of course, did not concern Captain Semmes on August 20, 1862, as he first saw his ship afloat in the harbor of Praya Bay. As *Alabama* lolled upon the sea, he approached her with excitement and anxiety. The ship "was of the most perfect symmetry, and she sat upon the water with the lightness and grace of a swan." Her masts "were of the best yellow pine, that would bend in a gale like a willow wand." *Alabama* "was to be not only my home, but my bride as it were for the next few years, and I was quite satisfied with her external appearance. She was, indeed, a beautiful thing to look upon."

Later, when he boarded her for the first time, he "was as much pleased with her internal appearance and arrangements" as he had been with her externally. A home, a love partner. The union between man and ship was complete, for that night, moved by the sensuous rolling of the waves, he took possession of her, and slept in her bosom, a sound restful, and peaceful sleep; he felt at one with her. It was a union that over the next twenty-two months would become ever more intimate as each learned more about the other and responded more readily to each other's demands. So close was the union that the two together—man and ship—would make naval history as sea-raiders that to this date has not been surpassed.

Their career together, like all good drama, was to end in tragedy. But those twenty-two months of romance carried the American Civil War throughout the world: from Liverpool, England, to the waters of the North and South Atlantic, from the Caribbean Sea and the Gulf of Mexico to the Indian Ocean and the China Sea, and finally to the coast of France. Everywhere they went, they sank United States merchant ships. Their sailings were reported in newspapers from London and Paris to Singapore and Capetown; from Rio de Janeiro to New York City, and finally, from Cherbourg, France. In her wake, *Alabama* left crowds of people cheering from sheer joy in her beauty and admiration for the audacious man who commanded her. Together ship and man made the American Civil War a worldwide event.

Raphael Semmes and *Alabama* in their audacity created for the world the drama that was the American Civil War.

How could the man not fall in love with the ship? Her very configurations revealed her as fast; she had a sharp bow and an elliptical stern. Not yet armed or supplied, she sat high in the water, and her rear draft was three feet deeper than her bow. Indeed, she seemed to be skimming across the sea's surface even as she remained at anchor. *Alabama* was 220 feet long and 32 feet across her beam. She had three masts, bark rigged, and six gun holes on either side. Her powerful engines propelled her through the waters at a speed, with her sails up, of thirteen knots; unlike the *Sumter*, a lifting device on her propeller enabled *Alabama* to sail without drag.

Two ships were servicing *Alabama:* the tender that had sailed with her from England and the *Bahama*, on which Bulloch and Semmes had come to her. The transfer of the enlisted personnel, "who had been picked up, promiscuously from the streets of Liverpool," the six thirty-two-pound cannon, other guns and ammunition, and extra parts for the engine and extra sails for the masts, extra masts and food supplies, medicines, and stores—in sum, all the necessities to sustain for unknown lengths of time between ports the lives of 110 men and 24 officers—all these things were transferred to *Alabama* within three days and without incident. It was a good portent of things to come.

All these necessities and more left *Alabama*'s decks "covered with coal dust and dirt and rubbish in every direction." Early on Sunday morning, August 24, 1862, Lieutenant Kell ordered all men, including officers as supervisors, to turn out to wash and holystone *Alabama*'s filth from her decks. Under Kell's guidance, *Alabama* became "sweet and clean, and when her awnings were snugly spread, her yards squared, and her rigging hauled taut, she looked like a bride, with the orange wreath about her brows, ready to be led to the altar." Still, she was not ready for the seas.

The seamen picked up from the streets of Liverpool had signed on only for a voyage to the Azores and back. Semmes faced the task of enlisting them in *Alabama*'s service, and he was worried because "no creature can be more whimsical, until you have bound him past recall, unless indeed it be a woman." Semmes decided he could only cast his die and await the men's reactions. In neutral waters he hoisted the flag of the newborn Confederate States and, with the officers all in dress uniforms, spoke to the men. He read President Davis's commission appointing him captain in the Confederate States Navy and the order of Secretary Mallory appointing him to the command of *Alabama*. Semmes spoke briefly to the men, explaining his object and purposes in putting the ship in commission. All eyes were on him as he read the official papers, and when he had finished, "with a wave of his hand" a gun was fired, the change of flags took place, and the "air was rent by a deafening cheer from all of the men, officers and seamen alike." Semmes was as impressed as were the common seamen, swept as they were by the emotional ceremony to sign on the *Alabama* for duty as a cruiser against Union shipping.

Eighty of the ninety seamen signed on for the cruise. But more than emotion prompted the English, Dutch, Irish, French, Italian, and Spanish sailors to accept Semmes's word or to become emotionally attached to the Confederate cause: It was the double pay in gold and the promise to share in the spoils of the ship's maritime victories. *Alabama*'s clerk was hard pressed to draw up the signing articles for so many men, who then had to wait in line to sign them. The moment that task was fulfilled, "the democratic part of the proceedings closed!"

> When I wanted a man to do anything after this, I did not talk to him about nationalities and liberties or double wages, but I gave him a rather sharp order, and if the order was not obeyed in double-quick, the delin-

quent found himself in limbo. Democracies may do very well for the land, but monarchies, and pretty absolute monarchies at that, are the only successful governments at sea.

Bulloch, who had given *Alabama* her birth, left her at about 11:00 P.M. to return to the *Bahama* and thence to Liverpool. Semmes praised him as an efficient and honest man, and so he was: honest and selfless. He had conceived *Alabama* in his mind, had nursed her to life, and had turned her over to Semmes. Bulloch was indeed the father of the Confederate navy in Europe. But it was Semmes who garnered the glory of the navy's achievements on the high seas.

Lieutenant Kell had been with Semmes in England and Nassau and remained with him to serve as first lieutenant of *Alabama*. He controlled the ship and its crew according to Semmes's orders. The two men became very close and remained friends long after the war. Kell, like Semmes, wrote an account of his service on both ships. He was not the only lieutenant from the *Sumter* to serve on *Alabama*. Lieutenant Richard F. Armstrong, whom Semmes had left on the *Sumter* in Gibraltar, joined Semmes in London and became *Alabama*'s second lieutenant. Midshipman Joseph D. Wilson of *Sumter* was promoted to be the third lieutenant on *Alabama*. Arthur Sinclair became the fourth lieutenant, and the fifth lieutenant was John Low of Georgia, "a capital seaman and an excellent officer." Semmes retained *Sumter*'s surgeon and added as assistant surgeon Dr. David Herbert Llewellyn, "an Englishman from Wiltshire." Acting Master Irvine S. Bulloch was the brother of *Alabama*'s creator. There was, then, a continuity of officer personnel from the *Sumter* to *Alabama* but also some who were new to Captain Semmes. Nonetheless, they soon learned to work together for the good of *Alabama* and the Confederate cause.

One other member of the crew saw more of Semmes than did even his first lieutenant; his name was A. G. Bartelli—simply called Bartelli. Semmes had first noticed him aboard the *Bahama* during his return trip from Nassau. Semmes had a streak of compassion for the common sailors. Though Bartelli was often too much under the influence of wine, he was an excellent cook and an accomplished waiter. When Semmes saw him aboard the *Bahama* en route to its rendezvous with *Alabama*, he offered him the position of the captain's steward, *if* he would swear off alcohol. Bartelli agreed, and he became Semmes's efficient and constant servant: He washed his clothes, cooked his meals (which the captain ate alone in his cabin), kept the cabin spotless, and in general saw to Semmes's good health. "He was faithful, and became attached to me, and kept his promise under strong temptation; for there was always in the cabin-lockers the best of wines and other liquors," wrote Semmes of Bartelli. The Italian steward served Semmes throughout the ship's lifetime.

Semmes always read newspaper accounts of the Civil War. As *Alabama* sailed alone into the ocean, he recalled the events of the war up to August 1862: the Union fleet's victories that gave it control of Pamlico Sound, on the coast of North Carolina; the North's capture of Bowling Green, Kentucky, that gave it control of the Cumberland and Tennessee Rivers, leading to the capture of the city of Nashville; the capture of New Orleans by the Union fleet under David G. Farragut and David D. Porter; the various army battles in Virginia where Northern movements threatened Norfolk and Richmond, balanced only by Thomas J. (Stonewall) Jackson's actions in the Shenandoah valley. Thus he took to the sea "with forebodings as well as hopes." Inasmuch as both belligerents were "thoroughly aroused," he felt "that a few blows, well struck on the water, might be of great assistance." This thought motivated him to "strike those blows."

On September 4, 1862, he found his first victim, a Northern whaling ship. He had sought it out very methodically. He knew that the movement of the warm Gulf Stream carried small sea nettles from the Caribbean Sea northward, then across the northern Atlantic eastward and southward toward the Azores, where they arrived in late summer and early fall. He knew also that sea nettles were a favorite food of whales, and thus in September New England whaling vessels, following prime whale feeding areas in the late summer and early fall, would be just off the Azores. It was late afternoon of September 4, 1862, when *Alabama*, just off the islands of Pico and Fayal, part of the Azores, sighted her first victim.

The ship was the *Ocmulgee*, a whaling vessel from Massachusetts. Semmes used the same technique of capture that he had developed on the *Sumter:* approach the other ship with neutral colors hoisted; if it answers with U.S. colors, simultaneously lower the neutral flag and raise the Confederate one, and fire a blank shot across the victim's bow. The technique worked perfectly: *Alabama* had captured her first of twenty-six Union ships sighted and hailed from September 4 to December 7, 1862, twenty-one of which Semmes burned on the high seas. The other five ships he released on bond because they carried neutral cargoes.

He did not immediately destroy the first four captures. Instead, he placed an armed boarding party on each of them, under command of an *Alabama* officer. If a ship carried food, clothing, or anything else his own men might be able to use, he took it all aboard *Alabama*. If the victim carried extra ropes, sails, or any items useful to *Alabama*, he transferred them also. The boarding officers sailed the ship to a near port and on one of the nearby islands discharged the captured crew members. On Tuesday, September 9, on the high seas, Semmes fired his next three victims: the *Starlight* at 9:00 A.M., the *Ocean Rover* at 11:00 A.M., and the *Alert* at 4:00 P.M.

As the flames of the *Alert* were still burning, at 5:00 P.M., he hailed the *Weather Gauge*, another Yankee whaler, which he burned the next day. During the next six days he captured and burned five additional New England whalers, sent their crews to nearby islands, and took on board *Alabama* additional supplies, especially food for her crew. He would never again have such good hunting in such a short period of time. Indeed, his knowledge of the Gulf Stream and of the eating habits of the sperm whales produced his most successful period of destroying American merchant ships.

One of the captured ship captains commented that when he saw the American flag flying from *Alabama's* mast, he assumed her to be a Northern gunboat sent to protect the whaling fleet. He had touched upon the basic Southern philosophy of sending ships against the American merchant fleet in order to draw American navy vessels from blockade duty and into the high seas to protect its merchant fleet. While, later, some ships did seek *Alabama*, the North never gave its merchant ships the kind of protection their captains had expected. The Washington government never saw fit to create a convoy system or to post ships in the areas of the high seas such as the whale feeding grounds, or at crossroads of the seas, to protect the American ships from Confederate raiders. The U.S. secretary of the navy obviously considered the blockade more important than the merchant ships. Given the North's development of its industrial base and its broad agricultural areas, U.S. Secretary of the Navy Gideon Welles just might have adopted the correct policy.

Semmes's success on the whaling waters was never again matched. Still, his overall success resulted from his knowledge of the prevailing winds and currents that created other crossroads at sea for merchantmen carrying goods between certain markets. Gradually moving northward and very slightly westward, but still in the whaling area, he captured two more whalers. Then he hailed the *Tonawanda*, a packet ship that created a new challenge: Seventy passengers were on board, including thirty women. What would he do with all these people if he burned the ship? He brought her master on board *Alabama* and sent an armed guard on her and kept her "in company for a few days," hoping to meet up with another ship to which he could transfer the passengers and the crew and then burn the *Tonawanda*.

But the plan failed to materialize, so he placed all of his prisoners—"some fifty or sixty of them"—aboard *Tonawanda*, bonded her, and allowed her to continue her voyage.

Moving ever northward, *Alabama* began to run into very bad weather, which did not deter Semmes from capturing Northern ships, burning most and bonding some. American vessels seemed to be traveling in pairs: Two more American ships were sighted on October 7. He burned one, but the other one, seeing the flames, required a chase. The "poor little afrighted fawn ahead of us, how its heart must have gone pit-a-pat, as it cast its timid eyes behind it, and saw its terrible pursuer looming up larger and larger, and coming nearer and nearer!" Inevitably, *Alabama* closed in, boarded the ship, and set her afire. One crewman was "a deserter from *Sumter*, whom we afterwards discharged from the Confederate service, in disgrace, instead of hanging him, as we might have done under the Articles of war."

Tonawanda had presented another opportunity before her release. One of the passengers had with him a "likely negro lad [named David] of about seventeen years of age—a slave until he was twenty-one under the laws of Delaware." Because *Alabama*'s officers needed servants, Semmes took him aboard. David was alarmed at first, but his reception by *Alabama* was pleasant, and after a few days he decided he was better off with the rebel crew than he would have been with his master. He became Dr. Galt's servant, "and there arose between the Virginia gentleman and the slave boy that sympathy of master and servant, which our ruder people of the North find it so impossible to comprehend." Semmes entered the boy's name upon the list of the ship as a servant and paid him accordingly. The slave boy remained happily with the ship until the end of her cruise.

Bad weather increased by October 15 into a gale, which did not deter Semmes from capturing the *Lamplighter*, out of Boston, just hours before the winds increased into a full-blown cyclone. *Alabama* was about 220 miles west of New York City when the storm struck. After explaining the scientific origin and nature of the cyclone, Semmes then described the effect of it on his ship and men. *Alabama* was first struck by its westward winds.

> The iron bolt on the weather-quarter, to which the standing part of the main-brace was made fast, gave way; away went the main-yard, parted at the slings, and, in a trice, the main topsail was whipped into fragments, and tied into a hundred curious knots. We were now under nothing but the small-storm staysail . . . the ship was pressed over and over until I feared she should be thrown upon her beam-ends. . . . The lee-quarter boat was wrenched from the davits, and dashed in pieces; and as the sea would strike

the ship, forward or aft, she would tremble in every fibre, as if she had been a living thing, in fear of momentary dissolution.

In the eye of the cyclone, Semmes breathed easier as the ship had behaved nobly during the first two hours of the storm and sat calmly in its eye. Still, "we knew that we were in the terrible vortex of the storm. . . . The aspects of the heavens were appalling. The clouds were writhing and twisting like so many serpents engaged in combat, and hung so low, in the thin air of the vortex, as to touch our mastheads."

Then the eastward winds struck *Alabama*. "It was impossible to raise one's head above the rail, and difficult to breathe for a few seconds." Finally, after another two hours of strong blowing, the cyclone moved on, leaving *Alabama* to sit calmly in the waters. It took five days for the crew to get her once again into shipshape; she then resumed her hunting. *Alabama*'s response during the cyclone strengthened the bond between man and ship.

In his memoirs Semmes explained his technique of determining the validity of a captured ship's papers regarding its cargo. Basically, he established himself as judge of an international court of law. In the case of the *Lafayette*, captured October 23, he examined her papers, which stated that the cargo was certified as English-owned by the British consul in New York City. He found that the cargo had not been ordered or paid for by a British subject in England but was only certified to that effect by the British consul. Consulting his copy of *3 Phillimore on International Law*, pages 610 and 612, Semmes determined that inasmuch as the goods had not yet been paid for, their ownership remained American, and he therefore ordered them destroyed along with the ship. From New York newspapers, taken off later victims, he learned that because of his *Lafayette* decision he was accused of piracy and was referred to as the "pirate Semmes." He strongly resented that accusation and in his memoirs went to great lengths to disprove it, citing always his handy copy of *Phillimore*. Indeed, although he was correct on international law, one can almost conclude that he wrote his memoirs not only to refute the charges of piracy but to justify all of his actions on the high seas. He used the same source on several other instances of claimed British ownership. After the war, the "Alabama Claims" made no charge against Semmes for burning the *Lafayette* cargo.

Semmes also engaged in another activity that skirted the edge of violating international law: He recruited seamen from his victims. These new crewmen, we are told, were well received by the original crew; they also enabled Semmes to man all of his guns.

As he headed southward leaving the Gulf Stream, toward a rendezvous with his coal tender, the weather improved. Semmes noticed the men "were fast becoming a well-disciplined crew." The young officers "had gained much experience in handling of their ship." The ship's captain "began in consequence to sleep more soundly" in his cot, even "when the weather was dark and stormy."

From one of his victims Semmes obtained "a batch of late New York papers" from which he learned "where all the enemy's gunboats were, and what they were doing," thus enabling him "to take better care of *Alabama*." He mused that "perhaps this was the only war in which the newspapers ever explained beforehand all the movements of armies and fleets to the enemy." He sometimes received the newspapers daily, including bags of private letters, which he considered to be his property. Under the "laws of war" he was correct. Apparently, he found in them little of use to him except enjoyable reading.

On October 19, when *Alabama* was about two hundred miles from New York City, Semmes captured the brig *Baron de Castine*, out of New York and bound for Cuba. She was an old vessel and of little use to Semmes except to empty *Alabama* of her many prisoners. He bonded the ship, put the prisoners aboard, and sent her back into the New York harbor. New York, Semmes later learned, was "all agog" when the *Baron* returned to that port. The released prisoners could little complain about their treatment aboard *Alabama*, so Semmes succeeded in delivering a blow not only to New York shipping interests but also to the newspapers' accusations of piracy. He felt rather smug about their confusion and privately gloated over it.

Alabama then headed for the island of Martinique to rendezvous with her coal tender by prearrangement made with Commander Bulloch before he sailed from the Azores. Martinique is one of the Leeward Islands that separate the Caribbean Sea from the Atlantic Ocean. Semmes had made the decision on October 30 when he had learned that *Alabama* then had only four days' supply of coal. As ship and crew headed southward, the weather became mild; the men changed from their cold-weather woolen clothing to their cotton duck frocks and trousers. New crew members worked at the guns with the older ones and relaxed with them during the evening hours, playing whatever musical instruments they had, singing, and dancing. The improved morale was matched by improved marksmanship of the gun crews.

On the morning of November 2, when Semmes least expected to see an American ship, *Alabama* captured a New England whaler. Bound for a voyage of thirty months hunting in the Pacific Ocean, she was well supplied for the long trip. *Alabama*'s crew took off the "store-ship . . . plenty of provisions, slops, and small stores," then burned her. From the recent newspapers aboard, Semmes learned "the latest news from the seat of war."

Five days later *Alabama* captured the *T. B. Wales.* An East India trader returning to Boston from Calcutta, her cargo consisted of jute, linseed, and saltpeter, all of which would enhance the North's war-making ability. On board also were several passengers, including the captain's wife and a former U.S. consul and his wife and three daughters. All were taken aboard *Alabama*. The passengers presented a new challenge to Semmes, for the five women were *Alabama*'s "first prisoners of the sex." Ever the romantic, Semmes received the ladies chivalrously:

> We treated the ladies . . . with all due consideration, of course: but I was forced to restrict them in the matter of baggage and furniture, for the want of room. I permitted them to bring on board their entire wardrobes, of course, without permitting it to be examined, but was forced to consign to the flames some fancy chairs and other articles of East India workmanship, which they seemed to prize very highly. I dare say they thought hard of it, at the time, though, I doubt not, they have long since forgiven me.

The captain of *Wales* also impressed Semmes, who, in describing the man, perhaps unconsciously revealed his concept of most Yankee skippers: "Though a Northern man, [he] had very few of the ear-marks of the Yankee skipper about him. He was devoid of the raw-bone angularity which characterizes most of them, and spoke very good English, through his mouth instead of his nose. His pronunciation and grammar were both good, quite an unusual circumstance among his class." Semmes was also favorably impressed with the former consul, George H. Fairchild, his English-born wife, and their daughters. Indeed, Fairchild made a very friendly gesture toward prisoner Semmes after the war. Semmes characterized him thus: "Though a New Englander, [he] was apparently an unbigoted gentleman, and observed all the gentlemanly proprieties, during his stay aboard my ship." After the war Semmes noted that "Mr. Fairchild was kind enough to write to me, in prison, and tender himself a witness in my behalf."

The *Wales* was perhaps Semmes's most fortunate capture: He not only enjoyed the company of the women and children, but *Alabama* received eight recruits from the ship. His crew then numbered 110 men, only 10 short of a full complement. Sails and other equipment he took from the *Wales* made it possible to heal *Alabama*'s wounds inflicted by the violent storms she had suffered while sailing in the Gulf Stream.

The greatest cruising captain in naval history, while writing about the *Wales*, left a touching and perhaps romantic description of his stateroom aboard *Alabama*. Referring to himself in the third person, Semmes wrote of an "interesting prisoner not paroled: a charming little canary-bird captured from a whaler" and the flowers that Bartelli kept in constant bloom, "growing in hanging pots that swayed with the rolling ship. When he awoke in the mornings to the sweet song of the canary and to the sweet odors of the geranium and the jessamine," he would "forget all about war's alarms" and think about "Home Sweet Home" with all its charms and would imagine that he was "clasping to his heart again the long-absent dear ones." But when Bartelli would awaken him at half past seven each morning, his thoughts would be "dispelled of such fantasies, whilst the Fairchilds were on board."

Such fantasies of his dear ones—Anne Elizabeth, the girls, and young Raphael—are not unusual for warriors serving at a great distance from home. Semmes's expression of such longing, therefore, makes it easy for every warrior who ever served far from home to identify with the captain of the CSS *Alabama*.

After the capture of the *T. B. Wales*, Semmes gave orders for *Alabama* to head for Martinique to meet the coal tender. As the ship rounded the northern tip of the island and sailed past the harbor of Saint Pierre, he recalled *Sumter*'s close encounter with the USS *Iroquois* and mused that aboard *Alabama* he now "cared very little about the *Iroquois* and vessels of her class." Thus unafraid, he sailed on to Fort-de-France, arriving there midmorning of November 18, 1862. He sent his *T. B. Wales* prisoners ashore, and happily, he found Captain Matthew J. Butcher and the tender *Agrippina* awaiting him.

Unhappily, he learned that Butcher had been in port for eight days and, under the influence of alcohol consumed in the French bars ashore, had talked freely of meeting the now famous *Alabama*. Fearing that news of their meeting could in the period of eight days have reached Union ears, he ordered Butcher to leave immediately and meet him later at an isolated island farther west in the Gulf of Mexico. Because *Alabama* was a faster vessel than the *Agrippina*, Semmes remained at Fort-de-France one day longer to get some supplies aboard and to give some of his men one-day passes to go ashore.

The USS *San Jacinto*, with fourteen guns, appeared off the harbor, and Semmes realized that he could not confront her. Cautious as he was brave, Semmes decided to leave earlier than he had planned, and on November 19 he ran out of Fort-de-France, fortunately avoiding the Yankee, and set sail for the second meeting with the *Agrippina*. At Cayos Arcas Islands, which he had previously visited while in the "Old Service," off the western coast of the Yucatan Peninsula, he found Captain Butcher awaiting him. After two and a half days of manually transferring 184 tons of coal from the *Agrippina*, *Alabama* had a total of 284 tons aboard. Semmes then felt that she could successfully meet the challenge he planned for her.

Semmes had read in captured Northern newspapers that U.S. General Nathaniel P. Banks was leading a flotilla of Northern troops to capture the city of Galveston, Texas; he learned even an expected date of arrival. Goaded by the same newspapers that accused him of fearing to fight a U.S. Navy vessel, Semmes developed a scheme to lure one of the enemy from the fleet escorting Banks and then to challenge the ship to a fight. Such a deed, he felt, would not only refute the newspapers but would also aid the Southern cause and might even save Galveston from capture. His only fear was that the Northern ship might well be one of the new ones, faster and more heavily armed even than *Alabama*.

Fully loaded with coal, he left Cayos Arcas on January 5, 1863, and set his course almost due north, expecting to intercept the Northern fleet just off the Texas coast. His calculations were slightly off; on January 11 his lookout shouted "Land ho! Sail ho!" However, no transport ships were in sight. Soon Semmes saw a shell fired by one of the ships burst over the city of Galveston. "Ah ha!" Semmes exclaimed to the officer of the deck. "There has been a change of programme here. The enemy would not be firing into his own people, and we must have recaptured Galveston, since our last advices." And so it was; but Semmes was placed in a quandary. As Semmes recalled in his memoirs:

> What was best to be done in this changed condition of affairs? I certainly had not come all the way into the Gulf of Mexico, to fight five ships of war, the least of which was probably my equal. And yet how could I run away in the face of the promises I had given my crew? For I had told them at the Arcas islands that they were, if the fates proved propitious, to have some sport off Galveston. Whilst I was pondering the difficulty, the enemy himself, happily, came to my relief; for pretty soon the look-out again called from aloft, and said, "One of the steamers, Sir, is coming out after us."

Alabama had given chase often, but this was the first time she had been chased. Her steam was up, and Semmes moved her to appear to be running from the enemy. When he had drawn the enemy vessel about twenty miles from the U.S. fleet, Semmes prepared the ship for action and ordered the crewmen to their combat posts. *Alabama* was about to take on a ship built to fight, not merely to capture an unarmed enemy merchant ship!

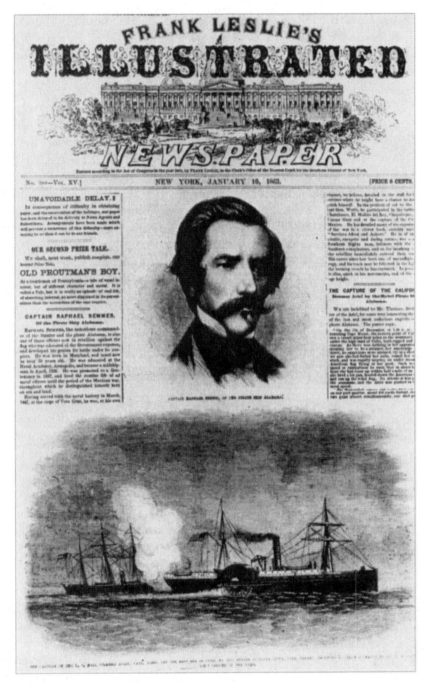

Semmes and the *Alabama* got full coverage in *Frank Leslie's Illustrated Newspaper* (January 10, 1863) after the capture of the California treasure steamer *Ariel*.

As the distance between the two ships diminished, they hailed one another; Semmes identified his ship as British, while the Union ship called herself the USS *Hatteras*. Semmes then raised the Confederate flag. In his memoirs Semmes reprinted the official report of the commander of the Union ship. At a distance of only about thirty yards, the two ships exchanged cannon and even pistol and musket shots. Soon, one of *Alabama*'s cannon shells penetrated the *Hatteras*'s side and exploded in an internal compartment, causing a fire, and within a few seconds another penetrated into the ship's engine room, causing an explosion. *Hatteras* surrendered then to *Alabama*. They had exchanged shots for only about twenty minutes. In order to prevent further deaths, the Union commander reported that he requested help from *Alabama* to save as many lives as possible. Throughout the report he referred several times to his ship's weaknesses.

In his memoirs Semmes questioned several points of Lieutenant H. C. Blake's report. First, writing after the war, he still resented Blake's references to *Alabama* as "a rebel steamer" and a "piratical craft." Blake, he maintained, should have been ashamed to use such terms, "especially after enjoying the hospitalities of my cabin for a couple of weeks." This thought led him to a general condemnation of all Union navy officers: "Must democrats necessarily be vulgarians? Must the howling demos devour everything gentle in the land and reduce us all to the common level of the pot-house politician, and compel us to use his slang? Radicalism seemed to be now just what it had been in the French Revolution, a sort of mad-dog virus; every one who was inoculated with it, becoming rabid."

Semmes also refuted Blake's claim that the *Hatteras* was an inferior ship to *Alabama*. The former, Semmes stated, was heavier by a ton than the latter; the number of crewmen aboard the two ships was almost equal—*Hatteras* had 108 men, while *Alabama* had 110; the number of guns was equal, except *Alabama*'s pivot gun was heavier than that of the *Hatteras*. There was, he wrote, a "considerable disparity between the two ships, in weight of their pivot guns, and the *Alabama* ought to have won the fight, and she did win it in thirteen minutes—taking care, too, though she sank her enemy at night, to see that none of his men were drowned—a fact which I shall have occasion to contrast, by and by, with another sinking."

Semmes seemed to be sympathetic with Blake, writing that "he behaved like a man of courage, and made the best fight he could, ill supported as he was by the 'volunteer' officers by whom he was surrounded." It was unlike Semmes to offer such a magnanimous gesture to a Yankee officer; why did he do it? Was it because the remarks reflected upon the U.S. Navy as a whole? Or was it because he, as victor, could readily afford to be lenient with the defeated officer?

In his memoirs Semmes omitted two other aspects of the battle: The sides of the *Hatteras* were covered with iron sheets; how had *Alabama*'s shells penetrated the enemy? Why were *Alabama*'s shells more effective against the enemy than those of the *Hatteras*? In neither his journal nor his memoirs does he address these questions, nor did Blake in his report.

Despite all of the unanswered questions, Semmes's plan to approach a large U.S. Navy fleet, lure one of the ships from the others, then turn upon it and destroy it was, in itself, pure audacity. It was also a high risk to *Alabama*, the ship he had come to love and with which he identified himself. Was it purely a reaction to the Northern accusations that he was nothing more than a pirate or at best a privateer? Was it, perhaps, a navy officer's frustration that he was assigned to destroy unarmed merchant vessels? Or was it an ego trip?

In many ways Semmes's victory resulted from pure luck—luck that the ship assigned to investigate the presence of an unknown vessel that had approached the Northern fleet was, except for the iron sides, inferior to *Alabama*. In his behalf, it must be noted that he did not brag about his victory; instead, he admitted that *Alabama* was a better ship than the *Hatteras* and that he should have defeated Blake.

Perhaps the historian must take Semmes at his word; he was proud that he had won, but he was also proud that none of the men of the *Hatteras* were lost in the sea after they abandoned ship. The questions and answers concerning *Alabama*'s victory are as complex as was Semmes; no single answer exists to any question concerning the encounter.

As soon as he ascertained that all of the men from the defeated ship were safely aboard *Alabama*, Semmes left the scene of the battle. He decided to sail for Jamaica, land his prisoners on parole, "patch up the two or three shot-holes the enemy had made above the water-line, re-coal, and proceed on my eastern cruise, against the enemy's commerce, as originally contemplated."

The voyage to Jamaica was unusually difficult. With more than a hundred enemy prisoners aboard who had to be guarded, and with strong countercurrents against the ship's movement, along with constantly raging storms, *Alabama*'s speed was slowed. Furthermore, the enemy was in full pursuit. From the site of the battle it took nine days to reach the harbor of Port Royal, near the eastern end of Jamaica. At last, Semmes could relax.

Semmes and his ship were warmly received by the British officials and residents of the island. He was allowed to release his prisoners on parole and to repair and replenish his ship. Realizing that he needed "a little rest and recreation to restore his wasted energies," he left Kell in command of the ship and with his "excellent friend, Mr. Fyfe," rode through a beautiful countryside to Fyfe's home, high on a mountain. Semmes feasted his inner soul on the beautiful vegetation and the scenery of the distant sea.

Semmes could not help but contrast the setting and the spaciousness with life on *Alabama*, especially considering the nine days he had shared his small cabin with Lieutenant Blake during the cruise to Jamaica. A new sense of freedom grew within him as he enjoyed the "delightful rides, and lunches and evening parties, where music and the bright eyes of fair women beguiled the senses." Indeed, he wrote, he could easily have "forgotten the war and *Alabama*" had Kell not sent a message on the fourth day informing him that his ship was nearly ready for sea. The Jamaican "vacation" had more effectively restored his health and vitality than had the week he spent at the Hotel Porto, in San Luis, Brazil, when he commanded the *Sumter*. He was ready to resume *Alabama*'s path of destruction.

Before *Alabama* could leave Port Royal, however, Semmes had to regain control over his crew. While he was enjoying the Jamaican countryside, his men had acted as most seamen did in those days: Granted shore leave, they fought the few Yankee sailors they encountered, got drunk on grog in the harbor bars, and indulged their sexual desires with the ever-present women at such bars. Even the paymaster, an officer of lower rank, had been drunk ever since he landed, and he frolicked with the common sailors from the various ships in the port, especially with Yankee sailors. Before Semmes's return, Kell had suspended the man from his duties and placed him under arrest. Upon his return, Semmes dismissed him from the Confederate service: sent him ashore, bag and baggage. Semmes waived the charges of misbehavior against the other sailors, fined them a few pence, and admonished them to shape up. The sailors appreciated this gesture and seemed more than ever willing to follow Semmes and *Alabama* wherever they sailed.

It was typical of *Alabama*'s captain to avoid severe punishment of his common sailors. He did so for several reasons: He understood the sailors, most of whom were not Southerners; he won their loyalty by mild punishment for small misdeeds; and he really had little choice, for *Alabama* could not operate without them. As he explained, "I accepted . . . when I sent my sailors on shore on liberty, that the result was to be a frolic, and I was always lenient to the mere concomitants of a frolic, but I never permitted them to abuse or maltreat the inhabitants, or perpetrate any malicious mischief."

While the mild punishment was being imposed, the lookout shouted "Sail ho!" Semmes soon hailed the *Golden Rule*, an American ship with a

CSS *Alabama* (*Frank Leslie's Illustrated History of the Civil War,* 1863)

mixed cargo, some of which was neutral, but with no sworn evidence to support the claim. Aboard ship was a complete set of rigging for the USS *Bainbridge* and additional ship masts and ropes, all of which Semmes took aboard *Alabama.* Then he burned the victim. He was particularly pleased to tie up "for a while longer, one of the enemy's gun-brigs for want of an outfit." Semmes headed for the port city of Santo Domingo, where on January 28, 1863, he landed his prisoners.

Semmes had visited the Dominican Republic, on the island of Hispaniola, as a lieutenant aboard the USS *Porpoise,* it will be recalled, shortly before the outbreak of the Mexican War. Since then, Spain had reestablished control over the Dominican Republic, and a friendly Spanish navy officer came aboard *Alabama* to visit him. Semmes soon went ashore and repeated the visit so ably described in his *Porpoise* journal. He could not restrain from describing once again the cathedral or from revisiting all the historical buildings in the city. And he could not help but comment that one of the ships in the harbor was American, flying the English flag. He took some satisfaction in the fact that he and the other Confederate cruisers were driving the American merchant ships from the U.S. flag.

Indeed, Semmes in early 1863 recognized the effect of the Confederate cruisers against Northern merchant shipping. By mid-1863, the *Sumter, Alabama, Florida,* and *Georgia* had together destroyed about 200 Union merchant ships. Furthermore, by mid-1863 many American merchant ships were sold to neutral countries. Even as early as November 1862, only 20 of 150 vessels loading in New York harbor for European ports were under the

U.S. flag. More than half of the U.S. merchant fleet was lost during the Civil War, either directly to Confederate raiders (110,000 tons) or indirectly by sale to neutrals (800,000 tons). Moreover, marine insurance rates for U.S. merchant ships increased by a factor of three between 1861 and 1863. All told, on his two cruisers Semmes captured 87 ships, of which he burned 62, thus accounting for about 32 percent of all Northern merchant ships destroyed. Those destroyed by the *Florida* (33) and the *Georgia* (5) were mostly small coastal vessels.[3]

It is remarkable that Semmes, as he wandered again through the remains of the history of Columbus in January 1863, was prompted by the lone U.S. ship flying a British flag in the Santo Domingo harbor to understand fully the impact of his wartime activity.

But the *Alabama* cruise was not yet over. Semmes never confided destinations even to his first lieutenant. His journal and memoirs, however, give the modern reader an advantage over Lieutenant Kell; *Alabama* was headed for the coast of Brazil, then across the South Atlantic Ocean to South Africa, en route ultimately to the waters of China, Indochina, and India—waters, as far as any records reveal, on which Semmes had never before sailed. To reach the Brazilian coast, *Alabama* had to sail wide eastwardly, at one point approaching halfway to the Azores Islands, where she had been transformed from an unarmed ship into a wartime raider, intent upon sinking peaceful ships. Between Santo Domingo and the point where *Alabama* was to turn southward, onto another "highway of the sea," she captured and destroyed three more Yankee ships and sighted many neutral ones. At the point where he planned to turn southward toward Brazil (that is, at latitude 30 degrees and longitude 40 degrees, known to seamen as "the crossing"), Semmes could see seven or eight ships. One was American and tried to outrun *Alabama*. She was obstinate and Semmes had to "wet the people on the poop, by the spray of a shot, before she would acknowledge that she was beaten." But Semmes had to release the ship because her cargo was certified neutral. He next stopped the *John A. Parks,* out of Maine with a cargo of lumber certified by the acting British consul in New York as being British property, but Semmes went through the ship's correspondence and found that the certificate of neutrality was false. The process took a while, so Semmes invited the captain of *Parks* to have a cup of coffee with him. As the two captains sipped their coffee, Semmes informed him that *Alabama* would burn his ship. What a shock it must have been to the Yankee skipper who thought the false certificate would protect him. Semmes took great delight in the flames that rose from the *John A. Parks;* undoubtedly, he graciously offered his guest another cup of coffee.

Alabama then turned southward and soon found another "crossing" at the equator. Of this hunting ground, Semmes wrote:

> We were never out of sight of ships. They were passing by in ones, and twos, and threes, in constant succession, wreathed in rain and mist, and presenting frequently the idea of a funeral procession. The honest traders were all there, except the most honest of them all—the Yankees—and they were a little afraid of the police. Still we managed to catch a rogue now and then.

Semmes headed south toward his next rendezvous with the *Agrippina,* which was the Brazilian island of Fernando de Noronha located some distance off the mainland. En route he sighted only a few Yankee vessels, but he did capture several Yankee merchant ships. All had false papers claiming the cargo to be neutral. In each case Semmes ruled the papers to be false and sank the ship. His prized victim was the *Louisa Hatch,* which was loaded with the best Cardiff coal and Semmes decided to transfer it to *Alabama.* The seas and the winds, however, were too high to effect the transfer at sea, so he ordered his boarding party to follow him to the island of Fernando de Noronha. On Friday, April 10, 1863, at sunset, *Alabama* towed the *Louisa Hatch* into the island's harbor and resumed transferring the coal to *Alabama.*

At the invitation of the governor, Semmes spent a very pleasant Sunday, April 12, on a tour of the island. During the next three days he arranged for the purchase of fresh meat and vegetables, which, he mentioned, his men sorely needed, sold some of the coal from the prize ship, landed his prisoners, and sent the *Louisa Hatch* out beyond the Brazilian waters and burned her. In the meantime several sailors from the prize had volunteered to sign up for *Alabama;* he accepted four of them, giving Semmes a full crew for the first time since leaving the Azores. He remained in the harbor six more days awaiting the *Agrippina.* On the morning of April 22, he decided that he could no longer passively await his tender, and he set out to cruise in the nearby waters.

About 45 miles east of Fernando de Noronha, he captured and burned three ships and had aboard *Alabama* 110 prisoners, equaling the number of her crewmen. He decided to go to a neutral port to land his prisoners, and he hoped to find the *Agrippina.* On May 11, 1863, he entered the Brazilian mainland port of Bahia, now known as Salvador, about 450 miles south of the island of Fernando de Noronha. He relieved *Alabama* of her many prisoners, but his tender was not in port. Semmes began to fear that "some disaster had befallen her."

On the morning of May 12, a messenger from the president of the Brazilian state, who resided in Bahia, boarded *Alabama* with a directive accusing Semmes of violating Brazilian neutrality at Fernando de Noronha and ordering him to leave the port the next day. Semmes successfully refuted the accusations and was then permitted to remain in the harbor.

On the next morning, as he looked around the harbor, Semmes saw a strange ship anchored about half a mile away. He raised the Confederate colors, and much to his surprise, so did the other ship. She was the CSS *Georgia* under Lieutenant Commander W. L. Maury, with whom Semmes had served in the "Old Navy," and with Lieutenants W. E. Evans and R. T. Chapman, who had served on the *Sumter* cruise with him.

Semmes was happy to see that his two former lieutenants were still in Confederate service, and he welcomed Maury as well. On May 14, officers from both Confederate ships, at the invitation of the manager of the local railway company, went on a tour by rail of the lower and upper portions of the city. Although Semmes undoubtedly had many questions to ask his former officers, he found time, as was his wont, to note the beauty of the countryside and of the city itself. Had he lived in the twentieth century he could very well have become an effective travel agent.

The English settlement in Bahia entertained Semmes and his officers at a dance, and his crew enjoyed shore leave in the same raucous fashion as they always did. But the president, anxious to prevent any violation of Brazilian neutrality, again accused Semmes of various acts in violation of that neutrality. Meeting with the president, Semmes successfully refuted each accusation. He even convinced the nervous young president to allow the *Georgia* coal from her tender and to permit *Alabama* to buy and receive coal from the shore. Finally, at 4:00 P.M. on May 21, *Alabama* steamed out of Bahia harbor, undoubtedly to the great relief of the president. As a parting shot, in his memoirs, Semmes speculated that the future of Brazil would be an unhappy one because of the amalgamation of the native Indians, the African freedmen, and the European Portuguese. That was his final word on Brazil.

Two days later Semmes reflected on his family: "I am now two long, long years and more absent from my family, and there are no signs of the abatement of the war. . . . On the contrary the Yankee devils seem to become more and more infuriated, and nothing short of a war of invasion is likely to bring them to terms, unless, indeed, it be the destruction of their commerce, and for this I fear we are as yet too weak. . . . We must sacrifice our natural yearnings on the altar of our country; for without a country we can have no home." As usual, he cast aside his innermost feelings and returned to the task of destroying Northern merchant ships.

The next day he captured two ships, destroying one and placing the prisoners aboard the other. Once again in the "crossing" of the South Atlantic Ocean, most of the ships he hailed were neutrals. Roughly about every four or five days he hailed, inspected, and burned an American ship. He learned from correspondence taken from his various victims that cargo insurance rates on American vessels was 5 percent higher than the rates for the same cargo shipped on neutral ships. He also hailed and boarded a ship that by her design was American made yet was flying an English flag—another testament to the effect the Confederate cruisers were having on the American merchant fleet.

Gale-strength winds and storms buffeted *Alabama* while in the southern "crossing," making the chases quite difficult and in some cases impossible. Nevertheless, Semmes did capture a number of American ships, and in each case he took off newspapers and personal correspondence. One American shipowner warned his captain that even if he were to make Liverpool safely, he would find difficulty in securing a return cargo because English shippers were more likely to use neutral vessels. From another letter he learned that there "was a large fleet in New York, and nothing for them to do, that will pay expenses, and more arriving daily." From still another shipowner he read: "I hope you will be as prudent and economical as possible in managing your ship matters, as your owners want all the money they can get hold of to aid in putting down this terrible rebellion of ours." Semmes knew, he wrote, that the money the Northern shipowner referred to would be used "to purchase gold bonds . . . and push on the war." He continued: "Hence our diligence in scouring the seas and applying the torch. Whenever we heard a Yankee howl go up over a burned ship, we knew that there were fewer dollars left, with which to hire the *canaille* of Europe to throttle liberty on the American continent."

On June 21, 1863, Semmes in his "diligence" captured the *Conrad*, of Philadelphia, sailing from Buenos Aires for New York, with part of a cargo of wool. To this ship he did not apply the torch. Instead, exercising a captain's right, he converted the Yankee ship into the Confederate States cruiser *Tuscaloosa*, named "after the pretty little town on the Black Warrior River in the State of Alabama." It was, Semmes thought, "meet that a child of the *Alabama* should be named after one of the towns of the State." He appointed Fourth Lieutenant John Low as captain and promoted Midshipman William H. Sinclair to be Low's first officer. Two crewmen, whom Semmes had observed to be excellent seamen, were designated to act as *Tuscaloosa*'s master mates, and twelve other crewmen from *Alabama* were assigned to the new Confederate ship. Low was a native of England, although at the outbreak of the war he was a resident of Savannah, Georgia. Semmes directed Low to cruise in the same shipping lane as *Alabama* in South African waters. By this unique and shrewd action he had quickly and easily added another Confederate cruiser to prey upon Northern shipping.

As *Alabama* turned toward the Cape of Good Hope, Semmes mused on the failure of Secretary of the U.S. Navy Welles to send some two or three of his warships in pursuit of *Alabama*. Any sailor would know that *Alabama* would eventually seek out the highways of the sea that merchant ships would almost have to use. He seemed disappointed that the Federal government cared so little that he was decimating the Northern merchant marine. He wrote:

> If Mr. Welles had stationed a heavier and faster ship than *Alabama*—and he had a number of heavier and faster ships—at the crossing of the 30th parallel, another at or near the equator, little to the eastward of Fernando Noronha, and a third off Bahia, he must have driven me off, or greatly crippled me in my movements. A few more ships in the other chief highways, and his commerce would have been pretty well protected. But the old gentleman does not seem once to have thought of so simple a policy as *stationing* a ship anywhere.

Semmes could not have known at the time he wrote those words that Secretary Welles had consciously adopted the policy of using his ships to blockade the Confederate coast, thus cutting the South off from the supply of European goods. In the long run, that policy served the North better than the stationing of ships would have done. But the Confederate navy captain in 1863 or even in 1867 had no way of knowing that; in 1867 he wrote that Welles's policy had "left the game entirely in my own hands."

"The game" from Semmes's point of view was really quite simple:

> My safety depended upon a simple calculation of times and distances. For instance, when I arrived off the coast of Brazil, I would take up my pencil and make some such estimate as this: I discharged my prisoners from the first ship captured, on such a day. It will take these prisoners a certain number of days to reach a given port. It will take a certain other number of days, for the news of the capture to travel thence to Washington.

This naval tactic, scientifically devised, was so successful that some forty-odd years later Emperor William II of Germany required his submarine commanders to read Semmes's memoirs. The U-2 boats were *almost* as successful in sinking Allied merchant ships as Semmes had been in sinking Yankee merchant ships.

Semmes's voyage to Cape Town was delayed not by enemy war vessels but by boll weevils in *Alabama*'s supply of bread. Semmes had no choice but to turn back toward Rio de Janeiro to visit the bakeries there. He was some 825 miles from the city, "some little distance to travel to a baker's shop," Semmes noted. But once again, the fates favored *Alabama*. On July 1, 1863, Semmes captured the U.S. merchant ship *Schmidt*, which had aboard not only ready-made hats and clothing for Semmes's crew but, more important, over thirty days' supply of bread. Semmes helped himself and ordered *Alabama* to do an about-face. The shortage of bread had delayed Semmes only a couple of days. As *Alabama* again sailed toward South Africa, she hailed many ships, but only one was a Northern vessel, whose cargo gave Semmes an opportunity to illustrate his knowledge of international law. The papers were improperly drawn. Semmes wrote a lawyer's brief to justify his decision to burn the ship. Again, it was upheld at the Geneva Convention.

On July 4, 1863, Semmes noted the special day in his journal, commenting that he should ignore it "because it was established in such bad company, and because we have to fight the battle of independence over again, against a greater tyranny than before." Nonetheless, he realized that "old feelings are strong, and it will not hurt Jack to give him an extra glass of grog." Finally, on the morning of July 28, 1863, *Alabama* ran into Saldanha Bay, some fifty miles north of Cape Town. Semmes had chosen that hideaway in order to reconnoiter the nearby waters before entering a harbor nearer Cape Town. No Yankee man-of-war was at the Cape, nor had one been there for some months: "Mr. Welles was asleep, the coast was all clear, and I could renew my depredations upon the enemy's commerce whenever I pleased."

It pleased him, however, to remain at Saldanha Bay for a week because *Alabama* needed some time for repairs. While mechanics overhauled her engine, other sailors repaired her hull and rigging. Semmes allowed the crew to take turns going ashore, where they found the few farmers to be friendly and generous with their fresh vegetables and meats. Semmes hunted ostriches on the rocky land. Unfortunately, *Alabama* also suffered the only casualty of the cruise: Third Assistant Engineer S. W. Cummings, while transferring from ship to boat to go hunting, accidentally shot himself. Semmes was deeply affected by this accident, writing in his memoirs that the curious visitor may still read on a marble slab "this mournful little episode of the cruise of *Alabama*."[4]

On August 5, 1863, *Alabama* sailed out of Saldanha Bay for Table Bay on the southern coast of which Cape Town is located. En route, she met up with *Tuscaloosa*, as previously planned. Lieutenant Low reported that he had captured an enemy ship from the East Indies, loaded with British-owned cargo, and thus had to release her on bond. Semmes directed Low to enter Simon's Bay to resupply his ship at Simon's Town, south of Cape Town.

As *Alabama* was hauling toward Cape Town, she captured the *Sea Bride* from New York. Semmes put a prize crew aboard the victim and ordered her to repair to Saldanha Bay by August 15. The capture created great excitement in Cape Town because it was made in full sight from that city, about four and a half or five miles distant from the land. The U.S. consul at Cape Town entered an official complaint that the capture was made in neutral waters, but the many eyewitnesses satisfied the South African government and the issue died away.

The famous cruiser's arrival in the evening of August 5 caused a great stir among the inhabitants of the city, especially among those who had witnessed the capture of the *Sea Bride*. Crowds that visited the ship favorably impressed Semmes; the crew and officers, dressed in their best uniforms, chatted with the visitors and served them refreshments in return for the flowers and food they had brought aboard *Alabama*. Bartelli, Semmes's "faithful steward," was "in his element during the continuance of this great *levee*." He greeted all the visitors at Semmes's cabin door, demanded a calling card, then allowed them to enter and to chat with his captain. "Fair women brought . . . bouquets with them, which they presented with a charming grace, and my cabin was soon garlanded with flowers." Semmes, resplendent in his captain's dress uniform and presenting his best demeanor, was a gracious Southern gentleman, bowing and kissing the hands of the ladies. The visits turned into a kind of mutual admiration society. "Dear ladies of the Cape of Good Hope!" Semmes loved every minute of it.

Alabama had to withstand a severe storm that swept into the harbor of Cape Town August 7–9. Semmes decided that his ship would be better protected in the inland bay of Simon's Town, south of Cape Town. En route, Semmes stopped an American merchant ship but had to release it when he discovered that he was within a league of a point of the South African shoreline. The captain profusely thanked Semmes, who replied that he had none to give him, "for I was only too sorry not to be able to burn him."

Simon's Town was the navy base of the British ships stationed in South Africa. Semmes enjoyed the British officers' hospitality during the five days his crew recaulked *Alabama* at "the bends," replaced copper sheathing about her waterline, and repaired her engine. Completely restored, on Saturday, August 15, 1863, *Alabama* sailed out of Simon's Bay, cruised a few days near the Cape, then headed north up the west coast of Africa. By prearrangement Semmes was to meet the CSS *Tuscaloosa* and the *Sea Bride* at an obscure bay on an isolated shore off West Africa. The location was in a part of Africa that at the time was unclaimed by any government; Semmes had carefully chosen it to avoid any violation of neutrality.

While in Cape Town Semmes had arranged to sell the *Sea Bride* for 3,500 pounds and to sell the wool that was aboard her. Money from the two transactions was to be turned over to a Confederate agent in Liverpool, with half of it deposited in a bank to the account of Raphael Semmes. It was one way that Semmes financed his voyage to the Far East.

Semmes ordered Lieutenant Low, commander of the *Tuscaloosa*, to proceed on a cruise off Brazil. Semmes was confident that, according to his calculations, sufficient time had passed since a Confederate cruiser had been in those waters so that U.S. shippers felt safe to sail in them. Back in Simon's Town harbor to repair *Alabama*'s freshwater converter, he learned that the USS *Vanderbilt*, under Captain Charles H. Baldwin, USN, had just left in search of *Alabama* and was cruising off Cape Agulhas, the southernmost tip of the African continent.

This news of the *Vanderbilt* disturbed Semmes. He knew that Baldwin's ship was considerably the faster ship and that her guns were larger than *Alabama*'s. Also, twelve *Alabama* crewmen had jumped ship in Simon's Town. Still, he did not mean to avoid the *Vanderbilt*; he just intended to assure *Alabama* of a fair fight with the Yankee. That meant, at least, he would have to replace the twelve missing seamen. According to international law, a belligerent may not recruit seamen in a neutral port. Semmes had a difficult moral decision to make. Nonetheless, he made a deal with a sailor-landlord for eleven men. He pacified his disturbed soul by some elaborate reasoning: If the eleven sailors want to leave Her Majesty's soil and go aboard the *Alabama*, which is legally Confederate soil, then decide they want to remain on that Confederate soil, he certainly would not be justified in compelling them to leave his ship. There, he had done it; he had violated international law! "What monstrous sophists we are, when interest prompts us," he chastised himself.

Alabama cruised in the sea lanes off the Cape of Good Hope without encountering the *Vanderbilt*, then headed eastward, where she ran into a series of high gales and rough waters but no enemy vessels to chase. Her commander began to look inward:

I am supremely disgusted with the sea and all its belongings. The fact is I am past the age when men ought to be subjected to the hardships and discomforts of the sea. Seagoing is one of those constant strifes which none but the vigorous, the hardy, and the hopeful—in short, the youthful, or at most the middle-aged—should be engaged in. The very roar of the

wind through the rigging with its accompaniments of its rolling and tum-
bling, hard, overcast skies, give me the blues.

On September 8 he recalled that it was the anniversary of his first orders
for sea service, as it was also the anniversary of General Worth's battle of
Molino del Rey in 1847 during the Mexican War. "How tiresome is the
routine of cruising becoming!" On Monday, September 27, 1863, *Alabama*
was "riding a heavy, confused sea," and Semmes realized that "today is the
fifty-fourth anniversary of the birth of the unworthy writer. How time flies
as we advance toward old age!" He prayed that God in his mercy would
"protect and preserve us" and "restore us, before another anniversary shall
roll around, in peace to our families." He reflected further on his life and
thought: "How strange seems the drama of human life when we look back
upon it; how transient, how unsatisfying!"

The black mood left him as *Alabama* turned eastward. Semmes noted
that "we were now about to make a long voyage, tedious to the unphilosophi-
cal mariner, but full of interest to one who has his eyes open to the wonders
and beauties of nature." It is obvious that he considered himself a "philosophical mariner" because he entered waters new to him not only with a lust
that lifted his black mood but also with a thirst for knowledge and new sea
experiences. Semmes chose a route across the South Indian Ocean that took
him so close to Antarctica that *Alabama* had to survive not only almost
constant winds and high seas but also something new: large and small icebergs.

The philosophical mariner, in his memoirs, educated the reader as he
sailed with him in the rough seas. The ever-present high waves tossed *Alabama* so that on occasions Semmes could not see the sea above her bow nor
beyond her stern. Semmes moved *Alabama* closer and closer to the icy continent; at one point, for several days among icebergs, the ship rode out those
winds and high waters just some 25 degrees above the shoreline of Antarctica. Semmes was fascinated by the rough weather: the constantly blowing
winds shifting 180 degrees on a regular schedule, the ever-present icebergs
threatening *Alabama*'s timbers. "This rough weather," Semmes noted in his
journal, "tries the ship badly, being so long in the heavy seas causes her to
complain and work in every timber. As yet she makes little more than her
accustomed water." Although *Alabama* bobbed on the waves like a cork,
Semmes relied on the ship's strength to survive the elements, and he was not
disappointed. On about October 12, 1863, at longitude 80 degrees, Semmes
turned northward and eastward toward the Strait of Sunda, between the
islands of Sumatra and Java. It was the entrance into the Java Sea, thence

into the South China Sea. It took the man and his ship from October 12 to October 27 to reach the strait.

At noon on October 26, *Alabama* hailed an English ship headed in the opposite direction. Semmes learned from her captain that the warship USS *Wyoming* was cruising in the strait, and he planned "to give her battle" if he could find her. If he were successful in finding her, it would be *Alabama's* second engagement with a U.S. warship. But the *Wyoming* was larger and more heavily armed than the USS *Hatteras,* which *Alabama* had sunk back in January. Semmes was concerned: "We will do our best, and trust the rest to Providence. May the Almighty crown my enterprise with success!" As he waited at the west end of the strait, Semmes had a gun transferred from one side of the ship to the other, to see if *Alabama* "could bear her battery thus." She could, and Semmes was satisfied that he could fight with seven guns on one side, and he was pleased with her. But still he hesitated to enter the strait; he chose to cruise in the open waters where he could more easily select an advantageous position should the *Wyoming* seek a battle.

On November 6 Semmes stopped an American merchant ship, boarded and condemned her, took the crew and some passengers aboard *Alabama,* then burned her. Tired of waiting for the *Wyoming,* on November 8, Semmes ran his ship into a port on the island of Sumatra, across the strait from Java. Failing to get fresh food from the natives, he got steam up and ran through the strait, seeing nothing of the *Wyoming.* He did, however, chase and burn a U.S. merchant ship just inside the Java Sea. That ship was the *Contest,* and her speed gave Semmes much concern; not until he moved the cannon from the bow to the stern of *Alabama* was he able, with steam and sail, to catch the American vessel. *Contest* was such a beauty and so obviously speedy that Semmes would have preferred to throw a crew aboard her and commission her into Confederate service as he had done with *Tuscaloosa;* but having no guns for her, he burned her. Knowing that the U.S. warships in the area were still looking for him, he sailed to the small island of Serutu, off the coast of Borneo, where he arrived on November 18. The next day, *Alabama* encountered a British ship, to which Semmes transferred his prisoners.

A passenger aboard the *Contest* wrote of the capture of the ship and of the time he spent aboard *Alabama.* His letter provides an excellent insight into the method and appearance of the men of *Alabama,* as well as the appearance of Captain Semmes.[5] "William" wrote to his father, describing the chase much as did Semmes; but his first-person account of the experience is unique:

In consideration of my illness I was permitted to take all my baggage, so that I lost very few articles of clothing. In the hurry and confusion however, many little things I failed to secure. I lost my chair, cushion, and all my books, a lot of knick knacks purchased in China and Japan, two small packages of Japan tea put up to order, together with a few articles of clothing that were in the soiled clothes bag, altogether not exceeding $150 in value. We remained on board the *Alabama* for eight days, during which time I was treated with the greatest kindness, one of the officers (Jeff Davis' brother-in-law) giving up his stateroom to my use. I messed with the officers and found them to be very pleasant and agreeable gentlemen.

William found Captain Semmes to be "villainous in appearance." He noted further that Semmes "keeps much to himself and is on deck very little. He neither spoke to me nor looked at me . . . although I frequently met him face to face."[6] This description and characterization of Semmes fits rather well the way Semmes saw himself: aloof, alone, and self-assured.

From November 18 to December 2 Semmes directed his ship northward, toward the coast of Indochina. The currents and winds were so strong that frequently he had to drag his anchor to prevent *Alabama* from being blown off course. Finally, late in the day of December 2, 1863, he reached the island of Condore, near the southern tip of present-day Vietnam. During the voyage from the Cape of Good Hope, the trying seas, contrary winds, and currents had sorely taxed the ship. It was Semmes's intention at Condore to repair and rest the ship and refresh her crew: they had been at sea constantly since August 31, almost three full months.

Much to the captain's surprise, the next morning he saw a small French man-of-war, which sent a boat to board *Alabama*. Semmes invited the French commander aboard, and the two had a long and friendly conversation in French. The Frenchman explained that France had taken over the island only recently and that he, himself, was the governor of it. The French ship led *Alabama* into a beautiful harbor, and the young governor placed no restrictions on the ship or her crew. The men and officers alike enjoyed freshwater swimming, hiking in the mountains, shooting game, catching the fresh fish of the harbor, and generally refreshing their spirits and regaining their land-legs after the rough voyage from South Africa. They also, as best they could, repaired *Alabama*'s engine and caulked her sides.

After two weeks in Condore harbor, *Alabama* left the little paradise December 15, heading southwestward toward Singapore. Semmes wondered, "Shall we ever reach our dear home, which we left nearly three years ago?"

Indeed, how were Anne Elizabeth, their daughters, and their young son?

Were they happy and safe in Cincinnati with the Spencer family? Anne Elizabeth could not, of course, write to Raphael; he had had no news of her or of their two older sons who were serving in the Confederate army since he had sailed the *Sumter* through the Union blockade at the mouth of the Mississippi River on that long-ago day in June 1861.

Nor could he have known until his return to Mobile that Anne Elizabeth and the three children endured much hardship in Cincinnati. The children could not attend school because their classmates teased and chided them because of their father's exploits; children and adults alike stood under their windows and shouted expletives until the Semmes children cried. The U.S. Army provost marshal repeatedly urged the government to force Mrs. Semmes and the three children to return to the South. Finally, while Semmes was in the eastern waters, a lieutenant of the army appeared at the door and ordered her and the children to prepare to leave Cincinnati, Anne Elizabeth's girlhood home, and go to Mobile, Alabama. The young lieutenant, she later wrote to her husband when he was back in England, was gentle during the journey and kind to her and the children but hardly let them out of his sight. They went to Philadelphia by train, then to the South by boat. It was a slow, long, and tiring trip.

Captain Raphael Semmes had been able on occasion to send money to them at Cincinnati, but when he finally discovered they were back in the South, such support was more difficult because of the increasingly more effective blockade. The welfare of his family must have been a constant worry, always in the back of his mind. But he was tough minded, and he put his family worries aside whenever *Alabama* demanded his full attention.

The voyage to Singapore was without incident. On the sixth day from Condore, *Alabama* reached the city's harbor. Semmes estimated about twenty-two American merchant ships were in the harbor, laid up without cargo. He felt some pride in that fact; his mere presence in the South China seas had forced the merchants to ship their products under neutral flags.

While his ship was receiving coal and provisions, Semmes, always curious about unfamiliar places, went into the city. Ever the observer, he noted that the multitude in the streets "comprises every shade of color, and every variety of the human race, and with every variety of dress." He rode outside the city proper and visited an English family. Thus refreshed, he returned to *Alabama*. Some good news and some bad news awaited him: The *Wyoming* had left twenty days earlier and was at the moment probably searching for *Alabama* in the China Sea; the bad news was that five crewmen had jumped ship. Semmes was, however, even in the neutral port able to replace them

Raphael Semmes (*Harper's Weekly*, volume 8, 1864)

with six new recruits. His violation of international law did not bother him this time; his conscience had become less sensitive.

Semmes was particularly happy to learn of *Wyoming*'s departure for the eastern part of the China Sea; it meant that his cruise in the western part of the sea had completely deceived the Yankee captain. Furthermore, the empty American merchant vessels in the harbor proved that *Alabama* had done her job—she had driven the American merchant ships from Chinese waters. *Alabama* could safely proceed westward to prey on enemy merchant ships and, more important, to receive some much-needed repairs on her boilers and to replace the copper stripping on her bottom. Semmes decided to "turn my ship's head westward from Singapore, run up into the Bay of Bengal, along the coast of Hindustan to Bombay through the Seychelles to the mouth of the Red Sea, thence to the Comoro Islands; from these to the Strait of Madagascar, and on to the Cape of Good Hope." He felt quite safe with that itinerary because the *Wyoming* was looking for *Alabama* in the eastern China waters.

Semmes was so pleased with his successes in the China waters that he indulged himself with a little fancy of the future. The industrious Chinese, who were then emigrating both west and east from their homeland, would, he maintained, soon overrun the western United States and then invade the Southern states:

> In the latter States their success will be most triumphant; for in these States, where the Negro is the chief laborer, the competition will be between frugality, forecast, and industry on the one hand, and wastefulness, indifference to the future, and laziness on the other. . . . Cheap labor must and will drive out dear labor. This law is as inexorable as any other of Nature's laws. This is the probable fate, which the Puritan has prepared for his friend the negro, on the American continent. Our system of slavery might have saved his race from destruction; nothing else can.

This racist statement undoubtedly was prompted by his observance of the hard-working Chinese in Singapore. It is one of the more extreme expressions of his low opinion of black people.[7] For a highly educated, widely read, intelligent man, this statement is most difficult to forgive.

His attention soon turned back to the ship and the sea. At about 8:30 on the morning of Christmas Eve 1863, *Alabama* sailed out of Singapore harbor and turned northward up the Strait of Malacca. Just after the noon hour, she overcame and stopped "an American-looking bark, under English colors, with the name *Martaban*." The captain refused to board *Alabama*, so Semmes, for the only time during the war, went aboard a captured vessel. As his boat approached the ship he became even more certain she was American built, probably in Maine; and as he boarded her he saw that everything looked ever more American, "even to the black greasy cook, who with his uncovered wooly head, naked breast and uprolled sleeves in the broiling sun, was peeling his Irish potatoes for his codfish." Semmes learned that the ship was the former *Texas Star*, with papers showing she was British owned. But there was no bill of sale and the cargo had no papers identifying it as British property except the usual bill of lading. Semmes, convinced the transfer was fraudulent, ordered the ship to be burned. When the merchant ship was in flames, her captain admitted he had "resorted to a sham sale in hope of saving my ship." Even so, the case of the *Texas Star,* alias *Martaban,* remained a live topic in the East. As recently as February 19, 1956, the Singapore *Sunday Times* printed an article on the burning of the *Martaban,* "which had been sold . . . to a British merchant," and reported that the Singapore newspapers "indignantly condemned Captain Semmes," writing that his "conduct savoured very much of downright piracy."[8] But the British never demanded compensation for the ship. When it came to questions of maritime law or international wartime law, Semmes was seldom, if ever, wrong.

At the turn of the new year *Alabama* continued her voyage westward into the North Indian Ocean. On New Year's Day 1864, Semmes commented in the ship's log: "Alas another year of war and toil and privation has passed over me, leaving its traces behind." He wondered again about his family in America: Were his sons still alive? Where were Anne Elizabeth and the younger children? He had no way of learning about them and so turned to the task at hand. On January 8, 1864, he stopped a British ship, identifying himself as the USS *Dacotah,* looking for the *Alabama.* The British captain replied: "It won't do; the *Alabama* is a bigger ship than you, and they say she is iron plated besides." Such legends grew during the war, and they made the history of the man and his ship all the more intriguing.

Semmes captured another American merchantman on January 14 as *Alabama* cruised among the islands off the tip of India for a few days. He then headed west by southwest and on February 6 reached the Comoro Islands that lie between the east coast of Africa and the island of Madagascar. He stopped off on one island to buy provisions.

There he entered into a conversation with one of the chiefs whose men had brought the provisions aboard, and he was delighted to learn that the "Black African Moslems, themselves, had black slaves." To learn that blacks enslaved other blacks reinforced his opinion that the black man everywhere lived better under slavery than he could as a free man.

Alabama's cruise was uneventful from Madagascar to the Cape of Good Hope. Semmes directed his ship into the harbor of Cape Town, arriving on March 20, 1864, almost six months after leaving the Cape to cruise in eastern waters. Immediately Semmes was faced with a question of international law: The governor of the Cape had received orders from Lord John Russell, foreign minister of England, to seize the CSS *Tuscaloosa.* Upon learning of this order on March 22, 1864, Semmes wrote a four-page, tightly reasoned refutation of England's right to seize the ship. Referring to international law, even citing British precedents to support his case, he demanded the restoration of *Tuscaloosa* to the Confederate States. The case was referred to London, where the decision was made to restore the ship to the Confederacy. Through his knowledge of international law Semmes had won the restoration of the ship. But it was too late, for by the time the case was decided, the war had ended. This obscure episode, however, reflects Semmes's knowledge of international law as well as his determination to adhere to that body of law to see justice done. The lawyer in him seemed to have enjoyed the legal debate, the results of which had no effect upon the outcome of the war.

Indeed, news from America was most discouraging to *Alabama*'s captain. He had earlier learned the results of the 1863 battles: the Confederate losses at Vicksburg, Chattanooga, Gettysburg. To his perceptive mind it was becoming obvious that the South could not win the war. But neither he nor *Alabama* would cease to fight it as diligently as they possibly could.

Semmes did not tarry in Cape Town. After getting coal and provisions aboard, on March 25 *Alabama* steamed out of Cape Town harbor, heading northward and slightly westward, to cruise in the vicinity of the island of Saint Helena. Semmes's ultimate destination was either England or France "for the purpose of docking, and thoroughly overhauling and repairing" *Alabama*. During the voyage, Semmes took time to read the many newspapers that had been taken aboard while at Cape Town. The signs of weakness among the Southerners, he wrote, which were becoming "for the first time painfully apparent after the battle of Gettysburg, and the surrender of Vicksburg, were multiplying." He became apprehensive "that the cruises of *Alabama* were drawing to a close."

After leaving the vicinity of Saint Helena, *Alabama* hailed "an unlucky Yankee, to whom we gave chase," which lasted the whole night and momentarily lifted the spirit of the still-despondent captain. The weather was good, with a bright moon, a gentle breeze, and a smooth sea. "The Yankee worked like a good fellow to get away, piling clouds of canvas upon his ship . . . but it was no use," Semmes wrote. "When the day dawned we were within a couple of miles of him. It was the old spectacle of the panting, breathless fawn, and the inexorable stag-hound." The thrill of the kill, however, soon turned to despair as Semmes read of Northern victories in the recent New York newspapers he took off the victim. "Might it not be," Semmes mused, "that after all our trials and sacrifices, the cause for which we were struggling would be lost? . . . The thought was hard to bear."

That ugly mood persisted as he recrossed the equator northward toward Cherbourg, and Semmes fell into a deep depression. Detached, he referred to himself in the third person—no longer the bright-eyed seaman who "gloated upon the spectacle" of the burning *Golden Rocket,* his first victim two and a half years earlier, and saw in those leaping flames the bright promise of a war easily won, but now only a man "upon whom stress and strain had laid, in the three years of war he had been afloat, a load of a dozen years on his shoulders." And he saw his ship just as clearly. The *Alabama* was no longer the "inexorable stag-hound" but now only a "wearied foxhound, limping back after a long chase, footsore and longing for quiet and repose." And above his visions of man and ship, he saw the "shadows of a sorrowful future" and knew that his cruise on board *Alabama* was "drawing to a close." The man and the ship were beaten not by the enemy on the high seas but by the seas themselves.

The bent and beaten seaman had pushed his ship, his sea bride, too long and too hard. The ship had answered his every demand: She had fought and defeated a U.S. war vessel; she had braved the storms of the Antarctic; she had survived the tropical waters of the East Indies; she had not been in dry dock since her launching in the River Mersey that fifteenth day of May so many nautical miles ago in 1862. As *Alabama* approached the coast of France on June 10, 1864, she "complained that her boilers were rusted and leaking, her copper sheathing was broken and dragging in the water, and her timbers—so tested by the raging seas infested with icebergs—were wearied by her long journeys." Her captain, too, was exhausted, not only from the "vigils by night and by day" but even more by a mental attitude: the lost cause for which he had "so struggled," "the shadows of a sorrowful future," his beloved *Alabama*'s cruise "drawing to a close."

On June 11, 1864, Semmes in his well-worn ship dropped anchor in Cherbourg harbor. Learning that Commodore James Barron was in Paris, the exhausted and depressed sailor grasped his pen in hand and wrote to his superior officer: "My health has suffered so much from a constant and harassing service of three years almost continuously at sea that I will have to ask for relief [from command of the *Alabama*]."[9] But he had no opportunity to relax because he heard rumors that the USS *Kearsarge* was in and out of the adjacent waters; when that ship sailed into Cherbourg harbor on June 14, all thought of resigning his command disappeared from his mind. *Alabama* still needed him. Soon the enemy vessel left the harbor and cruised off and on just outside the neutral limits.

What should Semmes do? He could hide *Alabama* safe behind the French flag; he could go about refreshing her with new boilers and copper sheathings. But such work takes time—time enough for other U.S. vessels to join the *Kearsarge.* Semmes knew that the CSS *Rappahannock* in Calais harbor was blocked from leaving by various U.S. warships. Semmes could not permit his gallant ship to be bottled up in Cherbourg as was the *Rappahannock* in Calais. What an inglorious end to her glorious cruise that would be! No, better that once again *Alabama* should ride the waves like a swan. She might win against the *Kearsarge:* The U.S. vessel possessed no visible advantage over *Alabama;* and if she failed, she would die as she had lived—gloriously. No, Semmes would never allow *Alabama* to become another *Rappahannock.*

Departing from custom, he summoned his first lieutenant into his cabin and announced: "Kell, I'm going to fight the *Kearsarge.* What do you think of it?" Somewhat taken aback to be asked his opinion, the loyal lieutenant dutifully reminded his captain that in target practice a few weeks earlier the gunpowder appeared to be weak and that one in three shells had failed to explode because of defective fuses. Semmes calmly replied: "I will take my chances of two in three."

Alabama's captain sent a message to *Kearsarge*'s Captain John A. Winslow, his former shipmate in the "Old Navy." Like a medieval knight, he threw down his gauntlet: "If you will give me time to recoal, I will come out and give you battle." And so the die was cast.

As romantic as Semmes's account of his decision to fight may appear, that decision nonetheless was a proper navy officer's determination to keep his ship afloat and active against the enemy. Semmes could do no otherwise. Loading 150 tons of coal took four days. During that time sailors holystoned the ship's decks, repaired or replaced her sails and riggings, and even freshened her paint. In the meantime, word of the impending battle had spread, and the curious and concerned took the train from Paris to Cherbourg or a boat from England to witness the upcoming battle. The artist Édouard Manet came and painted *Alabama* in her death throes; photographers and newspaper reporters arrived to record the event. Confederate naval officers from Paris tried to join her crew but were denied by the French officials who enforced their neutral obligations.

On Sunday morning, June 19, 1864, *Alabama*, with officers and crewmen in dress uniform, sailed out of Cherbourg harbor as if en route to a gala navy review. The crowds on the quays, housetops and hills, boats, and even the breakwater cheered as the proud ship steamed toward the waiting *Kearsarge.* *Alabama* responded to the gala occasion, once again riding the waves with the grace of a swan.

About three miles offshore, Semmes called his crew together to hear a rousing speech, reminiscent of Napoleon's First Order to his army in Italy: "The name of your ship has become a household word wherever civilization extends. Shall that name be tarnished by defeat? The thing is impossible!"

And *Alabama*'s crewmen, aroused at the word "defeat," answered: "Never! Never!" But Semmes himself was not so sure. Just earlier he had asked his fifth lieutenant, "How do you think it will turn out today, Mr. Sinclair?" Surprised to be asked his opinion, the lieutenant replied: "I cannot answer the question, Sir, but can assure you the men will do their full duty, and follow you to the death." Turning away, Semmes responded, "Yes, that is true." Knowing that new paint and sails had not corrected *Alabama*'s real needs—new boilers and sheathings—did Semmes mean that the crew that day would, literally, "follow [him] to the death"?

The story of the battle has been repeated often, from that day to this, by eyewitnesses, participants, popular writers, and scholars.[10] The plain facts— the "whats" of the battle—are clear: The two ships met about seven miles at sea, still in view of the spectators; Semmes opened fire about a mile from the *Kearsarge*, and the force of the fight threw the two ships into a circular pattern; after about sixty-five minutes of intense and continuous fighting, *Alabama* was foundering and sank stern first at 12:24 P.M. The "whys" of the battle are still disputed because eyewitnesses and participants recounted the events from their own scope of vision, personal allegiance, and mental conditions.

Depression struck Semmes early in the battle when he realized that *Alabama*'s shot and shell did little damage to the *Kearsarge*. He ordered his gunners to aim low so the shots would ricochet off the water into the enemy's hull. Finally, about thirty minutes into the fight, a lucky shot embedded a shell into the *Kearsarge*'s sternpost. A cheer went up from *Alabama*'s crew, but the shell failed to explode; it "was the only trophy they ever got from *Alabama! We* fought her until she could no longer swim, and then gave her to the waves."[11] As the ship began to settle stern first and the water engulfed the taffrails, Semmes and Kell prepared to abandon ship. Once again Semmes identified with his ship. At almost the last moment, in a subconscious gesture of defiance against the Yankee victor, Semmes cast his sword—a symbol of command—into the sea. Then he and Kell jumped and swam away to avoid the vortex of the waters.

It was an emotional moment for the two men as they swam in the water and saw their ship go down. Gallant losers often gain more renown than the winners. Whose name do we remember from the battle of Thermopylae? And whose name comes to mind when we hear the name Waterloo? Who remembers the name of the *Kearsarge*'s captain? It is from such stuff that legends grow.

Semmes later blamed his defeat on weak gunpowder and faulty percussion caps. But a sailor on board the *Kearsarge* claimed that *Alabama*'s shells failed to explode because the gunners had not removed the lead caps, which exposed the time fuses that in turn caused the shells to explode.[12] If that were true, then the blame should be placed on the gunners and not the gunpowder. Only about 8.5 percent of the 370 shots fired by Semmes's gunners even touched the *Kearsarge,* and more of these shots hit the rigging than the hull. Commander Bulloch, *Alabama*'s creator, analyzing the loss, wrote that the ship's crew had not been trained at judging distance, nor had they practiced "firing at a visible target and noting [the] effect," and he concluded that the "result of the action was determined by the superior accuracy of the firing of the *Kearsarge.*"

Semmes refused to criticize or lay blame on any of his officers or crew. Despite his earlier criticism of Jack Tar and the stern discipline he imposed during the cruise, after the battle Semmes wrote of his men with sentiments he had never before expressed: "When I looked upon my gory deck, toward the close of the action, and saw so many manly forms stretched upon it, with glazed eye of death, or agonizing with terrible wounds, I felt as a father feels who has lost his children."

It is true that of the twenty-one men who died in the action and in the waters, thirteen had served from the start of the cruise. It is also true that such a scene as the "gory deck" would impress itself on Semmes's mind as indelibly as that of his sinking ship. And Semmes's memoirs are impressionistic; but do his impressions convey any less truth than Édouard Manet's impressionistic painting of the death of *Alabama*? No, Semmes could not blame his crew any more than he could blame his ship:

> No one who is not a seaman can realize the blow that falls upon the heart of a commander, upon the sinking of his ship. It is not merely the loss of a battle—it is the overwhelming of his household, as it were, in a great catastrophe. *Alabama* had not only been my battlefield, but my home, in which I had lived two long years, and in which I had experienced many vicissitudes of pain and pleasure, sickness and health.

Before he wrote those words, he and Kell, as they swam in the waters, were picked up by a boat from an English yacht and were taken to Southampton, England. There and later he reflected upon *Alabama*'s duel with the *Kearsarge.* Two days after the battle Semmes composed his official report of the event to send to Commodore Barron. A wound to his left hand did not deter him from writing of the battle in his large and clear script. He referred first to the slight damage done by shells exploding against *Kearsarge*'s hull, but only in the context of his order to use shot alternately with shells; he did not mention weak gunpowder. Two paragraphs later, simply as a matter of information, he noted that his officers who went alongside the enemy ship reported that "her midship section on both sides was thoroughly iron-coated" by perpendicular chains covered by a thin outer planking. But he made no critical comment about the iron coating. Ten days later, on July 1, he wrote: "My defeat is due to two circumstances: the very thorough manner in which the enemy's ship was protected by her chain armor and the deterioration . . . of my powder and fuses." On July 5 he placed the loss on the condition of the powder and referred to the *Kearsarge*'s chain armor only by indirection. In neither letter did he criticize Captain Winslow for applying the chain armor or for covering it with planking. He did comment in the letters that his defeat had left him "overwhelmed" and "oppressed" with "mortification." His humiliation grew with the passing years, so that he wrote in his memoirs: "The plain fact is, without any varnish, the *Kearsarge*, though as effectively protected as if she had been armored with the best of iron plates, was to all appearance a wooden ship of war." The *Kearsarge* really had "concealed armour."[13]

The battle, then, had been unfair, won by deceit and trickery. The Semmes who wrote those words was not the navy officer who took the *Sumter* through the Union blockade in 1861, who destroyed more enemy merchant ships than any other raider captain in all of naval history, and who forced merchants to ship their goods under neutral flags, so wounding American merchant shipping that it has not yet recovered its pre–Civil War position among world merchant shipping. Nor was he the man who guided and molded a motley crew of various nationalities into fighting men who, despite defeat, left him glory. No, it was not Captain Raphael Semmes of the CSS *Alabama*, but a broken man whose pride, and perhaps self-respect, had been destroyed on that Sunday off Cherbourg in 1864.

Captain Raphael Semmes of the CSS *Alabama* was no more, but Captain Raphael Semmes of the Confederate States Navy did still live, and he would return to America to continue the fight for that cause he so ardently supported.

7

Survival after the *Alabama*

As *Alabama*, the staghound, settled into the Channel's murky waters, it was John Lancaster's *Deerhound* that leapt to pluck Semmes, Kell, and others out of those swirling waters and bore them to the safety of England's Southampton.

In that southern English city, despite his wounded left hand and the devastation he felt at the loss of his ship, Semmes set about the duty of paying off as many of his crew as he could locate. He also received a new fancy sword from English admirers, as well as visits from friends whom he had met after having laid up the CSS *Sumter* at Gibraltar. Among the latter was the Reverend Mr. Tremlett, whose friendship Semmes readily acknowledged. After completing his official acts as captain of *Alabama*, Semmes gratefully accepted Mr. Tremlett's invitation to a second visit at the latter's home at Belsize Park, London, where he rested under the tender ministrations of Miss Louisa Tremlett and began to regain some of the strength that had been sapped from him during and after the *Kearsarge* conflict.

The Tremletts decided that a trip to the Continent would hasten Semmes's recovery, so a party of six—three men and three women—from mid-July to the end of September traveled the Continent. Landing at Ostend, they traveled through Belgium, where the seaman visited the site of the battle of Waterloo, and then by boat on the Rhine River to Mayence, and then on to Geneva where they rested for several days. The fresh air and cleanliness of the city and the countryside helped restore Semmes's good health.

There is also the probability that the attentions of Miss Tremlett, who had taken an intense interest in the Confederate navy officer during his first visit to England, had something to do with his recovery. At any rate, when he returned to the Confederacy he was wearing a ring on his left third finger, along with his wedding ring, the former given to him by Miss Tremlett, much to the chagrin of Anne Elizabeth.

Semmes left his party on the Continent and returned alone to England. There he made his plans to return to the Confederacy by a circuitous route because "the very mention of my name had some such effect upon the Yankee Government as the shaking of a red flag before the blood-shot eyes of an infuriated bull." He planned his trip to avoid the Union blockade.[1] He took a British steamer to Havana, and from there a Yankee schooner, under the English flag, to the small Mexican port of Bagdad, and then a carriage to Matamoras. He was impressed by the "great revolution" that had transformed the sleepy Mexican port into a veritable beehive of activity. Because of the growing effectiveness of the Union blockade of Southern ports, a large percentage of the exported cotton went out through the Mexican port city, and the returning arms and munitions entered the Confederacy through that city. From his experiences during the Mexican War, it will be recalled, Semmes had little respect for the Mexicans, but now he saw them as an effective link in the lifeline of the Confederacy.

He crossed the Rio Grande in a skiff to the Texas city of Brownsville. As he touched the soil of the Confederacy, he "experienced, in their full force, the lines of the poet":

> Where shall that land, that spot of earth
>   be found?
> Art thou a man?—a patriot? Look around;
> Oh! thou shalt find, howe'er thy footsteps roam
> That land *thy* country, and that spot *thy* home!

His roaming footsteps had led him back to his country and soon to his home and to Anne Elizabeth.

The return to Mobile from Brownsville was an experience of extremes: From Brownsville he rode, with an escort of mounted soldiers, in a carriage that was provided "with a dozen bottles of excellent brandy, and cigars at discretion." His trip through Texas was not uneventful: Everywhere he was received with enthusiasm; the hotels gave him free rooms, and salutes of artillery greeted him at every town; he made short speeches to the townsfolk so they could hear "how the pirate talked." Semmes feared that he "drank a good many more mint juleps than were good for" him. He arrived at Shreveport, Louisiana, on November 27, 1864, where he was entertained by the inhabitants and "frequently importuned by a 'bevy of blooming lasses' to tell them 'how I did the Yankees.'"

He did not linger in Shreveport; he wanted to get on to Alexandria, Louisiana, where his son, Oliver J. Semmes, was serving as a major in the Confederate artillery.[2] He last had seen him, it will be recalled, when he was on his buying trip to New York; the son, then a cadet at West Point, had come downriver to visit with the father. Now, almost four years later, the two were together again, each with many tales of frightful wartime experiences to exchange. The commanding general arranged for Oliver to accompany his father to Mobile. The navy captain was delighted, and the remainder of the trip, difficult as it was, nonetheless was a happy one for Semmes.

Crossing the Mississippi River was the most dangerous part of Semmes's long journey home because the North controlled the river with its gunboats. And they had heard of Semmes's return, even of his journey through parts of Texas and Louisiana. Men of the Confederate mail service, however, had had much experience at avoiding the Yankee riverboats. The admiral and his son traveled through swamps where the water reached up to their waists and to the horses' bellies. It was not easy, but the mail personnel succeeded in conducting the navy captain and the army officer safely across the river to fresh horses, and the father and his son slept that night in the home of a Colonel Rose. They then went directly to Mobile, where they arrived about December 20, 1864. Raphael Semmes had been traveling for almost three full months; and he had not seen his wife, his three daughters, or his youngest son in almost four years.

At last, he and Anne Elizabeth were together again. It must have been at this time that she commented on the ring he now wore on the finger with his wedding band. Still, one can easily imagine the tear-filled embraces that greeted the husband and father. His name was as well known around the world as were those of Generals Lee and Grant, and his wife and daughters greeted him not only as a husband and father but also as a wartime hero.

A few days after his arrival in Mobile, Semmes received a telegram from Confederate Secretary of the Navy Stephen R. Mallory that arrived on Christmas Eve: "[I] congratulate you on your safe arrival. When ready to come on regard this as an order to report to Department."[3] Christmas 1864 could not have been a happy one for the people of the Confederacy: Soldiers of the Confederate armies were deserting daily and the armies of U.S. Generals William T. Sherman and Ulysses S. Grant were moving through the Southeast almost without opposition. The happiness of the Semmes family, so recently reunited, was tainted by Mallory's telegram. The war's demands still required his services; when would Anne Elizabeth see her husband again?

In his memoirs Semmes treated the telegram more as a request for him to report his activities afloat. Anne Elizabeth and the girls probably realized better than he that the war's end was near: They knew the difficulty in finding decent food; they had long dealt with the problems of high inflation; and they probably had heard of the widespread desertions from the Confederate armies. The wife and daughters knew that the husband and father soon would be leaving his home again. He did so on January 2, 1865, taking twelve-year-old Raphael, Jr., with him.

The trip took Semmes through that part of the Confederacy most devastated by Sherman's activities: "I was two weeks making my way to the capital of the Confederacy, owing to the many breaks which had been made in the roads by raiding parties of the enemy, and by Sherman's march through Georgia! Poor Georgia! she had suffered terribly during this Vandal march of conflagration and pillage, and I found her people terribly demoralized." Semmes remarked that he was "painfully struck with the changed aspect of things, since I had left the country in 1861." As he traveled through Georgia and South Carolina he saw ordinary people stealing and scavenging for food. "Reeling drunken soldiers passed in and out of dwellings, plundering and insulting their inmates." And the plunderers were not only the Yankee soldiers "but our own people":

> The civilians had taken themselves to speculation and money-getting, and the soldiers to drinking and debauchery. The *Alabama* had gone to her grave none too soon. If she had not been buried with the honors of war, with the howling winds of the British Channel to sing her requiem, she might soon have been handed over to the exultant Yankee to be exhibited at Boston, as a trophy of war!

It took two weeks for the captain and his twelve-year-old son to make the trip to Richmond, where they stayed with his cousin, Thomas J. Semmes, a senator from Louisiana. He called upon President Davis who, with his wife, received him cordially. As they talked about the state of things in the Confederacy, Semmes felt that Mrs. Davis had a firmer grasp of the realities in the South than did her husband. It was a pleasant interview, nothing more.

Soon after his arrival in Richmond, "near the end of January 1865," Semmes visited General Lee at his headquarters near Petersburg.[4] After a long chat about conditions prevailing in the Confederacy, Semmes realized that Lee knew all about them but felt powerless to change them. That very night 160 men deserted from Lee's own troops.

The Confederate Congress honored Semmes "with a distinction" that he felt he little deserved: It voted him a seat in Congress with the right of voice. The Virginia legislature also extended those honors to him. Within a matter of days, on Davis's recommendation, he was promoted to rear admiral (February 10, 1865) and eight days later assigned to command the James

River Fleet. He immediately arranged for Raphael, Jr., to be appointed a midshipman and assigned to his flagship, the ironclad CSS *Virginia II.*

For one who had sailed the *Alabama* halfway around the world and back, as he first inspected the ships of his newly assigned fleet, the waters of the James River seemed small indeed. The "fleet" was almost immobile, with the ships assigned to positions to prevent Northern ships from mounting the river. Semmes recognized the urgency of protecting the capital city of the Confederacy and entered no complaint in his memoirs. His fleet consisted of two ironclads in addition to the *Virginia,* each ironclad carrying four guns, and five wooden ships, each carrying two guns of smaller caliber. In addition to the ships, four shore batteries assisted in the defense of Richmond.

As he inspected the ships and men of his command, Semmes soon realized that the fleet was as demoralized as the army. Most of the enlisted personnel, he learned, were men from the army—men who had had little navy training, who were bored with their inactivity, and who used their free time to support each other's complaints. The new fleet commander attempted to remedy the poor morale by sending squadrons on shore to drill and march. But discontent continued to grow; enlisted personnel applied daily by the dozens for leave to visit their homes; some men who were Northern-born, known as the "Union element," agitated the Southern-born ones to leave or to neglect their duties aboard ship. Semmes noted that had the ships been at sea, discipline would have been easier; but it was almost impossible to prevent desertion with the ships lying so close to the riverbanks. Semmes realized that he faced the same problems General Lee faced, namely, constant desertion of the men under his command. It was not a pleasant command for Semmes.

On top of all these disturbing factors, Semmes himself was not well; suffering from a long-lingering cold he nonetheless forced himself to make his daily rounds, to insist upon the routine practices, and to shape up the ships and crew so they could defend Richmond from the sea. His duty was at best a time-consuming one that allowed him, from time to time, to forget the desperate situation the Confederacy faced.

Semmes's living and working quarters undoubtedly contributed to his poor health, which seemed to linger without improvement. His "office" was located in a barge tied to the side of his ship; to get to it, he had "to walk across a single balk of timbers which protruded" from the ship's side to reach the barge, then climb backwards down a ladder into the darkness and dampness of the barge. His living quarters were no better. The single room was dark and undoubtedly damp because it had no opening to the outside.[5] No wonder he and young Raphael were not well during those last weeks of the 1864–65 winter.[6]

As the 1865 spring weather dried the roads, the armies began to move: U.S. General Sherman cut a swath of destruction through South Carolina and into North Carolina, where Confederate Generals Braxton Bragg and Joseph E. Johnston temporarily checked the Union armies. In Virginia, Union General Philip Sheridan defeated Confederate General Jubal Early in the Shenandoah valley and joined his army of some 10,000 to 12,000 cavalrymen to Grant's 150,000-man army. Other Northern generals pressed into Virginia, giving Grant a total of some 260,000 men to oppose Lee's "half-starved, ragged army" of about 33,000 men. Semmes realized that his fleet would serve no purpose in the spring and summer fighting; yet his duty was with his ships, training his men, and planning his moves in case of a Union navy attack.

Semmes's thoughts turned to Anne Elizabeth and the girls, as the Northern forces began to concentrate in Virginia. He deposited 1,957 English pounds in the Richmond office of Fraser, Tremholm and Company, with the provision that fifty dollars were to be sent to "my family" each month.[7] It would not be a sufficient amount to sustain his wife and two daughters if paid in Confederate dollars; Semmes was obviously anticipating an end to the war because the pounds could be paid in U.S. dollars as easily as in Confederate ones. At least it would be some help to Anne Elizabeth when the war ended.

Meanwhile, his small and damp quarters contributed to his lingering illness. He reported no desertions from the fleet despite the growing threat from the Union armies. He was confident that Union navy vessels would not even attempt to move up the James River against his defenses, and he was just as sure that General Lee's constantly decreasing army could not long delay Grant's troops from entering the city of Richmond.

Finally, on Sunday, April 2, 1865, Grant began his move to dislodge Lee from his defense of Richmond. The battle began with a heavy artillery bombardment that was so effective Lee notified President Davis of his inability to protect the city. The government officials immediately began their withdrawal; Mallory notified Semmes of Lee's movement toward Danville, ordered him to sink his ships, and suggested that he coordinate his actions with Lee; but the admiral had no way of locating the general, so he had to act on his own. He scuttled the James River fleet and ordered his men to Richmond.

They arrived in Manchester, just across the James River from Richmond, about 2:00 or 3:00 A.M. on April 3 and found only pandemonium; crowds of civilians were wandering the streets seeking some sort of conveyance out of the city. The last locomotive had left some hours earlier, leaving not only Semmes and his sailors but also those civilians who then attached themselves to Semmes. Using his diary to refresh his memory, Semmes in his memoirs recreated the confusion as well as the resourcefulness of his sailors. The navy firemen were familiar with steam engines, so the admiral formed his sailors into columns and marched them to the Richmond railway station; but they found no steam engines there. He asked passing fugitives about the trains. "The trains!" said they. "The last train left at daylight this morning; it was filled with civil officers of the Government."

Semmes, the former commander of the CSS *Sumter* and the CSS *Alabama,* was at a loss. But his men were his responsibility, and he determined to do *something.* He sent his men to search for a steam engine, and they found a small one sitting on the tracks at the station, but there was no fuel. What to do? Looking about him, Semmes saw a picket fence nearby and set the sailors to work pulling off the pickets and then breaking them so they would fit into the small locomotive's little firebox. The only rail cars available were full of civilians confidently awaiting some authority to save them from the Yankees. Semmes ordered all civilians off the cars, had his men board them, then allowed as many civilians as there were seats to reboard the cars. Semmes, elaborating on his rather prosaic diary, in his *Memoirs of Service Afloat* pokes fun at himself: "All being in readiness, with the triumphant air of a man who had overcome a great difficulty, and who felt that he might snap his fingers at the Yankees once more, I gave the order to 'Go Ahead!' " The small engine with the poor fuel began to move slowly until it reached a slight incline just outside the station; then it stopped.

Semmes could see enemy cavalry across the river, on the Richmond side. He realized he and his "people" were in no danger because all the bridges were down. Still he had not solved the problem of the little engine that couldn't; but one of his engineers discovered another, larger engine. Firing both engines, the sailor/railway engineers, with better fuel, achieved normal speed. Along the way at various railway stations and small village way stations, they picked up unattached colonels and generals. After they had reached safety, railway conductors and engineers came forward and demanded that they take charge of the "Semmes Train." Semmes, of course, declined, firmly if not politely. The navy engineers had come through; they had fed the little engine, and it had responded. They reached Danville about midnight of April 4, 1865, joining President Davis and the various civilian and military officers who had arrived in the city earlier in the day.

Semmes, the steam engineers, and the two little engines operated by Confederate sailors had saved not only the naval personnel from capture but the many civilian passengers as well. Admiral Semmes had navigated them safely across the state of Virginia.

However, the war was not yet over. President Davis ordered Semmes to the command of an artillery unit composed of the sailors of the James River Fleet and appointed the admiral to the rank of brigadier general of artillery in the Confederate States Army. Semmes's navy rank of rear admiral was equal to the army rank of major-general but, he wrote, "It was folly, of course, to talk of rank in the circumstances in which we were placed." General Semmes carefully appointed his son, young Raphael, to the rank of second lieutenant and attached him to his own staff; he was not going to take any chances that his son would be captured by the enemy. From April 6 through April 10 Semmes and his men were busy preparing gun emplacements. On the latter date they received news of Lee's surrender the previous day at Appomattox Court House. "We all felt that the fate of the Confederacy was sealed." Davis in the meantime had left Danville for Charlotte, North Carolina, and from there to Abbeville, South Carolina, then into Georgia where he was later captured.

The first news Semmes had of Lee's surrender to Grant was from "the stream of fugitives which now came pressing into our lines at Danville." They were a sad-looking group of men, "some on horseback, some nearly famished for want of food, and others barely able to totter along from disease. It was, indeed, a rabble rout." The Confederates were completely at the mercy of the Northern army.

General Semmes with his artillery brigade was ordered to Greensboro, North Carolina, to join CSA General Joseph E. Johnston. En route from Danville, so many of his men deserted that on arrival at Greensboro Semmes's command, originally consisting of more than 400 men, then numbered only 250 men and officers. Johnston entered into negotiations at the invitation of USA General William T. Sherman to *disperse* the Confederate soldiers; Sherman did not take them as prisoners of war. While these negotiations were going on, news arrived of President Abraham Lincoln's assassination. In his memoirs Semmes recorded his reaction to that news:

> It seemed like a just retribution that he should be cut off in the midst of the hosannas that were being shouted in his ears, for all the destruction and ruin he had wrought upon twelve millions of people. . . . He had made a war of rapine and lust against eleven sovereign states. . . . These States had

not sought war, but peace, and they had found, at the hands of Abraham Lincoln, destruction. As a Christian, it is my duty to say, "Lord have mercy upon his soul!" but the devil will surely take care of his memory.

Raphael Semmes—intelligent, kind-hearted, honest, and capable—still could not contain his hatred of the North's leader against the Southern states. Was it a blindness to human rights that he had fought for slavery? Or was it a sincere conviction that the federal government was trampling the constitutional rights of the Southern states? Throughout his memoirs he showed repeated instances of his devotion to individual black persons, and that same individual devotion would reappear throughout his postwar life. There still remains in the South this white bifurcation of feelings toward black persons. Semmes, a strong-minded individualist in so many facets of his life, was nonetheless a typical Southerner on matters of race. In this light, combined with the viciousness of the lost war, his views on Lincoln are understandable if not acceptable.

U.S. General William T. Sherman, whose army had wreaked such havoc throughout the Southern states, offered a lenient parole to the leaders and men of the Southern armies. On May 1, 1865, Semmes, accompanied by his staff including young Raphael, met with Sherman's special commissioner, General William Hartsuff. The latter gave signed blank forms to Semmes for all of his officers and men. Semmes only had to write in the name of each individual. The guaranty for Semmes reads as follows:

> Greensboro, North Carolina, May 1, 1865
> In accordance with the terms of the Military Convention, entered into on the 26th day of April, 1865, between General Joseph E. Johnston, commanding the Confederate Army, and Major-General William T. Sherman, commanding the United States Army in North Carolina, R. Semmes, Rear Admiral, and Brigadier General, C.S. Navy and C.S. Army, commanding brigade, has given his solemn obligation not to take up arms against the Government of the United States, until properly re-leased from this obligation; and is permitted to return to his home, not to be disturbed by United States authorities, so long as he observes this obligation and obeys the laws where he may reside.
>
> R. Semmes
> Rear Admiral C.S. Navy, and
> Brigadier-General C.S. Army

Wm. Hartsuff
Brevet Brigadier-General U.S. Army
Special Commissioner[8]

This parole was to Semmes his passport to "life after the war." It failed, however, to protect him from the fury of U.S. Secretary of the Navy Gideon Welles.

Because of his high ranks in both the Confederate navy and the Confederate army, Semmes was allowed to have an armed escort of six of his officers on horseback as he and young Raphael rode in a wagon to Mobile. As usual, he kept a diary of the three-week trip; he recorded each village where they passed the nights, the admiral-general sleeping in a bedroll under the wagon while his escorts took turns guarding him and his son. The route he took followed very closely that of the present-day Interstate 85 highway. He veered from it about seventy miles northeast of Atlanta and passed through Athens, Georgia, which he described simply as a "quaint little college town." Continuing about ten miles further, he encamped that night at Farmville, Georgia. He devoted some three pages to a detailed description of the railway station, stores, and the various homes. Today Athens, the site of the University of Georgia with 30,000 students, has a population of almost 100,000 residents and is the commercial hub of northeast Georgia. Farmville, on the other hand, has suffered a decline: The railway station is empty and unused; there is one store; and the homes have dwindled to perhaps fifteen or twenty.

The Semmes entourage continued without mishap to Montgomery, Alabama, where Semmes dismissed his escort and with young Raphael took a steamer downriver to Mobile. Home at last! The reunion with Anne Elizabeth, at first, created in him more anxiety than pleasure: He found her hoeing a vegetable patch side by side with three black women who had been her house slaves. Semmes was astonished that food was so scarce that his wife had to work in the field alongside her former slaves. Later she explained that without their loyalty and help she and her two daughters still at home would have had nothing to eat. This very personal experience reinforced Semmes's feeling that the North had fought a war of attrition against the South.

Upon his safe arrival in Mobile, motivated by his shock at seeing the four women hoeing in the garden, Semmes immediately began to search for a way to support his family. He first sought employment in foreign navies. On May 31, 1865, he wrote to William Lindsay, an English friend, asking him to forward an enclosed letter to the Brazilian minister in London. Lindsay responded in a letter dated July 8, 1865, informing Semmes that because there was no Brazilian minister in London, he had given Semmes's letter to James Mason, the former Confederate diplomatic agent in London. Mason, in turn, sent the letter to John Slidell, former Confederate minister in Paris, who would present it to the Brazilian minister there. Brazil at the time was engaged in a war against Paraguay, a landlocked country. One wonders why the most successful raider captain of the American Civil War, whose fame was gained on the high seas, would offer his services to a country engaged in a war with a landlocked enemy. Perhaps he thought that Brazil could use his services somehow on the high seas; or perhaps he was willing to engage in naval activities limited to river actions. On the other hand, Brazil did maintain a decent high seas navy. Perhaps the real reason is simply that he was searching desperately for some means of providing for his family. But he heard nothing from Brazil.

The Brazilian minister to Paris, however, informed John Slidell that "no foreigner can be commissioned in the Brazilian service, unless he becomes a citizen, when a certain residency is required before naturalization, and this delay can only be dispensed with by an act of Congress." Semmes, of course, could not consider such a delay.

The Reverend Mr. Tremlett also got into the act. He confirmed what Mason had written and had taken upon himself the task of contacting other countries in Semmes's behalf. He wrote a long letter to the Argentine minister in London, in which he recited Raphael Semmes's career during the American Civil War. While an accurate account, it praised Semmes beyond the realities of his career. But nothing materialized from these efforts. In vain, he wrote not only to the government of Brazil but also those of Turkey, Argentina, and Prussia. In Berlin in June 1866, Otto von Bismarck asked the opinion of the United States minister to Prussia, Joseph A. Wright, on "the propriety of employing Captain Semmes in the Prussian navy." Wright replied that "Captain Semmes was one of the most objectionable men in the whole South to the loyal men of the Union." Bismarck quietly responded: "We want the respect and goodwill of the United States at all times, and we will not employ him."[9]

Indeed, that factor could well have been decisive in the refusal of other countries to commission Semmes in their navies. It was a factor that Semmes never understood; on October 15, 1865, he wrote to his son-in-law, Pendleton Colston: "I have determined after all to remain in Mobile. I have purchased a place four miles West of the city, and within ten minutes walk of the Spring Hill railroad. Spencer and his wife will reside with us, and he and myself will open a law office in town, and compete for a share of the business." Although he recognized that it would "be uphill work," many of his friends, he wrote, had promised them their business, as had the insurance companies in the city. He would arrange to live cheaply in the country, "until time shall enable us to accomplish results. So God willing, I shall manage to live, not as an Admiral perhaps, with his honors and large salary, but as a philosopher and a Christian of moderate views and few wants." Thus he had arranged a new life for himself, one in which he saw himself as an ordinary lawyer living comfortably off a small income.

About seven weeks later, he again wrote to Colston: "Spencer and I have been in practice a month, and though we have not yet *realized* anything, yet we have brought some half dozen suits in the courts, and have a dozen other claims in the courts for collection. Our friends speak encouragingly to us and I think we shall be able to take hold of a fair share of the practice of our one-horse city." He nonetheless feared that the federal "military misrule and plunder" would be maintained as long as possible. "But surely," he attested, "there is too much good sense and moderation in the people at large, to desire a further continuation of the present state of things. I feel no other interest in the matter than a desire to see the courts, and the law, once more in operation." Could the former "pirate" who had destroyed so many Northern merchant ships during the war achieve his goal? He soon was forbidden to practice law either in the state of Alabama or in the United States courts. His vision of a calm and peaceful life in the country with his family by his side was not to be.

Unlike other Confederate officers, he was not to be left alone. Seven and a half months after his parole at Greensboro, North Carolina, on December 15, 1865, Semmes was arrested. U.S. Secretary of the Navy Welles, whose ships throughout the war had been unable to capture Semmes aboard either the *Sumter* or the *Alabama,* had sent the U.S. Marines to do what the U.S. Navy had been unable to do: arrest Raphael Semmes.[10] According to his habit, Semmes kept a diary of his experiences related to the arrest.

> On the 15th of December 1865, whilst sitting with my family, a lieutenant of Marines and two sergeants entered my house, having first surrounded it by a guard of some 20 men, and presented me with an order for my arrest from the Secretary of the Navy, and a charge drawn by the same officer, and arrested me, and posted a sentinel over my door. Secretary's order dated 25 Nov. 1865.[11]

The next day, the lieutenant took Semmes into the city, "preparatory to my transfer to Washington." Semmes was allowed to "call upon the headquarters of the Commander of the Department of Alabama," where in vain he presented a protest of his arrest in light of the "convention entered into by General Johnston and General Sherman." After being permitted to call at his office for a few minutes, Semmes was taken to the *Louise,* preparing to leave for New Orleans. "Here I took leave of my afflicted wife and two sons who had repaired to the steamer for the purpose." On December 17, Semmes and his guards arrived at New Orleans and took rooms in the Saint Charles Hotel, where they remained for three days awaiting a ship for New York. Many of Semmes's friends and admirers were allowed to visit him during the next three days, which made the time awaiting transportation less unpleasant.

Ever the realist, Semmes also began to plan his defense and to seek legal representation. In a letter of December 19 to Pendleton Colston, his son-in-law and a lawyer in Baltimore, he mentioned several names for lawyers to act in his behalf. He referred to Winter Davis, who he thought would be sufficiently effective to act alone; he also mentioned Robert Brent, "an old friend from boyhood." Whoever agreed to represent him, Semmes wanted him to arrange the trial to be held as soon as possible. He assumed Colston would visit him as soon as he learned where Semmes was quartered.

On December 20, Semmes and his guards embarked on the steamer *Costa Rica* for New York. The next morning, at about 10:00 o'clock, the steamer passed out of the mouth of the Mississippi River; did the Confederate admiral recall his earlier passage on board the CSS *Sumter* four years ago? He made no comment in his diary.

Ever the seaman, Semmes could not help but record the ship's progress day by day. Christmas Day 1865 was "cloudy and gloomy, wind still fresh and much sea on." The next night they passed Cape Hatteras. On December 27, just after 9:00 P.M., the ship reached New York harbor amid a thick and heavy fog.

That night, as the ship reached its dock, he wrote a long letter to Anne Elizabeth.[12] He told her of the pleasant voyage from New Orleans to New York and of the courtesy with which he was treated during the voyage: "so far I have scarcely felt myself a prisoner." He felt confident that the charge under which he was arrested would not hold up in a court of law. His only offense, he wrote, was that he had "honestly and earnestly discharged his duty to his government, and in the midst of a sanguinary and exciting war never lost sight of the Christian and the gentleman."

> Do not permit yourself, my dear wife, to be unduly cast down by my arrest. I have no apprehension myself of being treated harshly or unfairly, except insofar as my arrest is in itself a violation of a solemn contract. The charge under which I was arrested—that I unlawfully escaped after my engagement with the *Kearsarge*—has no foundation in fact or in the law, and this I shall be able easily to prove, should the government proceed to trial upon

it. Encourage my dear daughters, to have patience and all no doubt will be well. Spencer of course will attend to his law business as usual. Oliver will be at home with you to assist in the cultivation of the pease [*sic*] and Ralph [Raphael, Jr.] must continue to make the best use of his time at the college. So cheer up and let the duties of the household go on as usual. Do not conjure up a thousand imaginary evils to make yourself unhappy. My imprisonment will be more a name than a reality, as I have no doubt that I shall be made comfortable, and have free access to books, and perhaps intercourse with my friends. My own greatest sense of unhappiness is my separation from my dear family, and its deprivation of my services at a time when those services have become so necessary to it.

Believe me, my dear wife,

Your most aff. husband.

Was he really as optimistic as he indicated in a letter designed to cheer his wife? Probably not, for he really did not yet know the charges Secretary Welles planned to bring against him. It was, however, appropriate under the circumstances for him to write an optimistic letter to Anne Elizabeth. It could only encourage her to believe in his ultimate release.

After breakfast on December 28, he was taken to the Astor House, where he had stayed on his buying trip just before the war broke out, to await the 11:00 A.M. train to Washington. He arrived in the capital city at 10:30 P.M. and was taken to the headquarters of the colonel of marines, and thence to the navy yard where he was placed in close confinement in the dispensary. There he spent his first night of a four-month imprisonment in the navy yard.

The next day Colston visited him; they undoubtedly discussed the question of a proper and effective counselor, because two days later he was visited again by his son-in-law and a certain "Judge [James] Hughes, my counselor." On January 3 he was moved to a building "containing the officers quarters at the Marine barracks, still under close guard." The details of the charges against Semmes were not yet prepared, so it was difficult for Hughes and Colston to prepare a defense. Judge Hughes did have an interview with President Andrew Johnson and discovered that "the arrest was by a cabal of the cabinet, unknown to the President!"

The chief charge that Welles intended to bring against Semmes was that after the *Kearsarge-Alabama* battle he escaped to a neutral ship. Welles maintained that Semmes had surrendered his ship when he ran up a white flag, which act required him to surrender himself and his sword to Captain Winslow. How could Semmes have maintained himself in the Channel waters with a sword in his hand? On its face the charge was ridiculous. Semmes had merely saved himself from drowning by allowing a boat from the English yacht *Deerhound* to pluck him from those waters.

Secretary Welles, although he was holding Semmes as a prisoner, really did not know what charges to bring against him and thus directed John A. Bolles, solicitor and naval judge advocate general of the Department of the Navy, to investigate Semmes's actions during his service aboard both the *Sumter* and the *Alabama*. Bolles clearly realized the significance of the assignment: "The exploits of Semmes were by no means forgotten by any one; and they rankled in the memories of thousands who had suffered from the depredations of the *Sumter* and the *Alabama*."[13]

Bolles consulted other experts on the laws of war and of the seas. As he began his investigation he was convinced that Semmes had violated many laws of war and usage of the seas, among which he considered Semmes's treatment of the prisoners on board his two ships, and he set out to confirm his beliefs. Many former prisoners, after being released by Semmes, had given lurid and horrible reports of their treatment on the Confederate ships. Bolles was an intellectually honest man and began his investigations by questioning as many former prisoners aboard Semmes's ships as he could locate.

Lurid stories told by released prisoners had inflamed the Northern public against the Confederate captain. Bolles cited the policy and orders of President James Madison and the U.S. secretary of the navy to U.S. ship captains during the War of 1812, and he found that Semmes's actions were in accord with those policies and orders. He also cited the order from Confederate Secretary of the Navy Mallory to "do the enemy's commerce the greatest injury in the shortest time" and commented that "never in naval history, has such an order been so signally obeyed, as that furnished by the *Sumter* and her successor, the *Alabama*, under the command of Semmes." He concluded "that neither treason nor piracy could be charged against Semmes."

Bolles then addressed the accusations of cruelty of Semmes's prisoners. He wrote letters to hundreds of persons who had been aboard Semmes's ships; he even brought to the United States an Englishman who had served on *Alabama* and who denied an accusation of cruelty in a specific event to which he had been an eyewitness. Concerning all the accusations of cruelty, Bolles found that

> In not one solitary instance was there furnished a particle of proof that "the pirate Semmes," as many of my correspondents called him, had ever maltreated his captives, or subjected them to needless or avoidable hard-

ships and deprivations, however much he may have offended them by taking their goods, burning their ships, and denouncing their country and its
government. . . . This chapter of complaint and suspicion was, therefore,
dismissed as composed of nothing but slanderous rumors and idle gossip.

Bolles then investigated the conduct of Semmes during and after *Alabama*'s sinking off Cherbourg. The charges were three in nature: "Fraudu-
lently obtaining a cessation of firing on the part of *Kearsarge* by showing
a white flag then reopening his own fire; perfidiously running away after overtures of surrender; re-entering the Rebel service without having
been exchanged." Captain Winslow, in reporting the battle, never accused
"Semmes of perfidy nor alluded to his escape." Furthermore, Winslow reported to Welles that he had requested the English yacht *Deerhound* to help
save *Alabama*'s men who were still in the water. Semmes claimed that it was
the duty of Winslow to capture him after he had jumped from the sinking
Alabama; the fact that Winslow did not do so, Semmes maintained, left him
free to seek salvation wherever he could find it; and the rescue just happened to be by a boat from the *Deerhound.* Nonetheless, Bolles concluded
that Semmes had, indeed, acted in an unmilitary way: He should have surrendered to Winslow. After the four-month-long investigation, Bolles concluded:

> And now, at last, it was determined that, because of his neglect to complete
> his surrender, and his return to the Rebel service, just at the end of the war,
> had produced no appreciable difference in the result of the Rebellion, but
> were practically of no consequence to either party of the strife, and be-
> cause the leaders of that Rebellion were still at large, and even the most
> red-handed raiders and "bushwhackers" and "jayhawkers" were left "un-
> whipped of justice," he should be set at liberty, and allowed to return, if
> he pleased, to his Southern home.

As soon as this conclusion was reached, Semmes was released from custody. Had he been hurried to trial as soon as arrested, his conviction would
have been certain. Without doubt the thorough investigation by Bolles
saved Semmes from imprisonment and most likely from execution. Bolles
was not shy in making that claim, which indeed, was quite self-serving.
Semmes, on the other hand, in his own notes and letters never mentioned
Bolles and never acknowledged his debt to the navy solicitor. Semmes died
in 1877, five years after Bolles's article was published.

During the long investigation, Semmes had not been passive. His attorney, Judge Hughes, visited President Johnson in his behalf but to no avail.
Semmes learned only that his arrest had been made by a "cabal of the cabi-

net, unknown to the President." On a second visit to the president, around March 8, 1866, Hughes learned that President Johnson reserved his opinion on Semmes until the matter was presented to the cabinet, at which time Hughes "expected a favorable result." That time came and went without result. Colston visited his father-in-law about every other day; Semmes looked forward to those visits, not so much to hear news of his case but to hear news of his family from his son-in-law. Colston was the only link to his family because Semmes did not correspond directly with Anne Elizabeth or his grown sons "as all letters, incoming as well as outgoing, were read by the Marine guards."

He did write a long letter to President Johnson in which he claimed that his actions after *Alabama*'s loss were proper ones at the moment; and he never failed to claim immunity from arrest based upon his parole at Greensboro, North Carolina. He apparently never considered that his arrest might be irrelevant to the pardon because it was founded upon his actions while at sea, not during his service in the navy and army within the Confederacy; and it related only to his failure to surrender himself to Winslow as *Alabama* was sinking. On January 15, 1866, he noted in his diary: "The days of the Louises and the Bastille are renewed in these republican states!"[14] On the next day he sentimentally wrote that his room was in the attic of the building and from one window he could see, looking eastward, "my good old native state of Maryland," and from his other window he could "see the city of Alexandria, Virginia." He often passed the time by speculating upon the past and the future: "such a past! such a future!"

He seems never to have become frustrated or downcast when he thought of the future. In a sense, he was basically an optimist: "A kind providence interposes his veil between us and the future." On January 17, he received from his son-in-law a letter from Anne Elizabeth: "She writes as if her heart were almost broken, but like a spirited woman withal." On January 19, he expected a visit from Judge Hughes, but he failed to appear. "And so the sun goeth down again upon this 'life deferred which maketh the heart sick.' " On the next day, Colston's visit "broke in upon the tediousness" of his confinement, as Colston spent some hours with the former admiral. The following day was Sunday: "solemn church bells are sounding in my ears, carrying me back in imagination to my own church, and home."

The confinement to a small room, however, began to gnaw at Semmes. A typical day consisted of arising at 8:30 A.M.

> when the drum under my window beats the first call for morning inspection and parade; my attendant in the meantime has made my fire. . . . I

have plenty of water, soap, and towels furnished me. I am usually ready for breakfast at a quarter past nine, at which hour my breakfast is brought in. I am supplied by a restaurant in the neighborhood. My meals are satisfactory. . . . My newspaper is brought in with my breakfast. It is the *National Intelligencer!* I read in it some such paragraph as this:

> Trial of Raphael Semmes: the trial of Raphael Semmes (it does not even call me the late admiral, or the so-called admiral, or the "so called" late admiral of the "so called" late Confederate States, or late commander of the steamer *Alabama*) it is generally believed will take place very shortly. The full detail for the court has not yet been made, but it is believed that the arrival in this city of Commodore Winslow has something to do with the subject.

> I do not believe I shall be speedily tried. This would not be in accordance with the Bastille system, imported from a bygone age and the French Revolution into the latter part of the nineteenth century and the American Revolution. Nor do I think I shall be tried at all for the government has no case and can make none. I shall be punished—have already been punished by a close confinement of 30 days.

Apparently, Bolles had informed the secretary of the navy that he could find no charges to make against Semmes. On January 27, Semmes was notified that if he made application to the Navy Department he would be released on parole. Semmes's reaction was typical and direct: "I have no application of any kind to make to the Navy Department." He would not grovel to Welles. And so he remained confined to his small attic room.

Even so, on the last day in January, Semmes applied to Secretary of the Navy Gideon Welles for release from confinement. He did so on the word of Colston, who had talked with Bolles. Semmes's request was for release from confinement, with permission to return to his family, "or with such other territorial restrictions as the Department may impose." If, indeed, Bolles had suggested this action to Colston, he was out of touch with Secretary Welles. Semmes's request was denied. His hopes had been raised, only to be destroyed. Semmes accurately concluded: "There is evidently confusion in the enemy's camp! They desire to let me go but do not know exactly how to do it." Then, in almost the same breath, as it were, he wrote: "Colston has brought me a beautiful little picture of my eldest grandson, whom he has named after me. Its sight breaks in agreeably upon the wavering anxieties of prison life and permits me to enjoy in imagination the pleasures of home and family."

On the same day, Colston informed Semmes that through a friend,

Mexican Emperor Maximilian had offered the former admiral the position of commissioner of immigration for the (then) state of Mahama. Semmes, confident of his early release, authorized his son-in-law to accept the position for him and to say that "I shall probably be at liberty in the course of a few weeks to enter upon the duties." Many former inhabitants of Southern states upon the end of the war had immigrated to South American states. Although Semmes did, in fact, later refuse the position, he would not have been unique had he gone to Mexico.

On February 3, 1866, he received a letter from home: His eldest son, Samuel Spencer, was elected solicitor of the city of Mobile. Semmes was proud of his son, and his anxiety over the financial welfare of his family was lessened by the news; he could wipe away that worry in connection with his imprisonment. The next day the restrictions on his movements were relaxed, and he was allowed to exercise outdoors; of course, an armed guard had to accompany him. It was the first time he had been allowed to leave his room in more than five weeks.

Finally, on April 6, 1866, Secretary Welles, apparently acting on the recommendations of Bolles, sent a short note to President Johnson recommending that Semmes "be unconditionally discharged from custody under his present arrest, and that he be remitted to his original written parole." In the end, then, Semmes had been right: The parole he had received in Greensboro was to be the instrument of his release through Bolles's findings. He had been under constant guard since December 15, 1865, almost four full months.

Semmes concluded his memoirs with ungracious comments about President Johnson. He did not write of regaining his freedom, or of his journey home, or of his reception by Anne Elizabeth and the children. In fact his pardon from the arrest came only in December 1868, when he was included in President Johnson's third amnesty proclamation. He still, however, was not allowed to practice law in Mobile or anywhere else.

His first trip after being released was to visit a fair in Baltimore, which he attended with Mrs. Virginia Tunstall Clay of Alabama. She wrote in her memoirs: "Admiral Semmes was present one day, and he and I promenaded the rooms together. Though not the 'pirate's bride,' I was proud of his company. Admiral Semmes," she continued, "was the most recent of the state prisoners to be released, and his presence at the fair was the signal for a lively enthusiasm."[15] Undoubtedly, Semmes was visiting Pendleton and Electra Colston in Baltimore, more perhaps to see his new grandson than his daughter. He soon left Baltimore for Mobile.

One must only imagine the happy reception by his family upon his return to Mobile. He immediately tried to open a law office in the city, but because his citizenship had not been restored by the presidential pardon, he was debarred from doing so; he could not take the test oath required for all lawyers. Soon, on May 7, 1866, the people of Mobile elected him to the office of probate judge of the county, the most lucrative state position; but the secretary of war declared him ineligible to hold that office. He was desperate to find some way to contribute to the support of his family, but to no avail.

His desperation was finally relieved. On October 24, 1866, the superintendent of the Louisiana State Seminary, later to become Louisiana State University, secured from the board of supervisors permission to offer former Admiral Raphael Semmes the chair of moral philosophy and English literature. Semmes, desperate to earn an income, accepted the position, which paid only $3,000 a year.[16] On January 1, 1867, Semmes once again left his family in Mobile and took a room in one of the seminary's buildings. The younger faculty members found him to be a gracious host (he always had a bottle of good whiskey on hand), dignified and easy to talk with, but they were unable to induce him to recount his wartime experiences. His teaching method consisted of formal lectures without much discussion. But even in that quiet academic setting, the Reconstruction leaders would not leave him alone. In the *Republican*, a Reconstruction newspaper published in New Orleans, Semmes read the following attack upon the seminary: "Among the faculty as it was organized in the fall of 1865, we counted no less than four rebel Majors, and to these, as if the spite were not stinging enough, the pirate Raphael Semmes was added—and added in derision of all decency, as Professor of Moral Philosophy."

Such public comments about him prompted Semmes to write a long letter to Anne Elizabeth expressing his dissatisfaction with life at the seminary:

> I am here at work playing school master in my old age, thanks to the bull-headed [man] who fills the President's chair [of the board of the institution]. I say bull-headed, but he is only bull-headed towards his friends, or those of his enemies who are weak and powerless to resist him. He is as timid as the coward that he is in the presence of the strong; and this is the basis of his whole conduct in my case. Like a whipped hound he is afraid to even bark in the presence of the radicals, who are kicking and spurning him.[17]

Semmes mentioned that personally he was comfortable enough, except that he was separated from his family, which made him "feel out of place."

He would not move his family to Louisiana but would retain his citizenship and domicile in Alabama: "I will never abandon my claim to my judgeship. . . . I cannot yet consent to regard my position here as permanent." It is not surprising, then, that when he was offered the editorship of a Memphis newspaper he accepted and left the seminary apparently only one month after he had joined the faculty. He also had submitted a manuscript of "his book" (he does not further identify it) but had not heard from the publisher; "if my present manuscript is not published, I will weave it into a new one."

Anne Elizabeth had mentioned in a letter that Semmes would be offered editorship of the *Memphis Bulletin,* a Southern-oriented newspaper. Semmes had heard nothing about it: "If such an offer were made to me, I should hardly know how to act. Memphis would undoubtedly be a better place to settle in, so far as the children are concerned, but it would be running a great risk to accept the place of a mere salaried editor." He would prefer to have a vested interest in the paper because "nothing is more uncertain than the newspaper business." If he could arrange to have "an interest in the paper at the same time I became its editor, this might tempt me." Anne Elizabeth and the children, however, would have to remain in Mobile because, again, he would not give up on his judgeship.

Semmes did, in fact, go to Memphis and succeeded in making an arrangement with the newspaper to secure a loan, to be repaid from the profits of the paper. He bought an interest in the company and accepted the position of editor of the *Memphis Bulletin.* In May 1867, Semmes informed Colonel Boyd, president of Louisiana State Seminary, that he would not be returning to the seminary. There were several inducements for him to go to Memphis. His Georgetown cousins, with whom he had lived as a boy, had earlier relocated in Memphis where they had established a successful brewery. Also, his salary as editor was $5,000 a year, $2,000 more than his seminary salary.

Nonetheless, he applied to the University of Kentucky for a faculty position; the president of that university replied that there were at that time no vacancies "in our corps of Professors."[18]

At the time, Semmes was receiving many requests from publishers and ordinary people to write a book on his wartime experiences. Indeed, some simply asked for an autograph or a short note in return for the request. Not long after his release from prison, J. Q. Adams of Georgetown, D. C., grandson of President John Quincy Adams, requested from Semmes "an autographed note to place with a collection of those gentlemen of the South, who have occupied positions of eminence, Civil, Military & Naval." Semmes seized the opportunity to express some of his ideas concerning the

Civil War. Correctly assuming from his name that the autograph seeker was a descendant of President John Quincy Adams, Semmes informed him that President Adams had appointed him to the U.S. Navy: "I did homage to the memory of your great ancestor by fighting for the principles of self-govern-ment, and constitutional liberty, embalmed in the Declaration of Indepen-dence, and handed down to us by the Jeffersons and Adamses of the Revo-lution."[19] Odd that Semmes, a Cavalier Southerner, should exchange such pleasant correspondence with a New England Puritan such as John Quincy Adams II.

Semmes, while serving as editor of the *Memphis Bulletin,* was consider-ing publishing his memoirs of the Civil War. Why not? His memoirs of the Mexican War had become a best-seller in the early 1850s; perhaps a second best-seller would enhance his income and enable him to return to Alabama and fight for his judgeship. Meanwhile, he brought his family to Memphis while maintaining his legal residency in Mobile. Memphis was a pleasant place for his family because his cousins from Georgetown were living there, and his two unmarried daughters found husbands in Memphis. Many of their descendants still live in that Mississippi River city. At any rate, he received several offers from various would-be publishers.

For the former Confederate admiral, however, the stay in Memphis was not all pleasantries and family reunions. Another Memphis newspaper, the *Daily Post,* which identified itself as a "Live Republican Paper," frequently attacked him by reprinting articles from Northern papers that still referred to him as a "pirate." Being the proud man that he was, he also got involved in quarrels with some men who criticized him for his wartime activities; some of the quarrels led to sharp exchanges bordering on duel challenges. Perhaps it was too much to expect a wartime leader to judge postwar activi-ties with objectivity.

One exchange of letters illustrates the atmosphere created about the per-son of Semmes as a newspaper editor. He apparently had written an edito-rial criticizing a certain James S. Brisbin, U.S. Army, for inciting blacks against the whites. Brisbin replied in a letter to another newspaper in a most vitriolic language, referring to Semmes as a "pirate and traitor." Semmes, of course, had to answer the vitriolic language and name calling. He referred to Brisbin as "one of those new men of the army, whose education has been defective; though I know nothing of your antecedents, never having heard of your name or fame until I read the incendiary speech delivered by you to the blacks, at Lexington, Ky, the other day." After further rebukes, Semmes mentioned the futility of argument with a person such as Brisbin: "I am wasting words on such a nice fellow as yourself, and so, if you will permit me, I will close our correspondence by telling you that, in my judgment, no officer of the United States army who entertained the sentiments of honor which should characterize a noble profession, could have written the coarse and slanderous attack upon my character which you have had the distinction of producing."[20] Such language and argumentation could not have been conducive to a calm life for the writing of his memoirs.

However, at the same time, Semmes was receiving many requests from various publishers to see a manuscript. Such requests forced Semmes to begin to develop his ideas concerning the theme of his yet unwritten memoirs. Indeed, just two days before writing to J. Q. Adams, Semmes had received from W. H. and O. H. Morrison, Book Sellers and Publishers, of Washington, D.C., a request to be the publishers of his rumored memoirs. On July 2, 1866, Semmes responded to the Morrisons:

> The announcement by the press that this work is already in course of preparation is a little premature, though I do intend at my leisure to prepare such a work. My journals and other materials necessary to perform the task are still in Europe, having been left by me in the custody of a friend when I sailed for the United States in the autumn of 1864. As soon as they shall be received I will commence the work. I think favorably of your proposition, and if, and when I shall be ready to treat with a publisher, I will give you the preference, as probably your position at the seat of government, and the facilities which this position gives you of pushing your publications into markets North and South, will be of advantage to us both.

Semmes was also invited in January 1867 to write an article for a magazine, *The Land We Love*. Obviously, he preferred the idea of writing a book rather than revealing some of his experiences in articles that might anticipate the theme of a book. He received an invitation, dated February 25, 1868, to correspond with the "Southern University Series of School and College Text-Books," of Atlanta, Georgia. But Semmes was not interested in such writing; no further correspondence exists on the subject.

Semmes soon found himself at odds with the other owners of the *Bulletin*, "my states-rights politics not suiting the changed views of the proprietors." By October 15, 1867, he had escaped the Memphis atmosphere and was back in Mobile. His judgeship never materialized, and he was still forbidden to practice law. What to do? He wrote to Colonel Boyd, still the superintendent of the Louisiana State Seminary, inquiring about the possibility of returning to his chair, but nothing came of it. He wrote to several insurance companies, including two in England, offering his services as an agent in Mobile. But Admiral Semmes of the C.S. Navy was not destined to be an insurance agent. As early as 1865, just after the war had ended, he had delivered several lectures on the *Alabama*'s cruise. The text of a lecture in Atlanta foreshadows some of the wording and structure of his memoirs, reflecting as they do even some of the same wording of his official ship logs. The lectures took him from Atlanta to Saint Louis and, after his return from Memphis, to a tour of Kentucky and Tennessee. The lectures, however, provided him with little profit. After one such tour, he returned to his home, after having given ten lectures, with a profit of only $500, an average of only $50 a lecture. Nonetheless, he continued his lectures well into the late 1860s.

When not on the lecture tour, or busy writing his memoirs, Semmes was busy trying to have his civil disabilities removed, for until that happened he could not pursue his profession of law. He wrote to various members of Congress arguing his case for the disabilities removal. The House of Representatives in May 1874 finally passed a bill removing them, but the Senate adjourned before taking action on its committee's report. Semmes seems to have been subjected to a particularly difficult punishment, because the state of Alabama had been readmitted into the Union in August of 1868 when it ratified the Fourteenth Amendment.

He managed to get his journal and other materials from England and began the task of writing *Memoirs of Service Afloat during the War Between the States*. It was first published in England in two volumes and then in one volume by the Baltimore firm of Kelly, Piet and Company in 1869, consisting of 833 pages.[21] There is nothing in his correspondence at this time concerning W. H. and O. H. Morrison publishers of Washington. As with his memoirs on the Mexican War, this set of memoirs is frequently cited as an original source by historians. It consists of his ideas and actions during the cruises of the CSS *Sumter* and the CSS *Alabama* and during his service within the Confederacy as admiral of the James River Fleet and as a brigadier general of artillery in the C.S. Army. Many sections are taken from his ships' logs, which in turn were published as *Official Records of the Union and Confederate Navies in the War of the Rebellion,* series 1, volumes 1 and 2, published in 1894 and 1895. By comparing the two works, historians have concluded that his memoirs are as accurate and unembellished as are the ships' logs. Unlike his Mexican War memoirs, his Civil War ones did not become a best-seller. Their republication in 1987, however, reflects an enduring value to historians of the Civil War naval activities.

Semmes's writing style in the American published book reflects his mid-nineteenth-century romantic nationalism. It also reflects the broad extent of his self-education. He had been an avid reader all of his life; he was familiar with the history and writings of the ancients and, as we have seen, made frequent references to them. He was also widely read in the science of the seas and in political and military history, and he was a devout Roman Catholic, all of which knowledge and convictions infuse his writings. None of the 833 pages of the memoirs contains any boring or irrelevant sections. The flowery expressions of nineteenth-century romanticism are refreshing, as is the accurate detail of his descriptions of mountains, stormy skies, ships, and seascapes. He wrote especially interesting sections on the sea storms he encountered and the prevailing movements of the oceans, their winds and currents, and their effects on his sailors and himself. His experiences as a prewar lawyer led to an accurate knowledge of international law, and he wrote long dissertations on the subject. The writings of Semmes, then, reflect the knowledge and ability of an acute observer and a highly trained mind.

One other factor impresses the reader. As of July 1866, the logs and journals of his cruises were still in England. There is no record as to the date he received them from Louisa Tremlett, but it could not have been much before the end of 1866. To write such a long book within two and a half years while at the same time editing a newspaper, writing almost constantly to politicians concerning the restoration of his political rights, and lecturing from Missouri to Kentucky and from Louisiana to Georgia, was quite a feat.

The January 2, 1869, edition of the *Mobile Weekly Register*, under the heading of "Admiral Semmes' Book," announced that "through the courtesy of its author we are in receipt of 'Memoirs of Service Afloat during the War Between the States.' " It highly commended the author, then indicated that Semmes had been requested by the publishers to act as their sales agent for the states of Alabama and Mississippi. In this author-salesman role, he placed a notice in the newspapers of the two states; it read: "Agents wanted! Agents wanted! In every county in the States of Alabama and Mississippi, for the sale of Admiral Semmes's NEW BOOK, entitled 'Memoirs of Service Afloat During the War Between the States.' This book can be purchased of duly authorized Agents only to whom a liberal percentage and exclusive territory will be given. Applicants will address the undersigned at Mobile. Signed: Raphael Semmes."

In the same edition, the *Mobile Register* carried this note on an article published in the *Boston Post*: "Semmes is lecturing, when he can get anyone to hear him and pay him, on 'The winds as water-carriers of the earth.' " The *Register* then commented on the Boston paper: "The *Post* is improving; a few weeks ago it was always 'the Pirate Semmes': in a few weeks it may learn to speak respectfully of him." Semmes had long become inured to such Northern criticism of his career and of his person; he took no notice of the paper's reference to him.

Indeed, at this time he was still busy setting up his sales network. He wrote to Mrs. C. C. Clay, as early as July 6, 1866 (she was the woman, it will be recalled, who had been proud to promenade with him at the Baltimore fair shortly after his release from prison): "Will you do me the favor to secure the services of some *reliable* person, to canvass Huntsville and the surrounding county? If the canvasser is at all capable, he will be amply repaid for his services." He added that he "had completed about two-thirds of my labor" and hoped "to get the book out in November next."[22]

On January 29, 1868, he sent a copy of the book to Mrs. Clay: "Do me the favor to accept this small offering, as an evidence of my regard for a lady who should have been born in the time of the old Romans; and when you shall have read it, give me the benefits from your pen in the Huntsville paper."[23]

His book obviously had attracted the attention of historians in the South. In June 1869 he was invited by Dr. Joseph Jones to deliver a lecture to the Southern Historical Society at its winter meeting. Illness, however, prevented him from doing so.[24] The attention of historians of the South has never slackened. Most university libraries contain at least two copies of *Memoirs of Service Afloat during the War Between the States.*

The success of his book and the restoration of his civil rights—the date of which is not noted by Semmes—finally provided the former admiral with sufficient income to support Anne Elizabeth and young Raphael, the only family members still financially dependent upon him. By 1869 he and his son Oliver had opened a law office in Mobile, and cases were sufficient to keep him busy. In 1874 Oliver was elected judge of the city court, a position he held for forty-four years. His father continued in practice of law, accepting only cases that most interested him, primarily those concerning maritime law. The people of Mobile honored Semmes in the late 1870s by presenting him a house in the city. It stands today with a historical marker to identify it as the home of Admiral Raphael Semmes, C.S. Navy, on Government Street. It is used by an adjacent church as an office building and is maintained in good condition.

Life in Mobile was a far cry from his treatment in Memphis. There were no disputes with the people of the city, as he had experienced in Memphis; on the contrary, he was treated with respect amounting almost to veneration. Most important, he was financially comfortable, and he was surrounded by his family, from whom he had for so many years of sea duty and imprisonment been separated. He now enjoyed his grandchildren, for even those who lived in Memphis visited him often, and Electra and her children, after Pendleton Colston's death, had come back to Mobile to live with her parents. For the first time in his married life, Semmes was at peace with himself because he was able to remain in the bosom of his family, uninterrupted by navy duty.

In October 1870 a yellow fever epidemic hit Mobile. Now sixty-one years old, Semmes hesitated to attend meetings or even to travel from his country residence into the city, especially at night: "As I live four miles in the country, and it might be imprudent to ride in and out, at night, during the prevalence of yellow fever, to attend the regular meeting of our Camp, will you be good enough to make this excuse for me to our brothers." The "Camp" was an organization of devoted Confederates. Semmes was the most noted of the Mobile Camp members.[25]

A devout member of the Roman Catholic Church, as we have seen, he was selected to address the "Grand Procession of Catholics in Mobile" on Sunday, June 18, 1871. The occasion was the celebration of "the Twenty-fifth Anniversary of the Election of Pius IX to the Pontifical Chair of St. Peter." Semmes's address consisted of fifteen single-spaced pages. Pius IX reigned from 1846 to 1878, the period of mid-nineteenth-century political and social upheavals and changes. In his address, Semmes emphasized the stability that Pius IX managed to maintain in his position as pope during the various changes in Europe: the reign of Napoleon III in France, the unifications of Germany and Italy, the socialist advocates of the revolutions of 1848 and afterward. His interpretation of the events and their effect on the papacy was obviously slanted in favor of the pope, but it also reveals a deep knowledge and understanding of the mid-nineteenth-century social and political events and philosophies that, including the American Civil War, wrought such vast changes throughout the Western world. It was, in fact, an excellent lecture on contemporary history.

In 1871, Semmes was appointed as attorney for the city of Mobile. Although Reconstruction in the state had ended in 1868, Alabama was still ruled predominantly by blacks and local scalawags. According to a notice in the *Mobile Register* of October 2, 1871, Semmes, then the city attorney, advised the mayor against endorsing the issue of railroad bonds because they were gold bonds: "The corporation of Mobile is not a joint stock company for the management of private enterprises; and except for purposes of government it has no power to tax the people. It cannot, therefore, vote money in aid of a railroad company, unless specifically authorized by the state." Two and a half years later, Raphael and Oliver Semmes, acting in behalf of two individuals, moved the court for a ruling against the Mobile and North-western Railroad Company, in which the city of Mobile, against Semmes's advice, had invested $1 million in bonds. The city was so deeply in debt that it was unable to pay interest on the debts. It lost its charter, ceased to be a city, and became a district under the control of the governor.[26]

During the month of November 1876, Semmes's health was poor. For five consecutive days (November 18–22) the *Mobile Daily Register* carried the notice that "R. Semmes being too unwell to attend to business, W. Boyles, Esq., 62 Conte Street, will attend to his legal business during his sickness. Signed, R. Semmes." Semmes had suffered from poor health ever since his return from Memphis to Mobile. Although he frequently had suffered from seasickness, he had had no serious illness during the cruises of the *Sumter* and the *Alabama* or in the years after the end of the war before going to Memphis.

In the meantime, two events occurred as a result of his cruise on the *Alabama* and the cruises of the other ships procured in the British Isles. The first was the "Alabama Claims" convention negotiated in Geneva, Switzerland. During the war, the United States had often accused Great Britain of unneutral acts, especially in the building of ships for the Confederacy. Because the *Alabama* was the most famous and successful of the Southern cruisers and had destroyed more U.S. shipping than any other cruiser, the negotiations at Geneva were called after Semmes's ship. After many diplomatic exchanges between Washington and London, commissioners from each country first met in Geneva on December 15, 1871. The commissioner from the United States was Charles Francis Adams, the father of John Quincy Adams II (who had requested Semmes's autograph). Each country submitted its case and the commissioners finally agreed on a settlement of the so-called "Alabama Claims." The Geneva Tribunal awarded $15.5 million in gold to be paid to the United States by Great Britain to reimburse the owners of the ships and cargoes destroyed by the Confederate cruisers whose origins were in the British Isles. Most of that amount was attributed to the actions of Semmes aboard the *Alabama*. Yet there is no mention of that decision in Semmes's papers. How could he have ignored the decision? Perhaps he was just too tired of hearing about his "piratical acts."

On the other hand, Semmes did become involved in the United States Court of Commissioners of the Alabama Claims. That court was established to determine which shipowners should share in the $15.5 million. On December 19, 1874, a Mr. J. Creswell, counsel of the United States before the court of commissioners, wrote to Semmes concerning the case of a certain William H. Whiting, because the claim did not result directly "from damage caused by the so-called insurgent cruisers *Alabama, Florida,* or their tenders; or by the *Shenandoah* after her departure from Melbourne on the 18th February, 1865, within the meaning and spirit" of the congressional act establishing the Commissioners of Alabama Claims. Then Creswell wrote:

> Should the demurer be overruled, I shall be obliged if you will furnish me with a statement of the facts contained in your letter, in due form of testimony, to be used at the trial.
>
> Would it be agreeable to you and your late first and second lieutenants, in case it should become necessary, to be summoned on behalf of the government?[27]

How ironic! How Semmes's relationship to the federal government had changed! He was no longer the "pirate Semmes" but now the lawyer Semmes who might be invited to testify on behalf of the United States government. When he read those words, the old sea captain must have had a good chuckle.

Yes, he was in 1874 an old sea captain. He was then sixty-five years old; he had served at sea ever since he was a teenager. The salt air undoubtedly had hardened his skin, still partly hidden by the mustache and goatee he wore all of his adult life. He had been accused of vile crimes, imprisoned, and exonerated; he had been deprived of his profession and forced into a struggle to support his family, and he was then successful.

Semmes in the latter half of the 1870s devoted most of his leisure time to his grandchildren, those who were visiting him as well as those who lived with him. They all called him "Big Papa." At home, he taught them to eat all that was placed before them; otherwise they could have no second helpings. He insisted that each grandchild should learn to phrase sentences correctly and to the point. But he was not only a disciplinarian. He took them for hikes in the woods, teaching them about the flora and fauna; he took them swimming in the waters near Mobile. He had acquired a small cabin at Point Clear, on the eastern shore of Mobile Bay. It was there that he taught his grandsons and granddaughters to swim. He himself never wore a bathing suit, preferring to swim in the nude, and he probably converted all his grandchildren to do the same. It was at that place, Point Clear, that he met his death. He had eaten some shrimp that made him ill. Physicians were sent to his small home, but their efforts to save him were in vain. Less than a month from his sixty-eighth birthday, he died at about 7:30 A.M. on August 30, 1877.

His life had been an exciting one: He had fought in the Mexican War on both the sea and land; he had sailed on five seas aboard *Alabama*, the ship with which his life became intimately identified. But he was much more than the captain of *Alabama:* He was a lawyer, an authority on the U.S. Constitution and maritime law; he was a self-educated master of the English language and was fluent in French and Spanish; he was a devoted husband, father, and grandfather, who nevertheless appreciated beautiful women of whatever color. He considered himself to be a "philosophical mariner," by which he meant a seaman who studied and understood the science of the seas with their various winds and currents. His appreciation of history was real, fed by his extensive reading. He was also a stubborn man. It was not only his Alabama citizenship that led him to side with the Confederacy in 1861 but also his conviction that the Southern states were constitutionally correct in maintaining their right to secede from a government they considered to be dogmatic in imposing its own peculiar interpretation on all the states of the Union. As to slavery, he often mentioned that he "did not hold much for it," but he had owned three household slaves. He also was prejudiced against men of a color different from his own, except for those whom he knew personally. A faithful Roman Catholic, he often railed against the narrow-minded New England "Puritans" who forced their own interpretation of the Constitution onto the Southern "Cavaliers." He was not a man to be easily placed into any one mental or philosophical category.

8

The Mariner's Legacy

Raphael Semmes left to subsequent generations a legacy that is still growing. It began with his service in both the U.S. Navy and the U.S. Army during the Mexican War, and it grew with his duty as a sea raider during the American Civil War. His memoirs of the Mexican War became a bestseller in the 1850s, and his service during the Civil War, when he destroyed more enemy merchant ships than any other sea raider in naval history, was publicized during that war by his victims. Inevitably, he was identified with the CSS *Alabama,* an identification that lives in American legend. As a popular ballad expresses it:

> Oh, Susannah, don't you cry for me:
> I still sail the Alabama with a banjo
>   on my knee.

> From the Eastern Isles he sailed forth;
> Roll, Alabama, roll.
> To destroy the commerce of the North.
> Oh, roll, Alabama, roll.
> And many a sailor saw his doom.
> Roll, Alabama, roll.
> As the Kearsarge hoved into view:
> Oh, roll, Alabama, roll.
> Off the three-mile limit in sixty-four.
> Roll, Alabama, roll.
> The Alabama was seen no more.
> Oh, roll Alabama, roll.

> Oh, Susannah, don't you cry for me:
> I still sail the Alabama with a banjo
>   on my knee.

And so despite defeat, or because of it, Semmes sailed on the *Alabama* into American popular legend. A well-known maxim states that "It is not so much who wins or loses, but how you play the game." Semmes always played his assigned game to win, be it in peacetime or wartime; and he always played it with intelligence and to the limit of his considerable abilities. This popular identification of Semmes and the *Alabama* does him an injustice because it praises him only as a sea captain. It fails to recognize his high intelligence; his linguistic abilities; his self-taught understanding of science, literature, history, and law, especially international law; and his devotion to his family and to his Roman Catholic faith.

It is nonetheless correct to identify the man with the ship. He had fought a horrible war to the extent of his abilities, and he had lost. That was a fact of life that he realistically accepted. A few years before his death, in April 1874, he spoke at the unveiling of a monument to the Confederate dead in Magnolia Cemetery, Mobile. A group of United States Army officers had contributed a wreath in memory of the departed soldiers. Semmes referred to the wreath: "It comes from the victor to the vanquished, in a spirit worthy of our age and our history." He continued: "The perfume of these sweet flowers, Federal soldiers, is the more sweet, as coming from your hands. It will surely be taken up by our gentle South winds and wafted to your homes in the North and West, as an emphatic declaration on your part, that, as between soldier and soldier, at least, the War Between the States is at an end." Turning to the statue of a Confederate soldier, he referred to it as a perpetual memory "of a band of gallant men, who perished in the greatest of modern wars, in obedience to the most powerful impulse that can move the human heart—the love of liberty." His ability to honor soldiers of both sides of the great war reflects his balanced approach, despite his personal participation in the war and his later imprisonment. It reflects also his ability to accept reality. There is no doubt that his remarks to the Union officers on that Confederate Memorial Day were honest and sincere.

Just after the loss of *Alabama* to the *Kearsarge* in June 1864, despite a wound to his left hand, Semmes had set about paying off his ship's crew. This devotion to duty was characteristic of the man; he always put duty before his personal needs. He had treated prisoners aboard his ships with kindness, as they later testified to John A. Bolles; it was his natural instinct. He wrote critically of only three men: General Winfield Scott during the Mexican War; President Abraham Lincoln; and U.S. Secretary of the Navy Gideon Welles. His criticisms of General Scott and of Secretary Welles probably were justified. In the case of President Lincoln, his criticism was based upon his own interpretation of the United States Constitution.

As a lawyer he saw the Constitution as a compact between the several states, a compact, as he viewed it, designed to protect the sovereignty of the individual states. This was a view held by many people in the country, especially in the South. He also criticized Lincoln on the question of slavery. As early as the Mexican War, he saw the Mexican peasants as being in a worse condition than the slaves in the United States, and he was undoubtedly right.

The one great flaw of Semmes's character was his conviction that blacks were inferior to whites. For them to achieve equality with whites was, in his mind, a corruption of nature. He never overcame that character flaw. "In this respect alone," a biographer has written, "he was a giver of bad counsel."[1] Nonetheless, he held real affection for individual blacks whom he knew well, such as the former house slaves with whom he found Anne Elizabeth hoeing the garden when he returned to Mobile at the war's end.

After the war, after he had survived arrest and imprisonment, and after his pardon, he returned to the practice of law in Mobile. His success reflected more the high esteem in which the people of the city held him than his brilliance as a lawyer. He did not make a fortune, but he did manage to support his family and to educate his children, especially his youngest one, Raphael, Jr. His family lived on after his death and all six of his children managed to live well and to prosper in their chosen avocations. They all were proud of him both as a man and as their father.

His six children, so capably raised almost single-handedly by their mother, were successful professionals or professionals' wives. Their successes, however, reflected their father's influence despite his long absences. Samuel Semmes (1838–1912) left his law practice in New Orleans to enlist as a second lieutenant in the Confederate army. He eventually was promoted to the rank of major, having seen action at Shiloh, Murfreesboro, Chickamauga, Missionary Ridge, and Lookout Mountain.

After the war he practiced law in Washington, Georgia, where he met and married his distant cousin, Pauline Semmes. Later he moved his family to Osceola, Arkansas, about sixty miles northwest of Memphis, Tennessee. He prospered there and became county judge. As a cofounder of the Bank of Osceola, he served several years as its president; he also served on the boards of several other businesses. His collection of books on the sea and the Confederacy developed into one of the largest libraries west of the Mississippi.

Samuel's younger brother, Oliver John Semmes (1839–1918), accompanied their father from Texas to Mobile in 1864. Oliver had a very distinguished career as captain of a riverboat during the fighting in the Louisiana bayous. He escaped after capture by leading a group of Confederate officers in overcoming a Northern crew of a small boat, then sailing to Confederate-controlled land and safety. In May 1865 he was paroled in Mobile, Alabama, and admitted to the bar in 1866. Later he was elected judge of the Mobile City Court and served as its judge for forty-three years, retiring one year before his death.

Anna Elizabeth Semmes (1847–1936) was educated at the Convent of the Sacred Heart in Philadelphia. She was in the North when the Civil War began but was able to make her way safely to Mobile. For most of her life after the war she was an active leader in the Daughters of the American Revolution, the United Daughters of the Confederacy, and various other patriotic organizations. There is no record of a marriage or a home location. She probably lived in Memphis, for the governor of Tennessee appointed her as a commissioner of the Jamestown Exposition.

Raphael Semmes, Jr. (1849–1918), accompanied his father to the James River Fleet. Near the end of the war he received the same parole from General Sherman as Admiral Semmes received. When he had completed his education, he went to Memphis to visit his sister Katherine and her husband, Luke Wright. Young Raphael went to work for the Memphis Street Railway, which his brother-in-law had helped to save from bankruptcy. By 1897, Raphael had moved back to Mobile, where he managed the city's electric rail system, apparently for the rest of his life.

Electra Louise Semmes (1843–1925) married Pendleton Colston in 1864. Her Memphis cousin described her as "the handsomest girl in the room" at her engagement party to Mr. Colston of Baltimore. She was also recognized as one of the most brilliant and cultured women of her day. Colston became judge advocate general of the navy. After their marriage another cousin described Colston as a "clever fellow and a good match." He certainly remained loyal to Electra's father during his imprisonment after the war.

The most successful marriage by a Semmes daughter was that of Katherine Middleton Semmes (1845–1937) to Luke Edward Wright of Memphis. He became one of Memphis's and the mid-South's most illustrious sons. He had fought against the Washington government during the Civil War. After the war, his law practice in Memphis developed rapidly, and it led him into other spheres of activity. In July 1901, President Theodore Roosevelt appointed him governor general of the Philippine Islands, where he served two years. Katherine accompanied him to the islands and then to Tokyo, where her husband was appointed the first American ambassador to Japan in 1905. Her stay in Tokyo inspired her to initiate the planting of the beautiful Japanese cherry trees that are still enjoyed around Washington's Tidal Basin.

The people of Raphael Semmes's adopted city, upon his death in August 1877, immediately took steps to pay him its highest honors. The public buildings were draped in mourning and their flags flew at half-mast, as did those on ships in the harbor. And it was not only the citizens of Mobile who publicly mourned his death: The *New Orleans Delta* characterized the deceased mariner as "one of the most chivalric leaders of the grand Confederate struggle for a separate nationality . . . as a naval commander, the Nelson of the Confederacy." Other Southern newspapers were just as flowery in their praise.

The funeral was held December 31, 1877, the day after his death. It was a military funeral: From morning to evening, an admiral's salute was fired at intervals of every half hour. The coffin rested in the Cathedral of the Immaculate Conception, where the "poet-priest" of the Confederacy, Father Abram J. Ryan, gave the funeral oration. Although it was a rainy, stormy day and the roads were muddy, hundreds of people, many on foot, processed behind the coffin to the Catholic cemetery, then some distance out of town, and watched as the coffin was lowered into a rain-filled grave. Perhaps the weather was appropriate because the lowering of the casket into the water-filled grave was suggestive of a burial at sea.

The citizens of Mobile remembered him some years later when, in the midst of a violent storm from the sea, on June 27, 1900, they unveiled a bronze statue of Raphael Semmes, portrayed in an admiral's uniform and with one hand on the hilt of his sword and the other holding a pair of binoculars, appropriately looking out to sea. The statue is at the intersection of Government and Royal Streets, at that time a very busy crossing. He stands there still, a bulwark-like guardian of the city against the fury of the sea.

Semmes was a man who saw his duty and fulfilled it to the extent of his rather formidable abilities. Without the benefit of a structured education, struggling almost to the end of his life to earn money to support his large family, Semmes remained true to his religious, philosophical, and intellectual values. It was the last of these values that served him best in times of stress. He referred to himself as a "Philosophical Mariner" because he had read and fully understood Matthew Fontaine Maury's writings on the sea's currents and winds and the resulting "crossroads" of the seas. Semmes understood Maury's theories, which have been substantiated by sea scientists with more modern technology. Not all of Semmes's seagoing contemporaries were so "philosophical." This self-conscious distinction probably accounts for his great success as a sea raider.

That success was so great that Emperor William II of Germany required all of his navy captains to read *Memoirs of Service Afloat during the War between the States*. Even so, with their more modern ships, none of them captured as many enemy merchant vessels as did Semmes. Furthermore, those he captured do not tell the full story of his impact on American merchant shipping. As he noted while at Singapore, insurance rates rose to such heights for cargoes carried in Northern ships that American merchant tonnage declined; American ships were stranded, empty, in foreign harbors while neutral ones were busy carrying neutral goods. Semmes's success in the war, then, so adversely affected American shipping that it lost its first place as a carrier of goods and has not yet reclaimed that place in international shipping.

Above all else, Raphael Semmes was an intellectual. His wide reading, his fluency in three languages, his observations on nature—the mountains and rivers in Mexico, the great storms at sea, and the beauty of a calm sea— all reflect a curiosity of humanity and nature greater than that of other people. He never tired of the beauties of nature; and, late in life, he took his small grandchildren into the forest to introduce them to those beauties, and that is why he always went swimming in the nude—to get as close to nature as he could. Other seamen, of course, had respect for the seas, but none developed that respect into a capacity to revel in the strength of waves and winds that treated his ship as if it were a cork, tossing it here and there on the waters, so that as *Alabama* traversed the South Atlantic Ocean, first her bow would be submerged in the waters so deeply as to be out of sight, and then her stern would disappear from view. He actually enjoyed such experiences.

While from all evidence he was faithful to Anne Elizabeth, he also appreciated feminine beauty, such as the Cuban women praying in the Havana cathedral. He enjoyed being with pretty and intelligent women, such as Louisa Tremlett in London and, just after his release from imprisonment in Washington, Virginia Tunstall Clay at the Baltimore fair. No matter how far from home he might be, his thoughts always turned to Anne Elizabeth; her welfare remained at the center of his being.

His second love was his ships, but especially *Alabama*, because she was the largest, sturdiest, and swiftest he ever commanded. She was also the ship on which he had his greatest successes at sea. He thought of the ship often as a living thing; she was his home for almost two years; and he "slept in her bosom, a quiet and peaceful sleep." He sailed her into the history books as the most successful raider in world naval history. He never forgot *Alabama* because his career was so thoroughly a part of her career. And that is why his name is still so closely related to her name: "Roll, *Alabama*, roll"!

Semmes's sea legacy cannot be separated from *Alabama* because their record of enemy ships destroyed stands to this day as the greatest achievement of a sea raider. He was her captain, her protector, and her lover all at once, their careers entwined. Their success, though, resulted from his experiences first on the little *Sumter*. It was aboard the former packet ship that he developed the sea strategy that he and *Alabama* rode to such success. As a philosophical mariner, Semmes exploited Maury's science of the seas. He knew where the whales, upon which Northern whaling ships and crews so depended, migrated to their feeding grounds. He also knew the tides and currents that other Northern merchant ships rode, and he lay in wait for them and destroyed them. But he never stayed long in one position because he carefully calculated the time required for his released prisoners to report his location and the time required for a U.S. Navy warship to find him and destroy him. He directed *Alabama* from crossroads to crossroads of the sea. That is why the Northern warships could never locate him on the high seas, and it is the reason he referred to himself as a philosophical mariner.

Semmes had taken many books with him on his cruises, and he read them extensively as Lieutenant John Kell controlled the ship. When he entered the South China Sea seeking a U.S. Navy warship, he read about the currents and the various harbors, and he used this information to sink U.S. merchant ships in that sea on which he had never before sailed. This knowledge of whatever sea he might be on gave him a distinct advantage over the enemy warships as well as merchant ships. Semmes took advantage of his knowledge of the winds and currents to overtake a U.S. merchant ship or to elude an enemy warship. He was not once surprised by the enemy. He even selected the time and place for his last battle at sea. Had *Alabama* been serviced in Cherbourg harbor, and had *Alabama*'s ammunition been fresh, the *Kearsarge* would never have sunk her. But armies on the land had already determined the outcome of the war. Semmes's last sea battle was a futile effort to prevent *Alabama* from being blockaded in a French port because he knew by that time that his war efforts, great as they were, could not determine the fate of the Confederacy. Why, then, did he not allow the ship to remain in the harbor and thus avoid the deaths of so many young men?

He wrote later that "the poor old *Alabama* was not now what she had been" and "her commander, like herself, was well-nigh worn down." He knew that neither the ship nor the man could contribute directly to the Confederate cause, as slim as that cause was in June 1864. He knew that had he kept his ship safely in the harbor of Cherbourg, there would be no improvement in the Confederate military position; he knew that if he offered battle, and somehow won, it would jolt the Southerners into greater efforts at home. He was willing to risk a sea battle, first to prevent his ship from being blockaded in the French port, and second to bolster the Southern people. He risked not only the lives of his crew but his own life as well; he was willing to make that sacrifice.

When Semmes was back in the South after the battle, he was shocked, first at seeing Anne Elizabeth hoeing in the garden with her former slaves, then at the destruction, the scarcity of food, the deserting soldiers scavenging for food and clothing, and the lack of transportation—in short, at the disintegration of the Southern society. The war, he realized, had never been so bad at sea as it was at home. His role, he knew when he arrived at Richmond, could only be a delaying tactic. Despite his promotion to rear admiral, he did not think the South could protect itself; yet as a brigadier general he fought until he was ordered to surrender to General Sherman's troops at Guilford Courthouse in North Carolina. What, one wonders, would he have done with *Alabama* had he won that battle? The philosophical mariner never speculated on that possibility, and it is today still futile to do so.

Semmes accepted his imprisonment after the war with less dignity than he had accepted the loss of *Alabama*. His diary of the imprisonment months, however, is upbeat in general. In it he only once indulged in self-pity, and that episode was representative of financial worries: How were Anne Elizabeth and his children? Did they have enough to eat? Were they safe from the occupying troops? He did not allow himself to dwell long on these negatives; it was more his style to be optimistic, to anticipate his early release. Still, the small room in which he was confined, as the days grew into weeks and the weeks into four long months, sapped his basic optimism, which had carried him over so many thousands of miles of ocean waters. His spirit was supported only by his strong religious beliefs and by his conviction that because of his Guilford Courthouse release his arrest had been illegal. In the end, he proved to be correct; but he suffered more in his small room than ever he did on the high seas.

His faith in the teachings of his church had helped to sustain him in prison. After his return to Mobile, he attended church services as regularly as his health would permit; he eulogized Pope Pius IX on an anniversary year, revealing understanding of the changes in Europe during the era from 1848 to the late 1870s and of his own staunch Catholicism.

During the postwar years he sought many ways to earn money for the support of his wife and younger children still at home. He began to write his memoirs, which when published never reached the "best-seller list" as had his Mexican War book. He extended himself also by lecturing in whatever town invited him. These were his most frustrating years because he was not allowed to practice law. He became bitter in his correspondence with the various members of Congress from whom he sought help in removing the civic restrictions placed upon him. Finally, after his pardon in 1868, he was free to practice law. His last years were peaceful and his income was sufficient for his family's needs. He became reconciled to life-after-the-war, enjoying his grandchildren, being at home with Anne Elizabeth, living the quiet life. He was at peace with himself and the world. He died a happy man.

It is difficult to reach a final analysis of Semmes's character because it was so diverse in nature. Each aspect of it rose to the surface in moments of stress or need, and its manifestation would change according to the need at the moment: He could be harsh on his sailors one moment and understanding and empathetic the next moment. His most dominant characteristic was his high intelligence; he seemed never to forget any book he had ever read or any experience he had ever felt. In times of stress, such as the hurricane *Alabama* endured off the coast of New England, he responded to the ship's changing needs immediately from moment to moment and thus saved her from the ravages of the storm. Normally he was calm in his dealings and evaluations of other persons, with the exceptions of Abraham Lincoln and U.S. Secretary of the Navy Gideon Welles whom he never forgave or forgot. He was thoroughly loyal to anyone whom he admired or who had accepted him with kindness, such as the Reverend Mr. Tremlett or the black boy whom he freed from slavery and assigned as steward to the ship's doctor. Yet he could not accept black persons as being equal to other races. His most telling remark on the subject of slavery was, perhaps, his delight in learning that black African Moslems held other black Africans as slaves. He was, of course, critical of anyone, white or black, who he thought to be inept or blundering; but he calmly accepted the decision of several of his children to leave Catholicism and join the Episcopal Church. He was loyal to his close friends and family, supporting them however much their decisions went counter to his opinions.

Raphael Semmes left a legacy to subsequent American generations through his total character and personality: intelligent, capable, self-taught; compassionate, loyal, sympathetic, determined, and effective. He never entered any enterprise unprepared, and thus he usually was successful. Despite his loss of *Alabama*, his name is better known in America today than is that of the man who destroyed his ship.

It may be right and proper that today his legacy is associated more with the *Alabama* than any of his other achievements. It was his success aboard that ship that led the Geneva conference in 1873 to require Great Britain to pay $15.5 million in gold to the United States; and it was that ship's career that led the great powers of Europe to convene the conference at that Swiss city, which still is the site of most important international conferences, and established Switzerland as perpetually a neutral state. Semmes and *Alabama* had sailed on six of the seven seas and literally carried the impact of the American Civil War to ports in all of the six seas. It was Semmes aboard *Alabama* that created the American Civil War, more so even than the impact of the cotton shortage in Europe, as a worldwide event. That achievement reflects Semmes's abilities, character, and intellect more clearly than any of his other achievements. And so his legacy to the world is identified rightly with the *Alabama:* "Roll, Alabama, roll"!

Notes

Chapter 1
The Student Mariner-
Philosopher

1. The material on the Semmes family and Raphael Semmes's early life is in Anderson Humphreys and Curt Guenther, *Semmes America* (Memphis, 1989), and Harry Wright Newman, *The Maryland Semmes and Kindred Families* (Baltimore, 1956).

2. Raphael Semmes, *Memoirs of Service Afloat and Ashore during the Mexican War* (Cincinnati, 1851), and idem, *Memoirs of Service Afloat during the War Between the States* (1869; reprint, Secaucus, N.J., 1987), hereafter cited, respectively, as *Service Afloat and Ashore* and *Service Afloat*.

3. For the training of a midshipman at sea, see Charles Lee Lewis, *Admiral Franklin Buchanan, Fearless Man of Action* (Baltimore, 1929), and Harold D. Langley, *Social Reform in the United States Navy, 1798–1862* (Urbana, 1967), 21–22.

4. Semmes's pre–Civil War U.S. Navy assignments are in National Archives, Washington, Record Group 24, Records of the Bureau of Naval Personnel, rolls 4–7, and National Archives, Publication #19, "Treasury Department Collection of Confederate Records."

5. National Archives, RG24, Records of the Bureau of Naval Personnel, rolls 4–7.

6. Charles Grayson Summersell, "The Career of Raphael Semmes Prior to the Cruise of the *Alabama*" (Ph.D. diss., Vanderbilt University, 1940), 8–9.

7. Ibid., 12, citing Ms. Statement of Sale of Lots at Pensacola in January 1837, and G. E. Chase, Plan of the New City of Pensacola, 1836, both in the P. K. Yonge Library, Pensacola, Fla.; Deed Book, 1836–37, 327, in the Office of the Clerk of the Circuit Court of Escambia County, Tallahassee, Fla.; *Pensacola Gazette,* April 29, October 15 and 21, 1836, and February 24 and May 6, 1837.

8. Humphreys and Guenther, *Semmes America,* 312.

9. Summersell, "Career of Raphael Semmes," 10–11.

10. The *Porpoise* Journal is in the Alabama State Department of Archives and History, Montgomery, Ala. It consists of 237 handwritten legal-size pages. The

following material concerning the *Porpoise* cruise and Semmes's experiences ashore are all taken from this journal.

11. See K. Jack Bauer, *The Mexican War 1846–1848* (New York, 1974), chap. 1, and Karl Schmitt, *Mexico and the United States, 1821–1973: Conflict and Coexistence* (New York, 1974), chaps. 2 and 3.

12. This *Porpoise* Journal is not cited in other books on Raphael Semmes.

13. This and the following quotes on Irving's biography of Columbus are in John Noble Wilford, *The Mysterious History of Columbus: An Exploration of the Man, the Myth, the Legacy* (New York, 1991), 39, 52, 253, and passim.

14. Gene M. Brack, *Mexico Views Manifest Destiny, 1821–1846* (Albuquerque, 1975).

15. Semmes, *Porpoise* Journal.

16. Ibid.

17. Ibid.

18. Ibid.

Chapter 2
The Mexican War: Navy Duty

1. Raphael Semmes, *Memoirs of Service Afloat and Ashore during the Mexican War* (Cincinnati, 1851).

2. See, for example, K. Jack Bauer, *The Mexican War 1846–1848* (New York, 1974); Alfred Hoyt Bill, *Rehearsal for Conflict: The War with Mexico, 1846–1848* (New York, 1947); Gene M. Brack, *Mexico Views Manifest Destiny, 1821–1846* (Albuquerque, 1975); Charles L. Dufour, *The Mexican War: A Compact History, 1846–1848* (New York, 1968). For an excellent survey of Mexican–United States relations, see Karl Schmitt, *Mexico and the United States, 1821–1973: Conflict and Coexistence* (New York, 1974).

3. Semmes, *Service Afloat and Ashore*, 41.

4. Ibid., 67–68.

5. Ibid., 54; see also William S. McFeely, *Grant: A Biography* (New York, 1982), 28–33.

6. Semmes, *Service Afloat and Ashore*, 76.

7. For this quotation and the following account of the *Somers*, see Philip McFarland, *Sea Dangers: The Affair of the* Somers (New York, 1985), 48 and passim.

8. Ibid.

9. Robert Self Henry, *The Story of the Mexican War* (New York, 1950), 262.

10. Semmes, *Service Afloat and Ashore*, 125–27.

11. Ibid.

12. Ibid., 145.

13. This and the shorter quotations that follow are in ibid., 154–55.

14. Ibid., 158–65.

Chapter 3
Off to the "Halls of the Montezumas": U.S. Army Duty

1. Raphael Semmes, *Memoirs of Service Afloat and Ashore during the Mexican War* (Cincinnati, 1851), 159–61.

2. For a further description of Semmes's horse, see ibid., 169–70.

3. Ibid., 171.

4. Ibid., 175.

5. Ibid., 180–82.

6. Ibid., 186.

7. Ibid., 190.

8. Ibid., 194–95.

9. Charles Winslow Elliot, *Winfield Scott: The Soldier and the Man* (New York, 1937), 484. Elliot presents an excellent account of the Trist mission and of the clash between Trist and Scott (486–87). Elliot, *Winfield Scott*, also presents an excellent account of the Worth-Scott controversy. Semmes, of course, supported Worth in his book.

10. Semmes, *Service Afloat and Ashore*, 212.

11. See Semmes, *Service Afloat and Ashore*, 244.

12. Ibid., 241.

13. Ibid., 250.

14. Ibid., 251.

15. Ibid. Chap. 13 is devoted primarily to descriptions of places, people, and social structure, 251–72.

16. Ibid., 284. The following pages describe the vain effort, with various humorous moments, to exchange prisoners with the Mexicans.

17. Ibid., 295.

18. Ibid., 315.

19. Ibid., 315–16.

20. Ibid., 317–19; see also Edward S. Wallace, *General William Jenkins Worth: Monterrey's Forgotten Hero* (Dallas, 1953), 136–37, and Elliot, *Winfield Scott*, 484.

21. These quotations and descriptions are from Semmes, *Service Afloat and Ashore*, chap. 16, 326 and chap. 17.

22. Ibid., chap. 17, esp. 357.

23. Ibid., 379.

24. Idib., 407.

25. Ibid., 408–10.

26. Semmes served as the U.S. interpreter during the peace negotiations; ibid., 414.

27. Ibid., 419–23. See also Elliot, *Winfield Scott*, 522–27.

28. Semmes, *Service Afloat and Ashore*, 429; see also Wallace, *General William Jenkins Worth*, and Elliot, *Winfield Scott*, 530.

29. Elliot, *Winfield Scott*, 549; also McFeely, *Grant*, 28–33.

Chapter 4
Light House Keeping

1. *Electra* Journal, kept by Raphael Semmes, January 15, 1848, to July 7, 1848. Alabama State Department of Archives and History, Montgomery, Ala.

2. For much of this information on Semmes during the late 1840s and 1850s I am indebted to the late Professor Charles Grayson Summersell of the University of Alabama. The material is derived from Semmes's Letterbooks (Manuscript Division, the Library of Congress, Washington, D.C.), which Frances Sharpley Summersell made available to me at her late husband's request.

3. For this account of Semmes's legal services at Kell's court-martial, I have relied upon John McIntosh Kell, *Recollections of a Naval Life* (Washington, D.C., 1900), and Norman C. Delaney, *John McIntosh Kell of the Raider* Alabama (Tuscaloosa, 1973). The trial occurred in July 1849.

4. In December 1850, with a new administration in Washington, the four passed midshipmen were reinstated as officers in the U.S. Navy (Delaney, *John McIntosh Kell*, 62).

5. Claude Banks Mayo, *Your Navy* (Los Angeles, n.d.), 18.

6. Francis Ross Holland, Jr., *America's Lighthouses: Their Illustrated History Since 1716* (Brattleboro, Vt., 1972), 34–36.

7. The above information and statistics are in J. G. Randall and David Donald, *The Civil War and Reconstruction*, 2d ed. (Boston, 1961), 1–28.

8. Secondary works tend to support Semmes's analysis of the South's economic plight during the two decades prior to the Civil War. See ibid., 80.

9. Many twentieth-century historians also tend to emphasize the sectional and economic differences as major causes of the Civil War. There remains today no unanimity among the twentieth-century histories. See the various essays in Kenneth M. Stamp, ed., *The Causes of the Civil War* (Englewood Cliffs, N.J., 1965).

Chapter 5
Secession, War, and the CSS *Sumter*

1. The other states seceded in the following order, all in 1861: Georgia, January 19; Louisiana, January 26; Texas, February 1; Virginia, April 17; Arkansas, May 6; North Carolina, May 20.

2. Alexander H. Stephens of Georgia had supported the various congressional acts of the 1850s on the grounds that compromise was the best way for the South to retain its institution of slavery, and after the election of Lincoln in Novem-

ber 1860 he maintained that position. The particular speech to which Semmes referred was in the same mode: Do not secede until the North forces it upon the South; cooperate with Lincoln's administration in order to maintain the Union; Lincoln was legally elected and therefore there were no grounds for secession. See Thomas E. Schott, *Alexander H. Stephens: A Biography* (Baton Rouge, 1988).

3. This letter and Stephens's reply are in the Semmes Papers, Alabama State Department of Archives and History, Montgomery, Ala.

4. See Walter L. Fleming, *Civil War and Reconstruction in Alabama* (1905; reprint, Spartanburg, S.C., 1978), 39–42.

5. The Curry to Semmes letter of February 1, 1861 and Semmes's reply of February 6 are in Semmes Papers, Alabama State Archives; Semmes's letter to Curry of January 24 is not in those papers, but its contents can be derived from Curry's letter of February 1.

6. See William Morrison Robinson, Jr., *The Confederate Privateers* (New Haven, 1928).

7. J. G. Randall and David Donald, *The Civil War and Reconstruction*, 2d ed. (Boston, 1961), 150.

8. Semmes's Refutation, 4, undated, in Semmes Papers, Alabama State Archives.

9. Semmes to his eldest daughter, Electra, March 26, 1861, in ibid.

10. Raphael Semmes, *Memoirs of Service Afloat during the War Between the States* (1869; reprint, Secaucus, N.J., 1987), 78. All quotations are from this book unless otherwise noted.

11. Davis to Semmes, Executive Department, Montgomery, Ala., February 21, 1861, in Semmes Papers, Alabama State Archives. Also in *The War of the Rebellion: A Compilation of the Official Records of the Union and Confederate Armies*, 128 vols. (Washington, D.C., 1880–1901), series 4, 1:106–07; hereafter cited as *ORA*.

12. Semmes to L. P. Walker, secretary of war, Richmond, Va., February 28, 1861, *ORA*, series 4, 1:118–19.

13. Morse to Davis, March 6, 1861, in ibid., 131–32.

14. The correspondence on Semmes's assignment to the CSS *Sumter* and her fitting-out in New Orleans is in Semmes Papers, Alabama State Archives. Ten of the letters, those dated April 18 and 22, May 23, and June 14, 16, 22, 23, 24, 25, and 30, are all in *Official Records of the Union and Confederate Navies in the War of the Rebellion* (hereafter cited as *ORN*), series 1, vol. 1, *The Operations of the Cruisers from January 19, 1861, to December 31, 1862* (Washington, D.C., 1894), 613–19.

15. See, for instance, Lynn M. Case and Warren F. Spencer, *The United States and France: Civil War Diplomacy* (Philadelphia, 1970), and Warren F. Spencer, *The Confederate Navy in Europe* (University, Ala., 1983), 8–10 and passim.

16. This and subsequent quotations are from Semmes, *Service Afloat*, unless otherwise noted. Much of this work is based on letters and official reports later published in *ORN*.

17. The account of *Sumter*'s experiences, including the problems with the river

pilots, in passing through the Northern blockade at the passages of the Mississippi River into the Gulf of Mexico are summarized by Semmes in *ORN*, series 1, vol. 2 (Washington, D.C., 1895), 628–37.

18. Porter's movements and Mahan's scheme are in ibid., 1:67–69, 87–88.

19. Semmes to Electra Semmes, New York City, April 26, and New Orleans, May 3, 1861; Semmes to Anne Elizabeth, Montgomery, Ala., April 9, 15, 18, and 25, and from New Orleans, May 28, 1861; Semmes to his son, Oliver J. Semmes, undated, all in the Semmes Papers, Alabama State Archives.

20. *Sumter* log, *ORN*, series 1, 1:725–28.

21. See Case and Spencer, *Civil War Diplomacy*, and Spencer, *Confederate Navy*. Neither author considered that the internal structure of foreign governments might affect their relations with Washington and/or Richmond during the Civil War.

Chapter 6
Semmes and the CSS *Alabama*

1. James D. Bulloch, *The Secret Service of the Confederate States in Europe: or How the Confederate Cruisers Were Equipped,* 2 vols. (1883; reprint, New York, 1959), 57–63 and passim; *ORN*, series 2 (Washington, D.C., 1921), 2:83–87. Bulloch was the most effective Southern agent in Europe. See below for his achievement in designing and building No. 290. North was less effective as an agent in Europe. See Spencer, *Confederate Navy*, 22, 24–25.

2. Raphael Semmes to the secretary of the Confederate States Navy, Nassau, New Providence, June 15, 1862, in Semmes, *Memoirs of Service Afloat during the War Between the States* (1869; reprint, Secaucus, N.J., 1987), 351–53, hereafter referred to as *Service Afloat.* All subsequent Semmes quotations are from this work unless otherwise noted.

3. George W. Dalzell, *The Flight from the Flag: The Continuing Effects of the Civil War upon the American Carrying Trade* (Chapel Hill, 1940), chap. I.

4. For these events, see Semmes, *Service Afloat,* 640 and passim.

5. William Williams was a passenger aboard the *Contest.* For the capture of the *Contest* and the description of *Alabama*'s crew as well as the conditions aboard *Alabama,* see *ORN*, series 1, 2:561–62.

6. Ibid.

7. Semmes, *Service Afloat,* 713–14.

8. *Singapore Sunday Times,* February 19, 1956.

9. Semmes to Barron, Cherbourg, June 13, 1864, *ORN*, series 1, vol. 3 (Washington, D.C., 1896), 651.

10. The best accounts remain those by participants and by Bulloch. Captain Semmes rendered an impressionistic report, in ibid., 649–51, and an even more subjective account in his *Service Afloat,* 751–65; Captain Winslow's reports were

matter of fact, *ORN*, series 1, 3:59–82, esp. 79–81; Lieutenant Arthur Sinclair of the *Alabama*, writing almost thirty years after Semmes, gave a subjective yet amazingly honest account in *Two Years on the* Alabama (Annapolis, 1989), 259–91; Commander Bulloch, writing with the aid of documents including the two captains' reports, presented an analytical and balanced account, *Secret Service*, 1:277–93. For accounts of eyewitnesses, see George T. Sinclair to Barron, Cherbourg, June 20, 1864, Whittle Papers, folder 10, no. 9, Norfolk Public Library, Norfolk, Va., and William M. Leary, Jr., "The *Alabama* vs. the *Kearsarge:* A Diplomatic View," *American Neptune* 29, no. 3 (1969): 167–68. Excellent illustrations are in Norman C. Delaney, "Showdown at Cherbourg," *Civil War Times Illustrated* 15, no. 3 (June 1976): 16–21. The best secondary accounts are Delaney, *John McIntosh Kell of the Raider* Alabama (Tuscaloosa, 1973), 164–68, and Charles Grayson Summersell, ed., *The Journal of George Townley Fullam* (Birmingham, 1973), 190–96. Other good secondary accounts are W. Adolphe Roberts, *Semmes of the* Alabama (New York, 1938), 195–211, and Edward Boykin, *Ghost Ship of the Confederacy: The Story of the* Alabama *and Her Captain, Raphael Semmes* (New York, 1957), 344–84. For the diplomacy of the pre- and postbattle days, see Lynn M. Case and Warren F. Spencer, *The United States and France: Civil War Diplomacy* (Philadelphia, 1970), 509–15.

11. Semmes, *Service Afloat*, 762.

12. Semmes to Barron, June 21, 1864, *ORN*, series 1, 3:650; Semmes to Slidell, July 1, 1864, ibid., 663, 664; Semmes, *Service Afloat*, 754, 761, 762.

13. Semmes, *Service Afloat*, 761–62.

Chapter 7
Survival after the *Alabama*

1. Semmes's departure from England created rumors that he was to meet another ship to resume his war against Northern merchant shipping.

2. Letter, L. G. Brent, chief of artillery and ordnance, District of Western Louisiana, to Major General Taylor, September 8, 1864, in Semmes Papers, Alabama State Department of Archives and History, Montgomery, Ala.

3. Mallory to Semmes, Telegraph, in ibid.

4. For Semmes's transportation to Lee's headquarters, see Frederick M. Colston, "Recollections of the Last Months in the Army of Northern Virginia," *Southern Historical Society Papers*, vol. 38, ed. R. A. Brock, Richmond, Va., January–December 1910, 4.

5. Nelson D. Lankford, ed., *An Irishman in Dixie: Thomas Connally's Diary of the Fall of the Confederacy* (Columbia, S. C., 1988), 63–64.

6. Although young Raphael joined his father aboard the *Virginia* only on April 7, 1865, he had visited his father every weekend; Semmes Papers, Manuscript Deparment, William R. Perkins Library, Duke University, Durham, N.C.

7. These financial arrangments are recorded in ibid., March 24, 1865.

8. The original of the parole obligation is in Semmes Papers, Alabama State Archives. Copy is also in Semmes, *Service Afloat*, 822–23.

9. Joseph A. Wright to William H. Seward, Berlin, June 7, 1866, in *Papers Relating to Foreign Affairs*, 39th Cong., 2d sess., 1866, pt. 2 (Washington, D.C., 1867), 26.

10. Semmes, *Service Afloat*, 822–23; see also *Diary of Gideon Welles, Secretary of the Navy under Lincoln and Johnson* (Boston, 1911), 2:476–77.

11. Semmes, *Service Afloat*, 824–25.

12. Semmes to Anne Elizabeth, New York Harbor, December 27, 1865, Semmes Papers, Alabama State Archives.

13. See the two-part article by John A. Bolles, "Why Semmes of the *Alabama* Was Not Tried," *Atlantic Monthly: A Magazine of Literature, Science, Art, and Politics* 30 (July 1872): 88–97 and (August 1872): 148–56. The account of the Bolles investigation is from this article.

14. Semmes's diary of his imprisonment, Semmes Papers, Alabama State Archives. All subsequent quotations of the period of his imprisonment are taken from this source unless otherwise indicated.

15. Elisabeth Joan Doyle, ed., "Notes and Documents: Eleven Letters of Raphael Semmes, 1867–1868," *Alabama Review* 5 (July 1952): 222–32. See also the C. C. Clay Papers, Perkins Library, Duke University.

16. W. Adolphe Roberts, *Semmes of the* Alabama (New York, 1938), 251–53.

17. Semmes to Anne Elizabeth, undated, Semmes Papers, Alabama State Archives.

18. President, University of Kentucky, to Raphael Semmes, Lexington, Ky., September 25, 1867, in Semmes Papers, Alabama State Archives.

19. J. Q. Adams to Raphael Semmes, Georgetown, D.C., June 22, 1866, in ibid., and the response by Semmes, draft, undated, also in ibid. For this J. Q. Adams, see James Truslow Adams, *The Adams Family* (New York, 1930), 236–37 and passim.

20. *Nashville Republican Banner*, July 28, 1867.

21. The two-volume edition is little more than the publication of the logs of the *Sumter* and *Alabama*. Semmes is referred to in the third person. The one-volume edition is in the first person and reveals Semmes's thoughts, as well as his commands, attitudes, and treatment of the common sailors aboard the two ships, and his asides on the seas and especially the violent storms his ships survived. Semmes's one-volume book was reproduced in a facsimile edition by the Blue and Grey Press, a Division of Book Sales of Secaucus, N.J., recopyrighted in 1987.

22. Semmes to Mrs. C. C. Clay, July 6, 1866, in the C. C. Clay Papers.

23. Semmes to Mrs. C. C. Clay, January 29, 1868, in ibid.

24. Semmes Papers, Perkins Library.

25. To an unknown fellow camp member, in ibid.

26. Walter L. Fleming, *Civil War and Reconstruction in Alabama* (1905; reprint, Spartanburg, S.C., 1978), 602.

27. J. Creswell to Semmes, Washington, D.C., December 19, 1874, in Semmes Papers, Alabama State Archives.

Chapter 8
The Mariner's Legacy

1. W. Adolphe Roberts, *Semmes of the* Alabama (New York, 1938), 261. The most recently published reference to Semmes and the *Alabama* is the article by Max Guerout, "The Wreck of the CSS *Alabama:* Avenging Angel of the Confederacy," *National Geographic* (December 1994). The author wrote of the results of the efforts that began in 1988 to raise the ship from where she had sunk during her battle with the USS *Kearsarge* in the English Channel off Cherbourg, France. Guerout describes the various artifacts that still remain in the sunken vessel, such as flush toilets, various paintings still recognizable, and pictures of Semmes and Kell. The article also includes an excellent map of *Alabama*'s cruise.

Bibliographical Essay

B ibliographies always begin with the most important material on which the author has based his or her work. In my case, that material has been Raphael Semmes's own writings, both published and unpublished.

Semmes wrote and published two books that recounted his experiences in two wars: *Memoirs of Service Afloat and Ashore during the Mexican War* (Cincinnati, 1851) and *Memoirs of Service Afloat during the War Between the States* (Baltimore, 1869). The two books have become important to historians of those wars: Semmes's Mexican War book is cited as an original source by writers on that war, and his Civil War book is considered so important as an original source that it was reprinted and republished in 1987 by the Blue and Grey Press (Secaucus, N.J.).

Both books are based on "journals" or notes that Semmes made as he traveled and served in the wars. A comparison of his published books with his unpublished memoirs and letters reveals his agile and analytical mind. In his published books he remained true to his unpublished journals; the one big difference is his choice of words and his ability to turn a phrase so that the words convey more than at first glance they appear to do. His writing style reflects his mid-nineteenth-century mind-set: a strong sense of nationalism, Victorian Puritanism, strong religious and moral convictions. Both books reveal Raphael Semmes to have been an exceptional product of his times.

As thorough as his two published works are, they fail to reflect all his experiences and thus cannot provide complete insight into the man and his mind-set. Those other experiences, however, have been preserved in his journals. The earliest one to come to light is his *Porpoise* Journal. It is in the Alabama State Department of Archives and History, Montgomery, Alabama, Semmes Papers. Semmes served as first lieutenant aboard the USS *Porpoise* just before the Mexican War began. Another unpublished journal is Semmes's diary of his postwar imprisonment in Washington,

D.C., in the Semmes Papers, Alabama State Archives. These records, as well as Semmes's letters, reflect portions of his career that have not appeared in any of the previously published biographies, and they provide a unique insight into his mental and psychological powers. They were invaluable in the effort to penetrate the mind of the man.

Semmes's arrest and imprisonment just after the South's capitulation was an unexpected event in his life. His diary during the imprisonment reflects not only his sad solitude but also his love for his family and his opinions of Northern officials and members of Congress. It was a true test of character for him, a test he passed with flying colors.

Secondary biographies of Semmes are numerous; some eight or nine exist. Each one listed in this bibliography contributed some insight into his life and his attitudes. However, the older ones tend to emphasize his wartime experiences and especially his command of the CSS *Alabama*. Because of his success in sinking Union merchant ships, that approach is somewhat justified. Even so, Raphael Semmes was more than a wartime celebrity. He was a family man, an honorable foe as well as friend, a devoted member of the Roman Catholic Church, and a scholar of religious as well as maritime history.

My purpose has been to get as close as possible to an understanding of the man's mind and spirit, given the sources available to me. For that reason I have not cited all of the books listed below, for they simply tell a story without analysis and in some cases are repetitious.

The best existing biography is John Taylor's *Confederate Raider: Raphael Semmes of the* Alabama (1994). He has consulted all the proper sources (original as well as secondary) and has written a very interesting biography. He also attempted, with a degree of success, to get at an understanding of the man; his is not just a book about a navy officer; it is rather a book about the mind-set of such an officer. It is an intriguing biography.

Among the older Semmes biographies are W. Adolphe Roberts, *Semmes of the* Alabama (1938), which romanticizes Semmes's life and career, and Edward Boykin, *Ghost Ship of the Confederacy: The Story of the* Alabama *and her Captain, Raphael Semmes* (1957), which treats Semmes's story as "the best out-and-out adventure story of the Civil War," and that theme characterizes the whole book. Professor Charles Grayson Summersell in his last work on Semmes, *CSS* Alabama: *Builder, Captain, and Plans* (1985), presented an excellent though brief analysis of Semmes the man.

The *Official Records of the Union and Confederate Navies in the War of the Rebellion,* series 1, vols. 1–3 (1894–96) and series 2, vols. 1 and 2 (1921), contain Semmes's ships' logs and his correspondence with Secretary of the

Navy Stephen R. Mallory. This correspondence was of great value to me, especially as it revealed the high esteem Mallory held for Semmes's successes aboard both the CSS *Sumter* and the CSS *Alabama*. Semmes's letters and reports to Mallory also provided a good insight into his ships' movements as well as Semmes's state of mind at various stages of both his cruises.

The secondary works on Semmes are voluminous. Some of them in the bibliography might appear to be redundant, but each author had an individual view or slant on the person or topic of his or her book. I have included the books I think would be most useful to the reader. Many of the entries are not cited in the notes; each of those listed, however, adds something to the topic that the others lack.

Finally, of the several biographies listed, each includes a unique fact or interpretation of Admiral Raphael Semmes. Comparative reading of the biographies is at times confusing but in the long run very informative. Semmes was a complex personality, and such personalities usually attract biographers. I trust my own effort to present a holistic account of the many-faceted personality of this nineteenth-century navy officer will be of help in understanding the man behind the heroic deeds.

The many secondary works on Semmes and the ships he commanded during two wars are too numerous to include in this bibliographical essay. Suffice it to say that within the context of his life span, I have drawn something—an idea or fact or interpretation—from each of the biographies listed in the section on secondary works. Several of Semmes's activities were completely new to me: his escapades on the high seas during the Mexican War; his service on the Lighthouse Board and later in the Light-House Bureau; his struggles to survive in the immediate postwar era; his practice of law in Mobile; his lecture tours; and the publication of his memoirs on the Mexican War as well as those famous ones on the American Civil War. All of these activities were new to me because they frequently are overlooked by his earlier biographers.

Other books and articles about Semmes are, again, too numerous to be included in this essay. I have listed those that I actually touched—held in my hand and perused to discern their value to this account of an officer in the Confederate States Navy.

Because Semmes's activities, acting alone on the high seas, were so successful in destroying the merchant marine of the United States, it does not follow that he was not a part of the regular Confederate States Navy. Indeed, the Southern navy's policy was a reaction to the Federal navy's activities. Thus Semmes should be placed in the overall history of the Civil War. George W. Dalzell, *The Flight from the Flag* (1940), has certified the long-range effect of Semmes's activities; the U.S. merchant marine has never recovered its esteemed prewar position in world maritime commerce. Semmes's Civil War activities perhaps established the longest lasting effects of any of the military operations during the war. Bern Anderson, *By Sea and by River: The Naval History of the Civil War* (1962), recounts the Confederate navy's activities during the war and their continuing impact after the war. In this context, the Washington government's postwar arrest and imprisonment of Semmes was totally unjustified.

The Civil War also created diplomatic and economic problems for the naval states of Europe. Lynn M. Case and I published *The United States and France: Civil War Diplomacy* (1970), intended as a companion volume to Ephraim Douglas Adams's *Great Britain and the American Civil War* (1925). My contribution to the book led me later to write *The Confederate Navy in Europe* (1983), which was designed as a companion work to Frank J. Merli, *Great Britain and the Confederate Navy, 1861–1865* (1970). In my work I had to describe the *Alabama-Kearsarge* battle, which occurred just off the coast of France in the English Channel. The defeat Semmes suffered in that battle, and his mental and emotional response to it, led me to see Semmes as a person whose character and mental strength were a cut above the average. All of these "accidents of history" led me to read more about the man, an activity that in turn has led to this biography.

Semmes's book on the Mexican War captivated me; his writing style was one of the best of Victorian literature I had ever read. Thus I became intrigued with his intellect, his broad knowledge of human nature, and his fascinating Victorian prose. First I had to learn about the Mexican War and the relations between the United States and Mexico from Karl Schmitt's *Mexico and the United States, 1821–1973: Conflict and Coexistence* (1974). I also had to read Philip McFarland, *Sea Dangers: The Affair of the* Somers (1985), because Semmes became captain of the *Somers* and lost her to a sudden wind change during a severe storm. Many of the crew lost their lives, but a Court of Inquiry exonerated Semmes of any fault. *Somers* was the second ship under his command that he lost to the waters. See the bibliography for other books on the Mexican War and Semmes's role on land as well as at sea. Semmes was bored with blockade duty, but his usual luck came to his rescue. He was ordered by the president of the United States to deliver a message to the president of Mexico. During his duty with the army he identified himself with General William J. Worth and served on his staff as the army marched northward to Mexico City. Semmes, in his book, supported Worth in that general's conflicts with General Winfield Scott, the commander of the army. See the bibliography for secondary works on Scott and Worth.

Although the Mexican War is at times considered a rehearsal for the Civil War (see Alfred Hoyt Bill, *Rehearsal for Conflict: The War with Mexico* [1947]), it was no such experience for Semmes because he spent half the Mexican War at sea and half on land; during the Civil War he spent nearly three full years at sea and only a few months on land.

The Confederate navy operations in American waters, both North and South, were limited by the North's superior navy-in-being. The South's ability to build a navy was sorely restricted by Northern naval activities. See David D. Porter, *Naval History of the Civil War* (1886); Clarence E. McCartney, *Mr. Lincoln's Admirals* (1956); Harold D. Langley, *Social Reform in the United States Navy, 1798–1862* (1967); Virgil C. Jones, *The Civil War at Sea, January 1861–March 1862*, 3 vols. (1960–62); William H. Parker, *Recollections of a Naval Officer* (1883); Frank Lawrence Owsley, Jr., *The CSS* Florida: *Her Building and Operations* (1965); and Richard S. West, Jr., *The Second Admiral* (1937) and *Mr. Lincoln's Navy* (1958).

For more on the most successful Confederate raider captain, see Charles Grayson Summersell, *The Cruise of the CSS* Sumter (1965); Harold Wilson, "The Cruise of the CSS *Alabama* in Southeast Asian Waters," *Journal of Confederate History* 4 (special commemorative issue, 1989); Arthur Sinclair, *Two Years on the* Alabama (1895; reprint 1989).

Officers who served with Semmes aboard the CSS *Alabama*, especially Semmes's first lieutenant, John McIntosh Kell, also wrote about the ship and her captain. See Kell, "Cruise and Combats of the *Alabama*," in *The Way to Appomattox: Battles and Leaders of the Civil War*, 4 vols., edited by R. H. Johnson (New York, 1959), 4:611; Kell also wrote his memoirs of service to Semmes aboard both the *Sumter* and the *Alabama*. Kell's greatest tribute to Semmes appeared in Kell's book: *Recollections of a Naval Life* (1900).

The one man whom Semmes considered to be a true hero was the one who came to be known as the "scientist of the seas": See Francis L. Williams, *Matthew Fontaine Maury* (1963). It was Semmes's self-understanding that led him to acknowledge Maury as a true scientist. He paid the scientist of the seas his highest acclaim: that of imitation. Semmes called himself an apostle to Maury, the ultimate scientist: thus "The Philosophical Mariner."

Bibliography

Original Unpublished Sources

Alabama State Department of Archives and History, Montgomery, Ala. Semmes Papers. Includes several journals: the *Porpoise* Journal, the postwar diary of his imprisonment, the *Electra* Journal, and the *Somers* Journal.

Library of Congress, Washington, D.C. Manuscript Division. Semmes's Letter-books.

National Archives, Washington, D.C. Record Group 24. Records of the Bureau of Naval Personnel. Rolls 4–7.

National Archives, Washington, D.C. Publication #19, "Treasury Department Collection of Confederate Records."

National Archives, Washington, D.C. Publication #169, "Department of the Navy. Department Collection of Confederate Records."

National Archives, Washington, D.C. State Department. Despatches: Calcutta and Singapore.

Office of the Clerk of the Circuit Court of Escambia County, Tallahassee, Fla.

P. K. Yonge Library, Pensacola, Fla. Ms. Statement of Sale of Lots at Pensacola in January 1837.

Public Records Office, Singapore. Governor's Papers: Miscellaneous Letters.

Whittle Papers. Norfolk Public Library. Norfolk, Va.

William R. Perkins Library, Duke University, Durham, N.C. Manuscript Department. C. C. Clay Papers; Semmes Papers.

Published Sources and Memoirs

Bolles, John A. "Why Semmes of the *Alabama* Was Not Tried." Part 1. In *Atlantic Monthly: A Magazine of Literature, Science, Art, and Politics* 30 (July 1872): 88–97.

———. "Why Semmes of the *Alabama* Was Not Tried." Part 2. *Atlantic Monthly: A Magazine of Literature, Science, Art, and Politics* 30 (August 1872): 148–56.

Bulloch, James D. *The Secret Service of the Confederate States in Europe: or How the*

Confederate Cruisers Were Equipped. 2 vols. 1883. Reprint. New York: Thomas Yoseloff, 1959.

Colston, Frederick M. "Recollections of the Last Months in the Army of Northern Virginia." *Southern Historical Society Papers* 38, edited by R. A. Brock. Richmond, Virginia: January–December 1910.

Doyle, Elisabeth Joan, ed. "Notes and Documents: Eleven Letters of Raphael Semmes, 1867–1868." *Alabama Review* 5 (July 1952): 222–32.

Kell, John McIntosh. *Recollections of a Naval Life.* Washington, D.C.: Neale, 1900.

Lankford, Nelson D., ed. *An Irishman in Dixie: Thomas Connally's Diary of the Fall of the Confederacy.* Columbia: University of South Carolina Press, 1988.

Low, John. *The Logs of the C.S.S.* Alabama *and the C.S.S.* Tuscaloosa. Edited with an introduction by W. Stanley Hoole. University, Ala.: Confederate Publishing, 1972.

Official Records of the Union and Confederate Navies in the War of the Rebellion. Series 1, vols. 1–3. Washington, D.C.: Government Printing Office, 1894–96. Series 2, vols. 1 and 2. Washington, D.C.: Government Printing Office, 1921.

Scott, Winfield. *Memoirs of Lieut.-Gen. Scott, L.L.D., Written by Himself.* 2 vols. N.p., 1864.

Semmes, Raphael. *Memoirs of Service Afloat and Ashore during the Mexican War.* Cincinnati: W. H. Moore, 1851.

———. *Memoirs of Service Afloat during the War Between the States.* Baltimore: Kelly, Piet, 1869.

Sterling, Ada, ed. *A Belle of the Fifties: Memoirs of Mrs. Clay of Alabama, Covering Social and Political Life in Washington and the South, 1853–1865.* New York: Doubleday, 1905.

Summersell, Charles Grayson ed., *The Journal of George Townley Fullam.* Birmingham: University of Alabama Press, 1973.

U.S. Congress *Papers Relating to Foreign Affairs.* 39th Cong., 2d sess., 1866, pt. 2. Washington, D.C.: Government Printing Office, 1867.

The War of the Rebellion: A Compilation of the Official Records of the Union and Confederate Armies. 128 vols. Washington, D.C.: Government Printing Office, 1880–1901.

Welles, Gideon. *Diary of Gideon Welles, Secretary of the Navy under Lincoln and Johnson.* Boston: Houghton Mifflin, 1911.

Secondary Sources

Adams, James Truslow. *The Adams Family.* New York: Literary Guild, 1930.

Alexander, Edward P. *Fighting for the Confederacy.* Chapel Hill: University of North Carolina Press, 1989.

Anderson, Bern. *By Sea and by River: The Naval History of the Civil War.* New York: Knopf, 1962. Reprint in paperback, New York: Da Capo Press, 1989.

Bauer, K. Jack. *The Mexican War 1846–1848.* New York: Macmillan, 1974.

Beaman, Charles C., Jr. *The National and Private "Alabama Claims" and their "Final and Amiable Settlement."* Washington, D.C.: W. H. Moore, 1871.

Bill, Alfred Hoyt. *Rehearsal for Conflict: The War with Mexico, 1846–1848.* New York: Knopf, 1947.

Boykin, Edward. *Ghost Ship of the Confederacy: The Story of the* Alabama *and Her Captain, Raphael Semmes.* New York: Funk and Wagnalls, 1957.

Brack, Gene M. *Mexico Views Manifest Destiny, 1821–1846.* Albuquerque: University of New Mexico Press, 1975.

Bradlee, Francis Bordman. *Blockade Running during the Civil War.* Reprinted from the historical collection of the Essex Institute, vols. 60 and 61. Salem, Mass.: Essex Institute, 1925.

———. *The* Kearsarge-Alabama: *The Story As Told to the Writer by James Magee of Marblehead, Seaman on the* Kearsarge. Salem, Mass.: Essex Institute, 1921.

Bradlow, Edna, and Frank Bradlow. *Here Comes the* Alabama: *The Career of a Confederate Raider.* Cape Town: A. A. Belkema, 1958.

Brodie, Bernard. *A Guide to Naval Strategy.* 4th ed. Princeton, N.J.: Princeton University Press, 1958. Reprint, Westport, Conn.: Greenwood Press, 1977.

Bronham, Alfred I. *'290': Story of the Sinking of the* Alabama, *1883.* Booklet form, 1930.

Brown, Lawrence, and Issac Colby. "The *Sonora* and the *Alabama.*" *Civil War Times Illustrated* 18, no. 3 (October 1971).

Browne, John M. "The Duel Between the Alabama and the Kearsarge." In *The Way to Appomattox: Battles and Leaders of the Civil War,* 4 vols., edited by R. H. Johnson. New York: Castle Books, 1959. 4:615–25.

Cable, George W. "New Orleans Before the Capture." In *The Way to Appomattox: Battles and Leaders of the Civil War,* 4 vols., edited by R. H. Johnson. New York: Castle Books, 1959. 1:11.

Carroll, Daniel B. *Henri Mercier and the American Civil War.* Princeton, N.J.: Princeton University Press, 1971.

Case, Lynn M., and Warren F. Spencer. *The United States and France: Civil War Diplomacy.* Philadelphia: University of Pennsylvania Press, 1970.

Cook, Adrian. *The Alabama Claims: American Politics and Anglo-American Relations, 1865–1872.* Ithaca: Cornell University Press, 1975.

Dalzell, George W. *The Flight from the Flag: The Continuing Effects of the Civil War upon the American Carrying Trade.* Chapel Hill: University of North Carolina Press, 1940.

Davis, Evangeline, and Burke Davis. *Rebel Raider: A Biography of Admiral Semmes.* New York: J. P. Lippincott, 1966.

Delaney, Coldwell, ed. *Raphael Semmes, Rear Admiral, Confederate States Navy, Brigadier, Confederate States Army: Documents Pertaining to the Charges Preferred Against Him by the United States Government.* Mobile: Museum of the City of Mobile, 1978.

Delaney, Norman C. "At Semmes' Hand." *Civil War Times Illustrated* 11, no. 18 (June 1979).

———. "Fight or Flee." *Journal of Confederate History* 4 (special commemorative issue, 1989): 27.

———. *John McIntosh Kell of the Raider* Alabama. Tuscaloosa: University of Alabama Press, 1973.

———. "Showdown at Cherbourg." *Civil War Times Illustrated* 15, no. 3 (June 1976): 16–21.

Dufour, Charles L. *The Mexican War: A Compact History, 1846–1848.* New York: Hawthorne Books, 1968.

Durkin, J. T. *Stephen R. Mallory: Confederate Navy Chief.* Chapel Hill: University of North Carolina Press, 1973.

Ellicott, John M. *The Life of John Ancrum Winslow, Rear-Admiral, United States Navy.* New York: G. P. Putnam's Sons, 1905.

Elliot, Charles Winslow. *Winfield Scott: The Soldier and the Man.* New York: Macmillan, 1937.

Ferris, Norman B. *Desperate Diplomacy: William H. Seward's Foreign Policy, 1861.* Knoxville: University of Tennessee Press, 1976.

Fleming, Walter L. *Civil War and Reconstruction in Alabama.* 1905. Reprint, with an introduction by Sarah Woolfolk Wiggins. Spartanburg, S.C.: Reprint Co., 1978.

Fowler, William M. *Under Two Flags.* New York: W. W. Norton, 1990.

Gosnell, Harpur Helen. *Rebel Raider.* Chapel Hill: University of North Carolina Press, 1948.

Guerout, Max. "The Wreck of the CSS *Alabama:* Avenging Angel of the Confederacy." *National Geographic* (December 1994): 67–83.

Hagen, Kenneth J. *This People's Navy.* New York: Free Press, 1991.

Haywood, Philip D. *The Cruise of the* Alabama, *by One of the Crew.* Boston: Houghton Mifflin, 1886.

Hearn, Chester G. *Gray Raider of the Sea.* Camden, Me.: International Marine Publishing, 1992.

Hendrick, Burton J. *Statesmen of the Lost Cause: Jefferson Davis and His Cabinet.* Boston: Little, Brown, 1939.

Henry, Robert Self. *The Story of The Mexican War.* New York: Bobbs-Merrill, 1950.

Holland, Francis Ross, Jr. *America's Lighthouses: Their Illustrated History Since 1716.* Brattleboro, Vt.: S. Greene Press, 1972.

Hoole, William Stanley. *Four Years in the Confederate Navy: The Career of Captain John Low on the C.S.S.* Fingal, Florida, Alabama, Tuscaloosa, *and* Ajax. Athens: University of Georgia Press, 1964.

———, ed. "Admiral on Horseback: The Diary of Brigadier General Raphael Semmes, February, May 1865." *Alabama Review* 28 (April 1975): 129–50.

———, ed. *The Logs of the CSS* Alabama *and CSS* Tuscaloosa *1862–1863 by Lieu-*

tenant (Captain) John Low, CSN. University, Ala.: Confederate Publishing, 1972.

Howarth, Stephen. *To Shining Sea: A History of the United States Navy.* New York: Random House, 1991.

Humphreys, Anderson, and Curt Guenther. *Semmes America.* Memphis: Humphreys, 1989.

Jones, Katherine M. *Ladies of Richmond.* New York: Bobbs-Merrill, 1962.

Jones, Virgil C. *The Civil War at Sea, January 1861–March 1862.* 3 vols. New York: Holt, Rinehart and Winston, 1960–62.

Kell, John M. "Cruise and Combats of the *Alabama.*" In *The Way to Appomattox: Battles and Leaders of the Civil War,* 4 vols., edited by R. H. Johnson (New York: Castle Books, 1959). 4:611. Also in *American History Illustrated* (October 1988).

Lambert, C. S. "The CSS *Alabama* Lost and Found." *American History Illustrated* (October 1988): 32–37.

Langley, Harold D. *Social Reform in the United States Navy, 1798–1862.* Urbana: University of Illinois Press, 1967.

Leary, William M. "The *Alabama* vs. the *Kearsarge:* A Diplomatic View." *American Neptune* 29, no. 3 (1969): 167–73.

Lewis, Charles Lee. *Admiral Franklin Buchanan, Fearless Man of Action.* Baltimore: Norman, Remington, 1929.

McCartney, Clarence E. *Mr. Lincoln's Admirals.* New York: Funk and Wagnalls, 1956.

McFarland, Philip. *Sea Dangers: The Affair of the* Somers. New York: Schocken Books, 1985.

McFeeley, William S. *Grant: A Biography.* New York: W. W. Norton, 1982.

Mahan, Alfred T. *Naval Strategy Compared and Contrasted with the Principles and Practice of Military Operations on Land.* 1911. Reprint. Westport, Conn.: Greenwood Press, 1975.

Mayo, Claude Banks. *Your Navy.* Los Angeles: Parker and Baird, n.d.

Meriwether, Colyer. *Raphael Semmes.* Philadelphia: George W. Jacobs, 1913.

Merli, Frank J. "Caribbean Confrontation." *Journal of Confederate History* 4 (1990).

———. *Great Britain and the Confederate Navy, 1861–1865.* Bloomington: Indiana University Press, 1970.

———, ed. "Letters on the *Alabama.*" *Mariners Mirror* (May 1972).

Nashville Republican Banner. July 28, 1867.

Newman, Harry Wright. *The Maryland Semmes and Kindred Families.* Baltimore: Maryland Historical Society, 1956.

Niven, John. *Gideon Welles.* New York: Oxford University Press, 1973.

Owsley, Frank Lawrence, Jr. *The C.S.S.* Florida: *Her Building and Operations.* Philadelphia: University of Pennsylvania Press, 1965.

Owsley, Frank Lawrence, Sr. *King Cotton Diplomacy: Foreign Relations of the Confederate States of America.* Chicago: University of Chicago Press, 1931.

Parker, William H. *Recollections of a Naval Officer.* New York: Charles Scribner's Sons, 1883.

Pensacola Gazette. April 29, October 15 and 21, 1836; February 24 and May 6, 1837.

Porter, David D. *Naval History of the Civil War.* New York: Sherman Publishing, 1886.

Randall, J. G., and David Donald. *The Civil War and Reconstruction.* 2d ed. Boston: D. C. Heath, 1961.

Roberts, W. Adolphe. *Semmes of the* Alabama. New York: Bobbs-Merrill, 1938.

Robinson, Charles M., III. *Shark of the Confederacy: The Story of the CSS* Alabama. Annapolis: Naval Institute Press, 1995.

Robinson, William Morrison, Jr. *The Confederate Privateers.* New Haven: Yale University Press, 1928.

Schmitt, Karl. *Mexico and the United States, 1821–1973: Conflict and Coexistence.* New York: Wiley, 1974.

Schott, Thomas E. *Alexander H. Stephens: A Biography.* Baton Rouge: Louisiana State University Press, 1988.

Semmes to Louisa Tremlett. *Journal of Confederate History* 4 (special commemorative edition, 1989): 58–59.

Sinclair, Arthur. *Two Years on the* Alabama. 1895. Reprint. Annapolis: Naval Institute Press, 1989.

Singapore Sunday Times. February 19, 1956.

Spencer, Warren F. *The Confederate Navy in Europe.* University: University of Alabama Press, 1983.

Stamp, Kenneth M., ed. *The Causes of the Civil War.* Englewood Cliffs, N.J.: Prentice-Hall, 1965.

Summersell, Charles Grayson. "The Career of Raphael Semmes Prior to the Cruise of the *Alabama.*" Ph.D. diss., Vanderbilt University, 1940.

———. *The Cruise of the CSS* Sumter. Tuscaloosa: Confederate Publishing, 1965.

———. *CSS* Alabama *Builder: Captain and Plans.* University: University of Alabama Press, 1985.

———, ed. *Journal of George Townley Fullam.* University: University of Alabama Press, Friends of Mobile Library, 1973.

Taylor, John M. *Confederate Raider: Raphael Semmes of the* Alabama. Washington, D.C.: Brassey's, 1994.

———. "The Fiery Trail of the *Alabama.*" *Military History Quarterly* (Summer 1991).

———. "Showdown off Cherbourg." *Yankee* (July 1984).

Valle, James E. *Rocks and Shoals.* Annapolis: Naval Institute Press, 1980.

Wade, William W. "The Man Who Stopped the Rams." *American Heritage* (April 1863).

Wallace, Edward S. *General William Jenkins Worth: Monterrey's Forgotten Hero.* Dallas: Southern Methodist University Press, 1953.

West, Richard S., Jr. *Gideon Welles, Lincoln's Navy Department.* Indianapolis: Bobbs-Merrill, 1943.

——. *Mr. Lincoln's Navy.* New York: Longman's, Green, 1958.

——. *The Second Admiral.* New York: Coward-McCann, 1937.

Wilford, John Noble. *The Mysterious History of Columbus: An Exploration of the Man, the Myth, the Legacy.* New York: Knopf, 1991.

Williams, Frances L. *Matthew Fontaine Maury.* New Brunswick, N.J.: Rutgers University Press, 1963.

Wilson, Harold. "The Cruise of the CSS *Alabama* in Southeast Asian Waters." *Journal of Confederate History* 4 (special commemorative issue, 1989).

Index